Library & Information Service
The Dementia Services
Development Centre
Iris Murdoch Building
University of Stirling
Stirling
FK9 4LA

# THE NEED FOR THEORY

# THE NEED FOR THEORY:
## Critical Approaches to
## Social Gerontology

*Edited by*

### *Simon Biggs*
*Centre for Social Gerontology, Keele University*

### *Ariela Lowenstein*
*Department of Gerontology and Center for Research
and Study of Aging, Faculty of Welfare and Health Studies,
University of Haifa*

### *Jon Hendricks*
*Dean, University Honors College, Oregon State University*

Jon Hendricks, Series Editor
### SOCIETY AND AGING SERIES

Baywood Publishing Company, Inc.
AMITYVILLE, NEW YORK

**Baywood Publishing Company, Inc.**
26 Austin Avenue
Amityville, NY 11701
(800) 638-7819
E-mail: baywood@baywood.com
Web site: baywood.com


Library of Congress Catalog Number: 2002038447
ISBN: 0-89503-277-5 (cloth)


**Library of Congress Cataloging-in-Publication Data**

The need for theory : critical approaches to social gerontology / edited by Simon Biggs, Ariela Lowenstein, and Jon Hendricks.
    p. cm. -- (Society and aging series)
    Includes bibliographical references and index.
    ISBN 0-89503-277-5 (cloth)
    1. Gerontology. 2. Aging. 3. Aged. I. Biggs, Simon, 1955- II. Lowenstein, Ariela. III. Hendricks, Jon, 1943- IV. Series.

HQ1061.N6 2003
305.26--dc21                                                                2002038447

# Table of Contents

INTRODUCTION
The Need for Theory in Gerontology . . . . . . . . . . . . . . . . . . 1
*Simon Biggs, Jon Hendricks, and Ariela Lowenstein*

## SECTION ONE
**Theorizing Gerontology**

CHAPTER 1 . . . . . . . . . . . . . . . . . . . . . . . . . . . . . . 15
Critical Gerontological Theory: Intellectual Fieldwork and
the Nomadic Life of Ideas
*Steven Katz*

CHAPTER 2 . . . . . . . . . . . . . . . . . . . . . . . . . . . . . . 33
The Perils and Possibilities of Theory
*Ruth E. Ray*

CHAPTER 3 . . . . . . . . . . . . . . . . . . . . . . . . . . . . . . 45
The Legacy of Social Constructionism for Social Gerontology
*Hans-Joachim von Kondratowitz*

CHAPTER 4 . . . . . . . . . . . . . . . . . . . . . . . . . . . . . . 63
Structure and Identity—Mind the Gap: Toward a Personal
Resource Model of Successful Aging
*Jon Hendricks*

## SECTION TWO
**Theorizing Micro Relations**

CHAPTER 5 . . . . . . . . . . . . . . . . . . . . . . . . . . . . . . 91
Sense and Structure: Toward a Sociology of Old Bodies
*Emmanuelle Tulle*

v

CHAPTER 6 . . . . . . . . . . . . . . . . . . . . . . . . . . . . 105
Contemporary Later-Life Family Transitions: Revisiting
Theoretical Perspectives on Aging and the Family—
Toward a Family Identity Framework
*Ariela Lowenstein*

CHAPTER 7 . . . . . . . . . . . . . . . . . . . . . . . . . . . . 127
The Aging Paradox: Toward Personal Meaning in
Gerontological Theory
*Gerben J. Westerhof, Freya Dittmann-Kohli, and Christina Bode*

CHAPTER 8 . . . . . . . . . . . . . . . . . . . . . . . . . . . . 145
Negotiating Aging Identity: Surface, Depth, and Masquerade
*Simon Biggs*

## SECTION THREE
### Theorizing Macro Relations

CHAPTER 9 . . . . . . . . . . . . . . . . . . . . . . . . . . . . 163
Globalization and the Reconstruction of Old Age: New Challenges
for Critical Gerontology
*Chris Phillipson*

CHAPTER 10 . . . . . . . . . . . . . . . . . . . . . . . . . . . 181
Theoretical Approaches to Problems of Families, Aging, and
Social Support in the Context of Modernization
*Merril Silverstein, Vern L. Bengtson, and Eugene Litwak*

CHAPTER 11 . . . . . . . . . . . . . . . . . . . . . . . . . . . 199
Theorizing Age Relations
*Toni Calasanti*

CHAPTER 12 . . . . . . . . . . . . . . . . . . . . . . . . . . . 219
Theoretical Perspectives on Old Age Policy: A Critique and a Proposal
*Carroll L. Estes*

CONCLUSION . . . . . . . . . . . . . . . . . . . . . . . . . . . 245
Where is Theory Headed?
*Simon Biggs, Jon Hendricks, and Ariela Lowenstein*


Contributors . . . . . . . . . . . . . . . . . . . . . . . . . . . 249
Index . . . . . . . . . . . . . . . . . . . . . . . . . . . . . . 251

INTRODUCTION

# The Need for Theory in Gerontology

## Simon Biggs, Jon Hendricks, and Ariela Lowenstein

## WHAT IS THEORY AND WHY SHOULD WE CARE?

Knowledge is more than an accumulation of so-called facts. At a fundamental level, knowledge is about explaining things and drawing associations. That is where theory comes in; theory also goes beyond the collection of data and tries to uncover the "why" as well as the "what" of occurrences and relationships. Theories are about the way we understand the world and about understanding the world differently. At an elemental level, theory is about the first order constructs that individuals use to explain events in their lives. At a more conceptual level, the second order constructs of gerontology supply the conceptual architecture we inhabit and the tools we use as part of the work of interpreting adult aging.

Some theories are more conceptual than others. At one end of the spectrum, there is accepted wisdom that hardly constitutes theory at all. These positions consist of exhortations to certain forms of conduct of the "be more active" or "keep on keeping on" variety. They may involve the classification of phenomena into increasingly refined and extensive categories, such as has arguably happened in the study of elder abuse, with, it must be said, little advancement in the understanding of abuse itself. The investigators have, in other words, become lost among the trees. This general approach also lends itself to meta-modeling, as a sort of theoretical stamp collecting. Different theories and traditions are grouped or re-grouped according to the collector's fancy, with little evident disciplinary progress and scant connection to the world of experience.

1

Sometimes intellectual work is called theory, but it is closer to modeling. The author has created a reflection, a model or copy of the world, which seeks to re-describe the systems under study. These approaches are rather like plani-spheres, brass models of the solar system so popular in eighteenth-century Europe. You can name the parts and watch them whirr and click. Nomothetic knowledge of this type is positivistic in nature, based on an assumption that the relationships described are images of naturally occurring patterns, discovered by the modeler. Often model metaphors are themselves borrowed from another discourse, such as computing to understand mental processes or economics to understand inter-personal exchanges. In each case modeling tends not to ask why a certain analogy is used, and how the assumptions that come with it affect our understanding.

Critical approaches are more likely to produce identifiably theoretical posi-tions insofar as they attempt to go beyond the surface of events and point to underlying processes. These theories often include a movement from theses, based on common-sensual or dominant explanations of events, to antitheses pointing out underlying power relations that maintain the status quo. Theory is seen to develop through a sort of dialectical spiral, as each antithesis becomes in its turn a thesis for the next generation of counter-theories (Hendricks, 1992). Carroll Estes' (1979) critique of *The Ageing Enterprise* is an apt example of critique building to a novel and antithetical understanding of the growth in services for older adults. It is suggested from Estes' view that the ostensive development of services to meet a growing need, in reality disguises the exploitation of new markets and the consolidation of new forms of professional power. At the extreme end of theory building, the ideas and explanations are infused with novelty and open new directions. They are less dependent upon the import of ideas from elsewhere or the critical comparison of existing ideas. They appear to arise from the first order constructs of the phenomenon under study, yet set them in an entirely new light, thus occasioning a paradigmatic shift in the way the issue is thought about. In gerontology we are still early in the process and have a way to go before we have such a sound grasp of the nature of aging.

We are, then, in the territory of ideas, their formulation and reformulation. And as Victor Marshall (1999) pointed out, data rarely leads to the resolution of debates in its own right. For Marshall one of the tests of a good theory is whether it lends greater logical coherence to a field or discipline. To this might be added the notion of zeitgeist—the spirit of the times, and whether a theory becomes popular because it fits its historical and social circumstances. To understand the growth and use of a particular perspective on aging, then, one would need to examine the social conditions together with the history of ideas that gave rise to new theoretical models.

James Birren (1988), now rather famously, opined that gerontology had become data rich, yet theory poor. There may be a number of reasons why this has been the case. First, contemporary gerontology cohered as a discipline shortly after the Second World War, when behavioral and structural-functional views of society held sway in Western social and human science. These positions left little room for critical analysis and have since been characterized as markedly unreflective on their own social and cultural assumptions (Lynott & Lynott, 1996). Second, the collection of knowledge at the time was seen as an almost exclusively empiricist endeavor, mirroring the methods, and it was hoped, the success of the physical sciences. Third, gerontology became part of the great push for social improvement that filled the post-war years. To this day, gerontology is closely, and possibly uncritically, allied to public policy on aging. This combination of factors has been succinctly expressed as "the union of science and advocacy" (Butler, in Moody, 1993), however it sometimes leads to the collection of data for data's sake and an overly pragmatic approach to the public presentation of knowledge. Neither of these trends facilitates critical reflection on how gerontology is developing, where it is heading, or the nature of adult aging beyond the concerns of established interests and habits of thought.

Moody (1993) noted that when it comes to philosophy, contemporary social gerontology reflects the influence of European rather than Anglo-American theory. Whether Moody's claim withstands close scrutiny or not, the influence appears slim when compared to the historical burden of structural-functionalism and the largely atheoretical and pragmatic empiricism of North American gerontology from which Western social gerontology takes its cue. There are, of course, a few notable exceptions to this a-theoretical blanket. A list would include: Marxism in the work of Estes (1979, 2001), Phillipson (1982), and Olson (1982); Psychoanalysis (Biggs, 1993; Woodward, 1991); Foucault (Frank, 1998; Katz, 1996; Powell & Biggs, 2000; Tulle-Winton, 2000); Existentialism (Cole, 1992; Tornstam, 1989); the Frankfurt School (Moody, 1993); and in Phillipson (1998) and Holstein and Gubrium (2000) who attempt a fusion of traditions. Undoubtedly there are others as well, but the point is that they stand as exceptions rather than the rule.

It is striking that the 1999 *Handbook of Theories of Aging* was marked by an absence of structure by theoretical orientation. Although the *Handbook* (Bengtson & Schaie, 1999) had become more extensive and inclusive than its predecessor, *Emergent Theories of Aging* (Birren & Bengtson, 1988), it retained essentially the same shape. This consisted of a mix of the progress within disciplines, method-driven, and problem- or site-based approaches. What emerged was a surprisingly atheoretical handbook on theory. Perhaps it is reflective of the historic nature of the field rather than the state of the art.

Does this mean, then, that social gerontology is creating its own theories and does not need to sit on the shoulders of these philosophical giants? Unfortunately not. The longevity of the disengagement versus activity debate, reflected in contemporary positions around gero-transcendence and productive aging, attests to both the poverty of homegrown theory as well as to the endurance of two key ideas that still speak to the construction of contemporary aging. Indeed, these trends may even repeat divisions and strengths noted at the first stirrings of the discipline in the late nineteenth century (Katz, 1996). Adapting this bifurcation as a facile characterization of the experience of aging is not likely to add insight or accumulate knowledge.

A close examination of how theory has developed suggests a picture of an emergent focus that has imported ideas from the wider social and medical sciences, plus politics and the humanities. It has generated debate and alternative interpretations of aging and contributed to the development of public policy and professional practice. What it has not yet done is generate convincing theorization from its own field of study. Hopefully this volume and similar efforts will redress that charge.

## GERONTOLOGY AS A FIELD FOR THEORY

If Manheimer (1993) is correct, then the study of adult aging begs the big philosophical questions: why are we here and to what purpose? What is a life well lived? It is also, and perhaps in part because of these questions, a meeting place of extraordinary disciplinary fecundity (Weiland, 2000). Gerontology has, in fact, been characterized as having certain key characteristics, including its multidisciplinarity, its applied nature and its preoccupation with the relationship between individual and social aging (Hendricks & Achenbaum, 1999).

First, gerontology is referred to as multidisciplinary and in its practical element, inter-professional. This focus may reflect the increasing interdependence of the social, soma, and psyche in later life. A mixing of disciplines can add richness, arising from different styles and paradigms. However, the notion of disciplinary interaction upon the ground that gerontology creates also raises questions about boundaries and dominance. With respect to boundaries, Katz (1996) has suggested that the multidisciplinarity of contemporary gerontology may include little dialogue. It may be a space that disciplines co-inhabit rather than one where they interact. Clair and Allman (2000) presented a catalogue of innovation by participatory disciplines, but regret the barriers that persistently resist meaningful collaboration on shared initiatives. Cole, Kastenbaum, and Ray (2000) made a plea for rapprochement between the critical and radical ends of social science and the humanities. While postmodernity has promised the erosion of professional boundaries, especially between health and social care workers and the older people that they assist, there appears to be little movement between disciplines (Biggs, 1997). Rather, contemporary gerontology may have experienced what Estes and Binney (1989) referred to as the bio-medicalization of old age. According to this view, powerful disciplinary and commercial lobbies have achieved a hegemony around policy thinking on aging, which then creates a particular momentum through the legitimation of its own research and program priorities. In other words, the power of a particular perspective, supported by research funding and commerce which then reinforces that very power, runs the risk of eclipsing the very possibilities that multidisciplinarity promises. One result can be seen in the increasingly close exchange of ideas between the social sciences and humanities, while such exchanges appear to have been met with indifference by the bio-medical sciences.

Second, gerontology has emerged largely as an applied focus and has been referred to as both a "problem oriented discipline" (Nydegger, 1981) and a "problem-solving discipline" (Morrow-Howell, Hinterlong, & Sherraden, 2001). This has become its great potential and its great curse in terms of theory building. The potential lies in the fact that in the study of aging one is never far away from real-life issues. Theorizing requires the examination of the way that certain aspects of aging come to be seen as problems while others do not. It requires dialogue between ideas and experience and between levels of conceptualization. It suggests that theoretical formulations should affect both professional practice and everyday aging. The downside is that applied approaches require ideas that are relatively quick and easy to comprehend, often at the expense of an understanding of complexity. They are subject to political and popular fashion and forms of short-termism that argue against debates that appear at first to have no obvious practical outcome. This is another way of saying that an applied gerontology pushes for models, rather than theories.

Two issues have dominated the application of gerontology to policy and practice; these have been social ageism and bodily decline. Both have had a longstanding presence in the developing discipline (Hendricks & Achenbaum, 1999; Katz, 1996), although concern with ageism is most commonly linked to Robert Butler's Pulitzer prize-winning *Why Survive? Being Old in America,* published in 1975. Butler has also been instrumental in advancing the cause of a challenge to ageism in the areas of policy and medical practice and takes an optimistic approach to gerontological progress through science. This is in contrast to Estes' (1979) equally seminal critique of the aging enterprise and observations on the near hegemony produced by biomedicalization. Moody (1993) claimed that the influence of instrumental reason, for example, reproduces structures of domination rather than confronting their underlying assumptions. This would suggest that the role of theory is as much to critically interrogate changes in policy and practice, as it is to act as an advocate. The surprising volte-faces of public policy, for example, from survivor to dependency, to burden, to victim, to consumer, to active citizen in the space of half a century, may require critical interrogation rather than being subsumed within a metaphor of scientific and social progress (Biggs & Powell, 2002).

Third, scholars, particularly in social gerontology, have attempted to explain aging through an understanding of the tension between the individual and the social, so much so that Ryff and Marshall (1999) have referred to it as "social gerontology's fascination." This fascination has taken the form of linking macro and micro influences on aging (Marshall, 1999; Marshall & Tindale, 1978), identity with social structure (Calasanti, 1999; Hendricks, 1992, 1999), individual inequality with political economy (Estes, 2001; Phillipson, 1998), personal experience and social attitudes (Biggs, 1999; Holstein & Gubrium, 2000), lifestyle and popular culture (Blaikie, 1998). In fact the list is virtually endless. There are sub-arguments around the role of the family (Silverstein & Bengtson, 1997), the relationship between social stereotyping and personal integration in later life (Cole, 1992; Tornstam, 1996), gender (Arber & Ginn, 1995; Holstein, 1992), and ethnicity (Blakemore & Boneham, 1994). Hendricks (1992) has even turned a gerontological fascination with generations on the discipline itself to suggest a genealogy of gerontological development. Generations of geron-tologists, have been studied: their social context, who followed whom and in what allegiances, creating paradigms of intellectual kinship. Marshall (1999) used this approach to great effect to examine the "debate" between disengagement and activity theories, both he suggested, "invented" by Cumming and Henry, with activity only later theorized. Lynott and Lynott (1996) claim that 1961 and the publication of Cumming and Henry's *Growing Old: The Process of Dis-engagement* marked the beginning of serious theorizing in gerontology. It was, of course, also the first attempt to theorize the relationship between personal and social aging.

There is a tension in any critical analysis of a field, between trying to "track" developments within the field itself and assessing its interaction and responsiveness to wider social trends and ideas. At the turn of the millennium, social gerontology has been marked by the wider debate concerning the relation-ship between modernity and post-modernity. Modernity is associated with a belief in progress, of mass social identities dependent on ones relationship to productivity and a scientific approach to the problems of aging. Postmodernity, it is argued, thinks in terms of spaces rather than time, looks to consumerism as a basis for identity and sees science as one of many, equally relevant narratives for explaining events. Polikva (2000) has argued that this debate is closely linked to globalization and the erosion of the welfare state, with relatively affluent older people gaining access to a complex series of lifestyle options, while poorer elders are left increasingly vulnerable and insecure. The debate over postmodernity has divided social gerontologists into optimists and pessimists, or as some might think, fools and angels. Optimists such as Murphy and Longino (1997) in the United States and Featherstone and Hepworth (1989) in the United Kingdom maintain that lifestyle flexibility and bio-technical innovation have removed many of the disadvantages that have previously accrued in later life. Other theorists, such as Phillipson and Biggs (1998) and Katz (1999) are more reserved, noting an avoidance of important life course issues, inequalities, and new risks in such a view. Whether one errs on the side of the advantages or disadvantages of con-temporary aging, the postmodern debate has had far-reaching effects on the way gerontologists think about later life. Polikva (2000) summarized one such effect as the perception of the life course as increasingly improvisational as older people cultivate the capacity to adjust to discontinuity. Old age has, in other words, become much less predictable, both as a social category and as a human experience. One outcome has become an acceptance that the claim that one can establish "facts" about aging itself depends upon a particular theoretical view of the nature of knowledge. Social gerontologists are increasingly likely to consider aging to be a narrative, a story to live by, as they are to see it as an objective process (Kenyon, Ruth, & Mader, 1999). An interesting twist in this development has been dissatisfaction with age as simply another source of relativism, and attempts to articulate what might be special about the aging experience. Tornstam (1996) has suggested that later life consists of a process of gerotranscendence, a combination of continued but disinterested concentration on self-development and social values. Others (Gullette, 2000; Westerhof, Dittmann-Kohli, & Thissen, 2001) have rediscovered age as a key element in defining social existence. An emergent contention of postmodernist perspectives on aging is that the types of theorizing espoused by social gerontologists in part, affect social control of the elderly.

## ADVANCING THEORETICAL FORMULATIONS

So what can a reader reasonably expect of a book extolling the need for theory in social gerontology? A critical awareness of the state of the discipline, certainly. That is, the volume should provide an outline of some of the key issues and contradictions surrounding adult aging, which have the power to project gerontology beyond the century of its birth. Also, a drawing out of implications, by degrees, for research policy and practice. And sometimes, if we are lucky, a glimpse of something more, a new way of thinking about adult aging. In the contributions to follow, the reader will encounter some of each of these agenda items and see that theorizing is neither ahistorical nor apolitical. The reader might also discern that theory is never just a form of conceptualization, like first order constructs, the theorizing of the scholars provides fundamental orienting perspectives for how questions are asked and solutions formulated.

Further, like the authors and editors, the reader should care about theory because it helps explain why we do what we do and may alert us to some of the currently unforeseen implications of unselfconscious assumptions about age. It may also provide conceptual tools to interpret complex events and critically evaluate the current state of aging. Most of all the contributions in this volume should help the reader to understand and imagine alternative possibilities. Without theory the findings of gerontology might actually be a disservice. By attending to how knowledge is created, the reader might also better grasp the course of their own thinking and that is perhaps the most that a reader can take away from an intellectual encounter.

Any division of the contributions presented here would be arbitrary as, with any critical approach, each contribution contains a wide variety of implications for personal and structural aspects of aging as well as for the discipline of gerontology itself. We have attempted, below, to order the contents in a way that reflects the principal concern of the authors.

The first section mostly concerns the theorizing of gerontology itself. In other words, authors examine the patterns and directions that can be discerned in contemporary gerontology as a discipline and offer observations on the strengths and weaknesses of current trends. This is followed by sections two and three where key areas are examined in detail. The second section addresses the theorizing of micro relations. In other words, one's entry point to aging issues is through, primarily but not exclusively, individual and interpersonal aging. The third section considers the power of macro or structural relations and their influence on the construction of aging. Again, the observations and critique developed by authors have implications for the issues raised in the other sections. Throughout we have attempted to bring together established and emerging contributors to critical gerontology in an attempt to explore adult aging in a new millennium.

## SECTION ONE:  THEORIZING GERONTOLOGY

Chapter 1. Stephen Katz looks at the development of gerontology as a discipline and notes the relationship between its "late arrival" within the social sciences and the influence of many different streams of thought that coexist within it. He suggests that critical thinking in gerontology is a nomadic enterprise and can be best understood as an exercise in what he calls "intellectual fieldwork."

Chapter 2. Ruth Ray explores the perils and possibilities of theory within gerontology. She draws on the experience of feminist thought in order that critical gerontologists might learn from its changing fortunes and avoid similar problems within their own discipline. Ray reports her own use of the work of Paulo Freire, and offers a radical perspective on teaching gerontologically.

Chapter 3. Hans Joachim von Kondratowitz considers the legacy of social construction in sociology and its implications for social gerontology. Writing of the German and Polish intellectual traditions, he makes critical observations on changes that have occurred in the development and diffusion of gerontological knowledge over time.

Chapter 4. Jon Hendricks critically examines a key distinction that has historically divided the study of adult ageing into structured inequalities on the one hand and experienced identity on the other. He argues that this theoretical gap has inhibited an understanding of the social meaning of old age and suggests an integrative model for successful ageing.

## SECTION TWO:  THEORIZING MICRO RELATIONS

Chapter 5. Emmanuelle Tulle points out that one of the most obvious aspect of adult aging, namely our relationship to our own bodies has, paradoxically, been one that has been underplayed by critical gerontology. She attempts to "map" the social nature of aging bodies and works toward a radical sociological perspective of the old body through an examination of athleticism.

Chapter 6. Ariela Lowenstein focuses on the importance of transitions in later life and the critical perspective that is thus allowed when static models of aging are examined. She argues that in order to understand age and identity within families an amalgam of individual, familial, and societal levels of analysis are required, and proposes an integrative framework for family identity.

Chapter 7. Gerben Westerhof, Freya Dittmann-Kohli, and Christina Bode begin by examining a contradiction between psychological stability across the life course despite adverse life conditions and social ageism. They suggest that both subjective experience and objective measures indicate that ageing is not as negative and experience not as positive as the original position assumes. Moreover, age is found to be a key source of meaning in itself and they argue that this should be reflected in gerontological theory.

Chapter 8. Simon Biggs relates age and identity to a wider debate on the post modernization of contemporary society. He argues that theories proposing that identities are becoming more fluid are challenged by the experience of adult aging. Key to understanding how older people negotiate intergenerational encounters is a distinction between surface impressions and deeper sources of the self.

## SECTION THREE: THEORIZING MACRO RELATIONS

Chapter 9. Chris Phillipson suggests that critical gerontology must take globalization and its effects on the reconstruction of old age into account. He argues that the resulting social, economic, and cultural changes will influence both national and international regulation of population ageing. The policies of trans-national organizations such as the World Bank will add significantly to the risks associated with ageing in the developed and developing worlds and should be the subject of radical critique.

Chapter 10. Merril Silverstein, Vern Bengtson, and Eugene Litwak propose that the context of modernization has created a series of challenges to understanding the problems faced by ageing families. They critically assess the value of task specificity and solidarity as theoretical approaches as a means of interrogating change in family systems with particular attention being paid to social support.

Chapter 11. Toni Calasanti criticizes the reluctance of social gerontologists to theorize power relations and the relationship between sources of inequality in later life. She argues that an increased sensitivity to diversity is not enough if similarities and differences between age based and other forms of oppression are not taken into account. Old age must be seen as a social location that is subject to intersecting relationships of power.

Chapter 12. Carroll Estes critically interrogates contemporary social policy toward aging. She examines the socio-cultural, economic, and political factors that underlie old age policy and uses this perspective to highlight to limitations of prevailing gerontological theory. Critical approaches should, she argues, be used to subvert social domination based on race, gender, class, and age.

Taken together, the contributions to this volume begin to map out some of the key issues, paradoxes, and contradictions facing gerontology now and in the future. Each of the contributors has placed themselves within a critical tradition that attempts to improve the lot of older adults in contemporary society. Crucially, this tradition does not accept prevailing orthodoxies. It works toward a radical reexamination of adult aging and will hopefully engage the readers' understanding and act as an impetus for critical practice.

## CONCLUDING COMMENTS

Knowledge advances to the extent that conceptual advancement and integration occur. Without theorizing and theoretical development social gerontology will stall-out with piecemeal empiricism but relatively few insights. We have to move beyond simplistic binary differentiation or the use of labels as explanations if we are to add insight to what we know and what we discover. Social experience and life course development do not simply happen, as if the course of nature were set and all that was required is putting life in motion. Rather, aging is a social construction and can unfold in myriad ways and follow numerous courses. The universality we think we see has as much to do with common institutional arrangements as it does with fate. For these reasons age will never become irrelevant, regardless of Neugarten's (1974) assertions. Behind the apparent obviousness of age categories and age-grades, political, economic and normative decisions shape the process. By the same token, any designs for intervention must take account of the underlying factors as well as the apparent age differentiation that society uses to organize itself. Social gerontologists face the task of explaining how the process unfolds as well as how the decisions take on the salience they do; neither are as transparent as they may at first appear. The quest for theories that help us make sense of what happens to people as they age is worthwhile. Hopefully it will be pushed forward by the theoretical formulations of those who have contributed to this volume, and further still by those who read them and make steps forward of their own.

## REFERENCES

Arber, S., & Ginn, J. (1995). *Connecting gender & ageing*. Bucks: Open University Press.

Bengtson, V. L., & Lowenstein, A. (Eds.). (2002). *International perspectives on families, aging & social support*. New York: Springer.

Bengtson, V. L., & Schaie, K. W. (1995). *Handbook of theories of aging*. New York: Springer.

Biggs, S. (1993). *Understanding ageing*. Bucks: Open University Press.

Biggs, S. (1997). User voice, interprofessionalism and postmodernity. *Journal of Inter-professional Care, 11*(2), 195-203.

Biggs, S. (1999). *The mature imagination.* Bucks: Open University Press.

Biggs, S., & Powell, J. (2002). Older people and family in social policy. In V. L. Bengtson & A. Lowenstein (Eds.), *Emergent theories of aging.* New York: Springer.

Birren, J. E., & Bengtson, V. L. (1988). *International perspectives on families, aging and social support.* New York: Springer.

Blaikie, A. (1998). *Ageing & popular culture.* Cambridge: Cambridge University Press.

Blakemore, K., & Boneham, M. (1994). *Age, race & ethnicity.* Bucks: Open University Press.

Butler, R. (1975). *Why survive? Being old in America.* San Francisco: Harper & Row.

Calasanti, T. M. (1999). Feminism and gerontology; Not just for women. *Hallym International Journal of Aging, 1*(1), 44-55.

Clair, J. M., & Allman R. M. (2000). *The gerontological prism: Developing interdisciplinary bridges.* New York: Baywood.

Cole, T. R. (1992). *The journey of life.* New York: Springer.

Cole, T. R., Kastenbaum, R., & Ray, R. (2000). *Handbook of the humanities & aging.* New York: Springer.

Estes, C. (1979). *The aging enterprise.* San Francisco: Jossey-Bass

Estes, C. (2001). *Social policy & aging.* Thousand Oaks: Sage.

Estes, C., & Binney, E. A. (1989). The bio-medicalisation of aging. *The Gerontologist, 29*(5), 587-596.

Featherstone, M., & Hepworth, M. (1989). Ageing and old age: Reflections on the postmodern lifecourse. In B. Bytheway, T. Keil, & P. Allatt (Eds.), *Becoming and being old: Sociological approaches to later life* (pp. 143-157). London: Sage.

Frank, A. W. (1998). Stories of illness as care of the self: A Foucauldian dialogue. *Health, 2*(3), 329-348.

Gullette, M. (2000). Age studies as cultural studies. In T. R. Cole, R. Kastenbaum, & R. Ray (Eds.), *Handbook of the humanities & aging.* New York: Springer.

Hendricks, J. (1992). Generations and the generation of theory in social gerontology. *International Journal of Aging and Human Development, 35,* 31-47.

Hendricks, J. (1999). Practical consciousness, social class and self concept; A view from sociology. In C. D. Ryff & V. W. Marshall (Eds.), *The self & society in aging processes.* New York: Springer.

Hendricks, J., & Achenbaum, A. (1999). Historical development of theories of aging. In V. L. Bengtson & K. W. Schaie (Eds.), *Handbook of theories of aging.* New York: Springer.

Holstein, J., & Gubrium, J. (2000). *The self we live by.* Oxford: Oxford University Press.

Holstein, M. (1992). Productive aging a feminist critique. *Journal of Aging & Social Policy, 4*(3), 17-34.

Katz, S. (1996). *Disciplining old age.* Charlottesville: University Press of Virginia.

Katz, S. (1999). Fashioning agehood: Lifestyle imagery and the commercial spirit of senoirs culture. In J. Povlsen (Ed.), *Childhood & old age.* Odense: Odense University Press.

Kenyon, G. M., Ruth, J., & Mader, W. (1999). Elements of a narrative gerontology. In V. L. Bengtson & K. W. Schaie (Eds.), *Handbook of theories of aging.* New York: Springer.

Lynott, R. J., & Lynott, P. P. (1996). Tracing the course of theoretical development in the sociology of aging. *The Gerontologist, 36*(6), 749-760.

Manheimer, R. J. (1993). Wisdom and method. In T. R. Cole, R. Van Tassel, & R. Kastenbaum (Eds.), *Handbook of the humanities & aging*. New York: Springer.

Marshall, V. W. (1999). Analysing social theories of aging. In V. L. Bengtson & K. W. Schaie (Eds.), *Handbook of theories of aging*. New York: Springer.

Marshall, V. W., & Tindale, J. A. (1978). Notes for a radical gerontology. *International Journal of Aging and Human Development, 9,* 163-175.

Moody, H. R. (1993). What is critical gerontology and why is it important? In T. R. Cole, W. A. Achenbaum, P. L. Jacobi, & R. Kastenbaum (Eds.), *Voices & visions of aging*. New York: Springer.

Morrow-Howell, N., Hinterlong, J., & Sherraden, M. (2001). *Productive aging concepts & challenges*. Baltimore: Johns Hopkins.

Murphy, J., & Longino, C. (1997). Toward a postmodern understanding of aging and identity. *Journal of Aging & Identity, 2*(2), 81-89.

Neugarten, B. (1974). Age groups in American society and the rise of the young-old. *Annals of the American Academy of Political and Social Science, 414,* 187-198.

Nydegger, C. N. (1981). Social gerontology and anthropology. In C. L. Fry (Ed.), *Aging, culture & health*. New York: Praeger.

Olson, L. K. (1982). *The political economy of aging*. New York: Columbia University Press.

Phillipson, C. (1982). *Capitalism & the construction of old age*. London: Macmillan.

Phillipson, C. (1998). *Reconstructing old age*. London: Sage.

Phillipson, C., & Biggs, S. (1998). Modernity and identity: Themes and perspectives in the study of older adults. *Journal of Aging & Identity, 3*(1), 11-23.

Polikva, L. (2000). Postmodern aging and the loss of meaning. *Journal of Aging & Identity, 5*(2), 225-235.

Powell, J., & Biggs, S. (2000). Managing old age: The disciplinary web of power, surveillance and normalisation. *Journal of Aging & Identity, 5*(1), 3-14.

Ryff, C. D., & Marshall, V. W. (1999). *The self & society in aging processes*. New York: Springer.

Silverstein, M., & Bengtson, V. L. (1997). Intergenerational solidarity and the structure of child parent relationships. *American Journal of Sociology, 103*(2), 429-460.

Tornstam, L. (1989). Gero-transcendence: A reformulation of disengagement theory. *Aging, Clinical & Experimental Research, 1*(1), 55-63

Tornstam, L. (1996). Gero-transcendence: A theory about maturing into old age. *Journal of Aging & Identity, 1*(1), 37-50.

Tulle-Winton, E. (2000). Old bodies. In P. Hancock (Ed.), *The body, culture & society*. Bucks: Open University Press.

Weiland, S. (2000). Social science toward the humanities. In T. R. Cole, R. Kastenbaum, & R. Ray (Eds.), *Handbook of the humanities & aging*. New York: Springer.

Westerhof, G., Dittmann-Kohli, F., & Thissen, T. (2001). Beyond life satisfaction: Lay conceptions of well being among middle aged and elderly adults. *Social Indicators Research, 14,* 1-25.

Woodward, K. (1991). *Aging & its discontents*. Indiana: Indiana University Press.

# SECTION ONE

# Theorizing Gerontology

## CHAPTER 1

# Critical Gerontological Theory: Intellectual Fieldwork and the Nomadic Life of Ideas

### Stephen Katz

In the past two decades critical gerontology has grown as a vibrant sub-field blending humanities and social science ideas to challenge the instrumentalism of mainstream gerontology and broaden aging studies beyond biomedical models. This hybridized literature has provided an important critique of prevailing social policies and practices around aging, while promoting the rise of new retirement cultures and positive identities in later life. There are also numerous approaches within critical gerontology, outlined below, that create an internal debate regarding the sub-field's constitution, accomplishments, and future directions. However, this debate has generally delimited criticality to research directly associated with radical theoretical traditions (e.g., Marxism, phenomenology, social constructivism) or radical social movements (e.g., feminist, anti-poverty, pension-reform), thus overlooking the intellectual and discursive contexts in which critical ideas attain their criticality within gerontology. This chapter steps outside of these associations to locate gerontological criticality within the contextual dynamics of its own development.

In this spirit of reflexivity I begin on a biographical note. Several years ago at a social science conference I participated in a session called, "After the Fall: New Directions in Critical Culture Theory." The "Fall" had several references: The fall of Soviet communist power and its many walls (both real and ideological), the fall of Marxism and Socialism as world political platforms, and the fall of politically-informed critical theory in the wake of postmodern scepticism. The invitation to present a paper on my area of research—gerontological theory— inspired me at the time to reflect on three questions that were related to the

15

session's theme. First, if Marxist political economy and affiliated critical discourses are *falling* by losing their prominent foundational and theoretical status in the social sciences, how is it that they are also resurfacing in rather unfamiliar places, such as gerontological studies of social aging? Second, in what ways does this resurfacing of major critical discourses serve to enliven professional fields; in this case the constitution of a critical gerontology? Third, compared to other established areas in the humanities and social sciences, what are the institutional and intellectual means by which new critical elements in the professional fields are incorporated and promoted?

Since the conference these questions have continued to be of great interest, and here I would like to highlight their relevance to a discussion of critical gerontological theory. This chapter's three sections and conclusions borrow from the theoretical work of French sociologist Pierre Bourdieu and philosophers Gilles Deleuze and Félix Guattari to address critical gerontology as a pragmatic and nomadic thought-space across which ideas flow and become exchanged, rather than as a kind of model, theory, or method. By depicting critical gerontology as a thought-space, a magnetic field where thought collects, converges, and transverses disciplines and traditions, I also wish to distance it from ongoing assumptions about multidisciplinarity in gerontology, especially the assumption that multidisciplinarity is a precondition for critical thinking. In many ways gerontology is unique because it has embraced the tenets of multidisciplinarity—diverse approaches, plural knowledges, and shared expertise. Indeed, these are seen as the fundamental intellectual resources by which gerontology grew as a profession since the early twentieth century (Achenbaum, 1995). It follows that much theoretical argument in gerontology today, concerned with the critical effectiveness of the field, questions whether or not gerontology has truly become multidisciplinary. However, multidisciplinarity has also furnished mainstream gerontology with a rhetoric of criticality with which to articulate its objectives. As such, since the postwar period multidisciplinarity has remained the critical hallmark of gerontology because practitioners draw upon its rhetorical appeal to shape their textbooks, curricula, journals, associations, funding organizations, and the overall cohesion of the field's "gerontological web" (Katz, 1996). As Bryan Green says,

> The unproblematic collection of multiple perspectives on aging and the aged into unitary handbooks, textbooks, and readers asserts the objective unity of what they are about. Maximization of variant perspective is indispensable to gerontology in ensuring the objectivity and coherence of its subject matter. (1993, p. 167)

Despite the critical ideals that characterize multidisciplinary studies, therefore, multidisciplinarity can limit rather than enrich critical thinking about aging in professional and institutional practices. Hence, this chapter looks to other theoretical stories about gerontology, beginning with the one about its "data-rich but theory-poor" state of affairs.

## I. DATA-RICH BUT THEORY-POOR: THEORY AND CRITIQUE IN GERONTOLOGY

James Birren and Vern Bengtson introduced their 1988 text, *Emergent Theories of Aging,* by claiming that gerontology is "data-rich but theory-poor" (1988, p. ix). In the same text Harry R. Moody further states "the paucity of theory in social gerontology is an embarrassment to academic students of human aging" (1998b, p. 21). Since that time, responsive gerontologists have enhanced the scope and quality of theories in aging in two main ways. First, they have revisited the development of gerontological theory in order to review or debunk its traditional knowledge claims. In the 1990s critical writers produced a series of instructive studies on the various schools of thought, "generations," "phases," or "periods" of theorizing that have emerged in gerontology especially since the postwar period (Bengtson, Burgess, & Parrott, 1997; Bengtson, Parrott, & Burgess, 1996; Bengtson & Schaie, 1999; Bond, Biggs, & Coleman, 1990; Hendricks, 1992; Lynott & Lynott, 1996; Marshall, 1999a). From these we learn how structural functionalism informed disengagement, modernization, and age stratification theories; symbolic interactionism influenced activity and subculture theories; social constructivist theories of aging built on phenomenology and ethnomethodology; and life course studies combined macro-micro perspectives in the social sciences. Or, as Victor Marshall points out in his creative interpretation of the Kansas City Studies that produced disengagement theory, gerontological theory can be understood in terms of "stories about theories, theorizing and theorists" (1999a, p. 435).

Second, certain gerontological thinkers (discussed below) have introduced ideas from political economy, feminism, the humanities, and cultural studies into their work to establish their critical stance. In the process these thinkers have turned to structural models of social inequality, interpretive and deconstructive methodologies, and international and cross-cultural frameworks to contest gerontology's longstanding emphases on individual roles, masculinist life course models, biomedical frameworks, and liberal political agendas. The resulting books and papers produced through these critiques vary according to their authors' approaches to critical thinking within gerontology. For example, when Canadian gerontologist Victor Marshall first called for "radical" methods in gerontology in the late 1970s, he had in mind the adaptation of symbolic interactionist, phenomenological, and ethnomethodological sociologies (Marshall, 1978). In the early 1980s, when the decline of Marxism dominated the agendas of most of the social sciences, British writers such as Alan Walker (1981) and Chris Phillipson (1982), Americans such as Meredith Minkler and Carroll Estes (1984), and Canadians such as John Myles (1984) along with others (Olson, 1982) broke with traditional gerontological studies by establishing a political economy of aging. Specifically, their work focused on the history of capitalist production and the division of labor, and the political foundations of population aging and the welfare state. They criticized as well what Carroll Estes calls the "aging enterprise"; that is, the conglomeration of experts, institutions, and professions that arose in the latter half of the twentieth century to cater to individual needs while neglecting their underlying historical and structural sources (Estes, 1979). However, the political economy of aging does not represent a meta-theoretical endorsement of Marxism; indeed Marx is hardly referred to in the literature. Rather, the political economists merge selected aspects of Marxist theory with gerontological concerns in a creative bridging of theoretical discourse with professional practice.

In the late 1980s and 1990s the political economy of aging expanded by underscoring gender, regional, racial, and ethnic inequalities. This move gave gerontological theorists a wider foundation on which to build the parameters of a critical gerontology. An early example is the paper by Chris Phillipson and Alan Walker, "The Case for a Critical Gerontology" (1987), where the authors outline a number of feminist, discursive, and micropolitical issues typically neglected in formal political economy treatments. Two journals begun in the 1980s, *The Journal of Aging Studies* and *Journal of Women and Aging,* and later *Journal of Aging and Identity,* also radiated a widely critical approach. The influential text, *Voices and Visions of Aging: Towards a Critical Gerontology* published in 1993, further established critical gerontology with a potent mix of philosophical, literary, postmodern, historical, and scientific commentary. In the text's "Overview," Harry R. Moody defines critical gerontology in the tradition of the Marxist-inspired Frankfurt School and its sustained critiques of instrumental reason, and "by its [critical gerontology's] intention of locating actual 'openings' or spaces for potential emancipation within the social order" (1993, p. xvii). This is also a direction Moody initiated in his earlier writings (1988a, 1988b) where he explored new critical directions in policy analysis by taking aboard Jurgen Habermas' ideas on the rationalistic colonization of the "life-world." Habermas uses the idea of "life-world" in much of his work to indicate a vaguely traditional realm of human resources, communicative practices, and domestic spaces that has become subject to incursions by modern forms of "system" (Habermas, 1991). To support his thesis that modernity has been a process whereby rationalizing systems "colonize the life-world," Habermas points to new social movements whose leaderships use life-world issues such as human rights and environmental protection (in place of labor demands for equitable economic distribution) to resist global corporate domination. Thus, as Moody and others (Scambler, 2001) have discovered, Habermas' ideas have great value in the area of critical health studies.

More recently, the collection of essays in *Critical Gerontology: Perspectives from Political and Moral Economy* (1999), edited by Meredith Minkler and Carroll Estes, compels its readers to think politically and ethically about age-based inequality, poverty, and injustice as widespread structural problems. As with their former text, *Critical Perspectives on Aging: The Political and Moral Economy of Growing Old* (1991), here the editors fortify their political economy framework with E. P. Thompson's ideas on moral economy and include research papers that target the mostly American state agencies, healt hcare systems, and social security policies that perpetuate these structural problems. In the "Introduction" to *Critical Gerontology* Minkler notes that critical gerontology consists of two paths: the political economy of aging, and the more "humanistic path" where the accent is on meaning, metaphor, textuality, and imagery in aging and old age. *Critical Gerontology* regards the second humanistic path as "an important supplement to political economy perspectives" (1999, p. 2; see also Minkler, 1996), hence the text appeals more directly to those interested in how political economy research strengthens critical studies of age and gender, race, disability, and class. Students interested in humanistic studies must turn to approaches innovated by Kathleen Woodward (1991) in the United States, Mike Featherstone and Mike Hepworth in Britain (1991), and others who elucidate the new cultural processes redefining later life based on retirement lifestyles, cosmetic and body technologies, popular imagery, and consumer-marketing (Biggs, 1999; Blaikie, 1999; Cohen, 1998; Cole & Ray, 2000; Featherstone & Wernick, 1995;Gilleard & Higgs, 2000; Gullette, 1997; Hepworth, 2000; Hockey & James, 1993; Woodward, 1999). Chris Phillipson's *Reconstructing Old Age* (1998) expands Minkler's synopsis of critical gerontology by identifying a third critical path or stream consisting of biographical and narrative perspectives that draw upon metaphysical humanist concepts of self, memory, meaning, and wisdom. In a parallel fashion, Achenbaum (1997), Brown (1998), Katz (1999), Laws (1995), and Ray (1996, 1999) discuss the co-development of critical and feminist gerontologies. I would also include within the critical gerontological fold those who work in the area of *Age Studies* and explore the alternative, performative, artistic, fictional, trans-sexual, poetic, and futuristic conditions of aging and their radical contributions (Basting-Davis, 1998; Gullette, 2000; Squier, 1995; Woodward, 1999).

Studies of metaphorical development and terminology in gerontology have also been important in shaking up conventions about aging (see Kenyon, Birren, & Schroots, 1991). For example, metaphors-turned-concepts such as "male menopause" or "midlife crisis" signify how individual and social aging are intertwined. The term social or cultural "lag" is used by many gerontologists to indicate that negative social expectations of older people lag behind the more positive realities of aging (Riley, 1994). However, when Chicago sociologist William F. Ogburn came up with the idea of "cultural lag" in the 1920s he used it to discuss his observations on the lag between changing women's economic roles inside and outside the home (1957). Nevertheless, the metaphorical strength of "cultural lag" created a theoretical opportunity for gerontology to borrow and critically use the term for other purposes.

On the one hand, these kinds of organizational exercises and reflections reaffirm that gerontological theory is potentially more expansive, flexible, and inventive than the typically instrumental purposes to which it is put in research applications. Although, as Lawrence Cohen insightfully remarks on critical gero-anthropology, the traditions of Habermas, Horkheimer, Marx, and others are often invoked in critical gerontology, but rarely engaged (1994, p. 139). Cohen warns that, "through the mobilization of anger and ambiguity, a disciplinary ethos emerges that envisions itself as mission practice against an empty past and writes itself through a mix of applied sociology and romanticized narrative" (p. 146). In other words, to account for its criticality gerontology cannot rely solely on its protective and positive mandate to liberate aging and older people from an ageist world, if it neglects to engage the theories and theorists it invokes in theoretically sophisticated ways. This not only romanticizes the narrative of gerontology's development but can also justify weak theoretical and historical approaches. Rather, we need to extend critical ideas to new areas in aging studies while being wary of relegating critical status to the scholarly politics of a benevolent "mission practice."

On the other hand, these exercises reveal that gerontological criticality is shaped by a destabilizing pattern unrelated to its horizon of critical positions. It seems that the more critical gerontologists attempt to "discipline" (or multi-discipline) the sub-field by refining its theories of stratification, exchange, social construction, feminism, and political economy, the less stable and more open critical gerontology becomes. In my view, it is this theoretical instability and indeterminacy that articulates gerontological criticality; that is, ideas become critical when they overflow their contextual boundaries, resist theoretical stasis, and accommodate emancipatory projects aside from professional pronouncements about their value and utility. Indeed, the critical force of ideas has much to do with the unpredictable life of the ideas themselves and the careers of those who conceive them, areas to which this chapter now turns.

## II. INTELLECTUAL FIELDWORK AND THE LIFE OF IDEAS

While social theory appears confined within the covers of texts, biographical or genealogical treatments depict a more contingent and political story about social theory as a form of practice, especially where professional and intellectual worlds meet. The crises and experiments that produce theoretical knowledge involve material contexts where ideas emerge, travel, and mutate. There are many examples in the theoretical traditions to which gerontologists look for inspiration. Antonio Gramsci's *Prison Notebooks* would not have existed without the covert work and risks taken by his partner Giulia and her sister Tatiania while Gramsci was imprisoned (de Lauretis, 1987). Max and Marianne Weber wrote and spoke in Germany about religious cults, race relations, the rights of women, and the moral dilemmas of democratic society after their transformative visit to America in 1904 where they met W. E. B. Dubois and William James (Scaff, 1998). Talcott Parsons' analysis of professional and institutional relationships in his *The Structure of Social Action* (1937) reflects the work of Elton Mayo and Lawrence J. Henderson, the two Harvard researchers in the 1930s with whom Parsons worked and whose Rockefeller-funded program on industrial hazards linked professional sociology to medical and industrial know-how (Buxton & Turner, 1992). Early twentieth-century urban sociology developed with Georg Simmel and Louis Wirth because Simmel lived in central Berlin, the largest metropolis in Europe, when he wrote "The Metropolis and Mental Life" in 1903 and other urban papers, and Wirth lived and worked in bustling, multicultural, and agonistic Chicago when he wrote "Urbanism as a Way of Life" in 1938.

Similarly, there is a great deal to learn about the making of gerontological theory from the lives of its leaders; for example, Bernice Neugarten's account of her career (Neugarten, 1988) or Nathan Shock's intellectual history (Baker & Achenbaum, 1992). Gerontological historians W. Andrew Achenbaum (1995) and Thomas R. Cole (1992, 1993) also revisit the biographies of pioneering gerontologists Elie Metchnikoff and G. Stanley Hall to explain how they approached problems of aging with more intellectual curiosity, interdisciplinary boldness, and philosophical imagination than those who followed. The political lives of gerontological thinkers certainly play a role. For instance, Robert N. Butler, during a housing dispute in 1968 when he was Chair of the District of Columbia Advising Committee on Aging, introduced the idea of "ageism" to signal the widespread bigotry and injustices faced by older persons (Butler, 1969, 1990). While Butler went on to become the first director of the American National Institute on Aging in 1976, ageism has joined racism and sexism as a valuable critical sociological term.

These are not just biographical details; they illustrate the lived and practical realities behind the social and theoretical questions that we continue to ask today. In a related and very relevant sense sociologist Pierre Bourdieu claims that much of what he does as a theorist can be conceptualized as "fieldwork in philosophy," a phrase he borrows from philosopher John Austin (1990a). Philosophical fieldwork has two aspects. First, it is a way of discovering how sociological ideas are composites of different sources and sites. For example, Bourdieu admits his own notion of *habitus* echoes strongly in the works of Hegel, Husserl, Weber, Durkheim, and Mauss (p. 12). *Habitus* is a complex mode of socialization that inscribes structural relations into the personal and bodily lifeways of different subjects. To write about it, however, Bourdieu deliberately takes a philosophical ethnographic path to see *habitus* as a compromise between phenomenology, Marxism, and structuralism. Second, for Bourdieu, the philosophical or intellectual fieldworker who traces ideas to the source-worlds of their thinkers, also discovers the dynamic qualities of the ideas themselves. Thus Bourdieu believes that studying theory as a practice and closing the gap between lived and abstracted worlds are crucial to understanding and using theory effectively, reflexively, and critically.

The work of Berkeley anthropologist Paul Rabinow is a good illustration. Rabinow combines aspects of Bourdieu's philosophical fieldwork with Foucault's ideas on the power/knowledge foundations of modern forms of truth. Rabinow then ethnographically traces the theoretical components associated with the Human Genome Project in his book, *Making PCR: The Story of Biotechnology* (1996). In an earlier historical text, *French Modern: Norms and Forms of the Social Environment* (1989), Rabinow sketches out the spatializing and professionalizing practices through which *reason* circulated in the making of French modernity in the nineteenth century. Here, along with the police and the state's bureaucracies, the philosophical enterprise of reason and related quasi-philosophical sociologies created the enduring political problems of "the social." Likewise, Barbara Marshall conceptually follows "the travels of gender" as a way of understanding sociology's sexualization of modernity (2001, p. 98).

If we take Bourdieu's attitude of philosophical fieldwork back to explore critical gerontological theory, apart from the weaknesses of its multidisciplinary rhetoric, identification with radical traditions, and "mission" practices to liberate old age, what kind of alternative story about criticality might we find?

## III. "THE GERSCHENKRON EFFECT" AND THE NOMADIC QUALITIES OF CRITICAL GERONTOLOGY

At first glance, the overall ethnographic story of critical thinking in gerontology would appear to be a case of what Pierre Bourdieu calls "The Gerschenkron Effect." Alexander Gerschenkron was the Russian economic historian who explained that capitalism was unique in Russia because it arrived so late relative to Western Europe. By analogy, Bourdieu suggests that the social sciences "owe a great number of their characteristics and their difficulties to the fact that they too only got going a lot later than the others, so that, for example, they can use consciously or unconsciously the model of more advanced sciences in order to simulate scientific rigour" (1990b, p. 37). For Bourdieu, sociology's characteristics are due in part to the "lateness" of its advancement as a discipline and its problems in translating the precision and (assumed) consistency of the hard sciences into the social field. Similarly, one can see that the gerontological study of aging, in its embrace of Marxist political economy and related critical models, has theoretically lagged behind the other major human sciences which had long ago elaborated such models only to repudiate them during the 1980s and 1990s in favor of other perspectives. Indeed, one advantage gerontology has had in developing half a century behind the major social sciences, and thus trailing in critical and theoretical maturity, is that it can recuperate their theoretical innovations unburdened by their disciplinary constraints.

However, as social gerontology enters its critical phase, it is only partially in the time warp of the "The Gerschenkron Effect" since such an effect is really a feature of *before-the-fall* rather than *after-the-fall* theories, to return to my earlier discussion. In other words, *before-the-fall* theories such as Marxism are still very much with us but they are based on the general project of disciplinary progress, unity of knowledge, and universality of representation. By contrast, *after-the-fall* theoretical formations derive their criticality less from a cohesive disciplinarity than from the creative tension effected by the interplay of plural and dislocated discursive fragments. In this sense, contemporary criticality has been structured in the shadow of the postmodern fracturing of the moral and intellectual foundations of modern knowledge formations. This postmodern fracturing features in a number of intellectual contexts, such as François Lyotard's attack on modernity's "master-narratives" (1984), feminist critiques of biased "malestream-ism" across intellectual traditions, Foucaultian subversions of institutionalized knowledges as stratagems of power, and university programs that engage in poststructuralist renunciations of Western canons and methodologies. Social gerontology's theoretical transformation, in its political economy and critical developments during the last two decades, therefore, may be an interesting case of how critical theory in general operates in an *after-the-fall* sort of way. In brief, the discourse of critical gerontology pragmatically recombines *before-the-fall* fragments to recast formerly uncritical ways of knowing. And this process, rather than through multidisciplinary studies alone, is how and where critical gerontology is becoming a promising new genre that challenges mainstream gerontology.

To refine and speculate further on the dynamics of critical gerontology in the terms presented above, the discussion shifts to the work of French philosophers' Gilles Deleuze and Félix Guattari, in particular their ideas about *nomad science* and *minor literature*. Deleuze and Guattari are members of the wider poststructuralist camp that has celebrated the fall of Marxist and psychoanalytical meta-theory (which Deleuze considers to be an "intellectual bureaucracy"). However, their own way of radicalizing critical thinking is germane to our concerns with gerontological criticality.

*Nomad science* is a term developed by Deleuze and Guattari in *A Thousand Plateaus*, where they envision distinct "nomad" and "state (or royal)" sciences, separated by a "constantly moving borderline." State science perpetually appropriates the contents of nomad science, while nomad science "continually cuts the contents of royal science loose" (1987, p. 367). State science reproduces state power through the formalization of universal laws and the separation of intellectual from manual labour, as was the case of Gothic architecture. In contrast, nomad science, "which presents itself as an art as much as a technique" (p. 369), is heterogeneous, flowing, discontinuous, indefinite, ambulatory, and potentially radical in its undoing of state science, as was the case of the practices of medieval building associations and guilds. Deleuze and Guattari define the two kinds of science by way of historical example. For instance, differential calculus, had only parascientific status and was labeled a "Gothic hypothesis;" royal science only accorded it the value of a convenient convention or a well-rounded fiction. The great State mathematicians did their best to improve its status, but precisely on condition that all the dynamic, nomadic notions—such as becoming, heterogeneity, infinitesimal, passage to the limit, continuous variation—be eliminated and civil, static, and ordinal rules be imposed upon it. (1987, p. 363)

Another case is bridge-building in eighteenth-century France, where roadways (royal science) "were under a well-centralized administration while bridges [nomad science] were still the object of active, dynamic and collective experimentation" (1987, p. 365). Hence bridge-building became subordinated to the State and subsumed under its architectural and administrative authorities. In these and their other historical examples, Deleuze and Guattari maintain that:

In the field of interaction of the two sciences, the ambulant [nomad] sciences confine themselves to *inventing problems* whose solution is tied to a whole set of collective, nonscientific activities but whose *scientific solution* depends, on the contrary, on royal science and the way it has transformed the problem by introducing it into its theorematic apparatus and its organization of work. (1987, p. 374)

The distinction between state and nomad science is paralleled by one between *major* and *minor* languages which Deleuze and Guattari formulate in their work on Franz Kafka (1986, 1990). Major language is homogenizing and tries to stabilize the relationships among meanings, grammatical structures, literary figures, and national subjects. Minor language disrupts major language by creatively using non-major terms and forms of expression, politicizing literature, and inventing new genres. In turn, minor writing becomes revolutionary because it allows marginalized peoples to articulate their contradictory relationship to major cultures in a collective fashion. Hence, Kafka, in mixing Czech and Yiddish with German, develops a minor language in his writing that challenges the major status of German. In theorizing Kafka's work, Deleuze and Guattari praise the minoritarian status of his writing, saying that "there is nothing that is major or revolutionary except the minor" (1990, p. 67) since minor writing provides an escape for language. The authors advise their readers not to "dream" about major writing, but to "create the opposite dream: know how to create a becoming-minor" (1990, p. 68). Furthermore, according to Ronald Bogue, minor languages act "as a literature that has an immediately social and political function; that fosters collective rather than individual utterances; and that uses a language 'with a strong coefficient of deterritorialization'" (1989, p. 116). Hence, a language or a theoretical discourse whose sources are nomadic and minor, and whose form is incomplete and lateral, gains in criticality what it loses in stability and majoritarian legitimation (see Patton, 2000).

The Deleuzoguattarian (Bogue's term, 1989, p. 108) position on nomadic and minor discourses is unique because it suggests that *after-the-fall* theoretical ideas and fragments can be critically empowering without resorting to their reorganization along the disciplinary lines of *before-the-fall* schools of thought. Such ideas and fragments can be brought to bear on new investigative areas traditionally regarded as minor and peripheral to dominant fields, and enhance their critical stature and social importance. Examples have been the study of accounting, nursing, the history of statistics, and urban planning. Social gerontology is also such an area because it developed its critical incarnation first through its openness to Marxist political economy and feminism, and later by adding other theoretical fragments to open a critical thought-space for the study of age. But what continues to fill this space does not follow any particular agenda since the nomadic filling of this space is the agenda. Thus, critical gerontological projects and texts appear rather messy (Katz, 2000a; Weiland, 2000). They are amalgams of seemingly multidisciplinary but fragmented collections of often unrelated research. Their chapters range from empirical biological and psychological studies, to basic political economy investigations, to cultural speculations on the postmodern life course. This was clearly the case in the development of critical gerontology during the 1980s and early 1990s. For example, *The Journal of Aging Studies* in its editorial policy announces that "it highlights innovation and critique—new directions in general—regardless of theoretical or methodological orientation, or academic discipline." In *Critical Perspectives on Aging,* editor Carroll Estes says that the political economy perspective draws on "all varieties of neo-Weberian and neo-Marxist theoretical developments" (1991, p. 21). The critical work begun in the humanities also took aboard plural and heterogeneous theoretical elements from cultural and literary studies in order to portray the plural and heterogeneous realities of the human life course.

Hence, arguments leveled at framing the constitution of critical gerontology as a special theoretical intervention are difficult to make. Jan Baars, in his paper "The Challenge of Critical Gerontology: The Problem of Social Constitution," tries to formalize critical gerontology by stating:

> Critical gerontology can be understood as a study of aging that takes methodological problems seriously but doesn't *restrict* its criticism to such issues. It includes in its critical analyses normative questions, material interests, the functioning of gerontology itself and other factors that are regarded by the mainstream as only of 'contextual' importance. (1991, p. 221)

But Baars misses a point, which is that critical gerontology's criticality does not derive from the coherent, disciplinary, and scholastic attributes characteristic of *before-the-fall* paradigms. Rather, and despite the haphazard and eclectic textual organizations of critical gerontology, criticality is an accumulative effect of deterritorialized political economy, cultural theoretical, and related remnants, which are fractured, diluted, transfigured, and reordered to create a critical resonance within gerontological studies.

Bourdieu, Deleuze, and Guattari offer an active theoretical model where ideas live, mobilize, and nomadically congregate in minor discourses to produce radical critiques of state and major systems of representation. Their work implies that the fragmentation of meta-theory need not be apolitical, ineffective, or permanently and postmodernly crisis-ridden, and that the "fall" of major social science theories can also theoretically revitalize other minor areas. In the process, peripheral areas such as gerontology can and do become important critical zones through which new ideas flow against the grain of scientific tradition and the status of theory itself (see Gubrium & Wallace, 1990), and where new theoretical inquiries into the social construction of aging in late capitalist society are raised. In our case the demographic changes effected by growing aging populations in Western society are set to transform every social institution from the family to the state and resonate through every social and political register. Sorting out the prospects and problems caused by these changes will require both critically powerful theoretical ideas and a strong sense of how they can be sustained in the gerontological field. In the same way G. Stanley Hall in writing *Senescence: The Last Half of Life* (1922) struggled to understand old age by combining elements from poetry, fiction, psychology, religion, ethnography, and autobiographies, today critical thinking continues to be an open exchange between fields of thought, practice, and imagination. When Simon Biggs explains social policy from a narrative perspective (2001), Julia Twigg examines eldercare "bodywork" and bathing by way of cultural studies of the body (2000), Russell, Hill, and Basser question health promotion programs through critical discourse analysis (1996), and Victor Marshall rethinks the concept of "case study" from a reflective and interpretive position (1999b), they along with the other critical gerontologists discussed in this chapter join Hall's legacy in making gerontology an inventive thought-space where theoretical solutions to the complexities of an aging society can identified and advanced.

## CONCLUSIONS

W. Andrew Achenbaum agrees that "'critical gerontology' shapes some investigations of ageing-related problems," but he cautions that "its influence thus far has been marginal" (1997, p. 17). The reasons behind this marginality are not simply intellectual. The predominance of biomedically-driven funding policies, the privatization of health care resources, the priorities of corporate and pharmaceutical research, and the popularity of an alarmist demography that blames growing aging populations for the fiscal collapse of social programs, all contribute to the marginalization of critical thought. At the same time, much gerontological research is increasingly affiliated with governmental projects to *responsibilize* a new senior citizenry to care for itself in the wake of neoliberal programs that divest

Western welfare states of their health, educational, and domestic life course commitments and extend their political power to new areas of micro-social management and community affairs (Katz, 2000b). Examples are certain health promotion and risk-management campaigns, lifestyle and activity regimes, and self-improvement and lifelong learning programs. The HMOs (Health Management Organizations) in the United States are the most obvious illustration of these forces, but they are also becoming more influential in countries with more socialized public service traditions as well, such as Britain (Bunton, Nettleton, & Burrows, 1995; Gilleard & Higgs, 1998) and Canada (Broad & Antony, 1999). Thus, social conditions challenge gerontological criticality today just as they did 10 years ago when Carroll Estes wrote, "academic gerontology is in danger of 'selling its soul' to mindless, theory less positivism without retaining or regenerating the reflexivity that is essential to the resurgence of the 'gerontological imagination'" (1992, p. 60). This chapter has argued that, to counter the *danger* of a soul-less, mind-less, and theory-less gerontology, we need to recognize gerontology's critical and practical configurations and spaces (however marginal and minor), and link them to the boundary-crossing nomads, knowledge-hybridizing practitioners, and intellectual fieldworkers who would imagine new forms of expertise and advocacy for a new age. Understanding the internal strengths of critical gerontology as a resourceful thought-space is key to accomplishing this task and tackling the political and ideological forces that govern aging and old age in the twenty-first century.

## ACKNOWLEDGMENTS

I wish to thank Trent University's Committee on Research for its support of this research. A preliminary essay exploring some of the ideas in this chapter appeared in *The Discourse of Sociological Practice,* Volume 3, Issue 1, 2000.

## REFERENCES

Achenbaum, W. A. (1995). *Crossing frontiers: Gerontology emerges as a science.* New York: Cambridge University Press.

Achenbaum, W. A. (1997). Critical gerontology. In A. Jamieson, S. Harper, & C. Victor (Eds.), *Critical Approaches to Ageing and Later Life* (pp. 16-26). Buckingham: Open University Press.

Baars, J. (1991). The challenge of critical gerontology: The problem of social constitution. *Journal of Aging Studies, 5*(3), 219-243.

Baker, G. T., & Achenbaum, W. A. (1992). A historical perspective on research on the biology of aging from Nathan W. Shock. *Experimental Gerontology, 27,* 261-273.

Basting-Davis, A. D. (1998). *The stages of age: Performing age in contemporary American culture.* Ann Arbor: University of Michigan Press.

Bengtson, V. L., Burgess, E. O, & Parrott, T. M. (1997). Theory, explanation, and a third generation of theoretical development in social gerontology. *Journal of Gerontology, 52B*(2), S72-S88.

Bengtson, V. L., Parrott, T. M., & Burgess, E. O. (1996). Progress and pitfalls in gerontological theorizing. *The Gerontologist, 36*(6), 768-722.

Bengtson, V. L., & Schaie, K. W. (Eds.) (1999). *Handbook of theories of aging.* New York: Springer.

Biggs, S. (1999). *The mature imagination,* Buckingham: Open University Press;

Biggs, S. (2001). Toward critical narrativity. Stories of aging in contemporary social policy. *Journal of Aging Studies, 15*(4), 303-316.

Birren, J., & Bengtson, V. L. (Eds.). (1988). *Emergent theories of aging.* New York: Springer.

Blaikie, A. (1999). *Ageing and popular culture.* Cambridge: Cambridge University Press.

Bogue, R. (1989). *Deleuze and Guattari.* London & New York: Routledge.

Bond, J., Biggs, R., & Coleman, P. (1990). The Study of Aging. In J. Bond & P. Coleman (Eds.), *Aging in society: An introduction to social gerontology* (pp. 17-47). London: Sage.

Bourdieu, P. (1990a). "Fieldwork in philosophy" (Interview). In *In other words: Towards a reflexive sociology* (pp. 3-33). Stanford: Stanford University Press.

Bourdieu, P. (1990b). Landmarks. In *In other words: Essays towards a reflexive sociology* (pp. 34-55). Stanford: Stanford University Press.

Broad, D., & Antony, W. (1999). *Citizens or consumers? Social policy in a market society.* Halifax: Fernwood.

Brown, C. V. (1998). *Women, feminism, and aging.* New York: Springer.

Bunton, R., Nettleton, S., & Burrows, R. (Eds.) (1995). *The sociology of health promotion: Critical analysis of consumption, lifestyle and risk.* London & New York: Routledge.

Butler, R. N. (1969). Age-Ism: Another form of bigotry. *The Gerontologist, 9,* 143-466.

Butler, R. N. (1990). A disease called ageism. *Journal of the American Geriatrics Society, 38,* 178-180.

Buxton, W., & Turner, S. (1992). From education to expertise: Sociology as a "profession." In T. C. Halliday & M. Janowitz (Eds.), *Sociology and its publics* (pp. 373-407). Chicago: University of Chicago Press.

Cohen, L. (1994). Old age: Cultural and critical perspectives. *Annual Review of Anthropology, 23,* 137-158.

Cohen, L. (1998). *No aging in India: Alzheimer's, the bad family, and other modern things.* Berkeley: University of California Press.

Cole, T. R. (1992). *The journey of life: A cultural history of aging in America.* Cambridge: Cambridge University Press.

Cole, T. R. (1993). The prophecy of *senescence:* G. Stanley Hall and the reconstruction of old age in twentieth century America. In W. K. Schaie & W. A. Achenbaum (Eds.), *Societal impact on aging: Historical perspectives* (pp. 165-181). New York: Springer.

Cole, T. R., Achenbaum, W. A., Jakobi, P. L., & Kastenbaum, R. (Eds.). (1993). *Voices and visions of aging: Toward a critical gerontology.* New York: Springer.

Cole, T. R., & Ray, R. E. (Eds.). (2000). *Handbook of the humanities and aging* (2nd ed.). New York: Springer.

de Lauretis, T. (1987). Gramsci notwithstanding, or, the left hand of history. In T. de Lauretis (Ed.), *Technologies of gender* (pp. 84-94). Bloomington and Indianapolis: Indiana University Press.

Deleuze, G., & Guattari, F. (1986). *Kafka: For a minor literature* (D. Polan, Trans.). Minneapolis: University of Minnesota Press.

Deleuze, G., & Guattari, F. (1987). *A thousand plateaus* (B. Massumi, Trans.). Minneapolis: University of Minnesota Press.

Deleuze, G., & Guattari, F. (1990). What is a minor literature? In R. Ferguson, M. Gever, T. T. Minh-ha, & C. West (Eds.), *Out there: Marginalization and contemporary cultures* (pp. 59-69). Cambridge, MA: MIT Press.

Estes, C. L. (1979). *The aging enterprise.* San Francisco: Jossey-Bass.

Estes, C. L. (1991). The new political economy of aging: Introduction and critique. In M. Minkler & C. L. Estes (Eds.), *Critical perspectives on aging: The political and moral economy of growing old* (pp. 19-36). Amityville, NY: Baywood.

Estes, C. L., Binney, E. A., & Culbertson, R. A. (1992). The gerontological imagination: Social influences on the development of gerontology, 1945-present. *International Journal of Aging and Human Development, 35*(1), 49-65.

Featherstone, M., & Hepworth, M. (1991). The mask of ageing and the postmodern life course. In M. Featherstone, M. Hepworth, & B. S. Turner (Eds.), *The body: Social process and cultural theory* (pp. 371-389). London: Sage.

Featherstone, M., & Wernick, A. (Eds.) (1995). *Images of aging: Cultural representations of later life.* London & New York: Routledge.

Gilleard, C., & Higgs, P. (1998). Old people as users and consumers of healthcare: A third age rhetoric for a fourth age reality? *Ageing and Society, 18*(2), 233-248.

Gilleard, C., & Higgs, P. (2000). *Cultures of ageing: Self, citizen and the body.* Harlow: Prentice-Hall.

Green, B. (1993). *Gerontology and the construction of old age.* Hawthorne, NY: Aldine de Gruyter.

Gubrium, J. F., & Wallace, J. B. (1990). Who theorises age? *Ageing and Society, 10*(2), 131-149.

Gullette, M. M. (1997). *Declining to decline: Cultural combat and the politics of midlife.* Charlottesville: University Press of Virginia.

Gullette, M. M. (2000). Age studies as cultural studies. In T. R. Cole & R. E. Ray (Eds.), *Handbook of the humanities and aging* (2nd ed., pp. 214-234). New York: Springer.

Habermas, J. (1991). *The theory of communicative action, Volume 2: Lifeworld and system: A critique of functionalist reason.* Cambridge: Polity Press.

Hall, G. S. (1922). *Senescence: The last half of life.* New York: D. Appleton.

Hendricks, J. (1992). Generations and the generation of theory in social gerontology. *International Journal of Aging and Human Development, 35*(1), 31-47.

Hepworth, M. (2000). *Stories of ageing.* Buckingham: Open University Press.

Hockey, J., & James, A. (1993). *Growing up and growing old: Ageing and dependency in the life course.* London: Sage.

Katz, S. (1996). *Disciplining old age: The formation of gerontological knowledge.* Charlottesville: University Press of Virginia.

Katz, S. (1999). Charcot's older women: Bodies of knowledge at the interface of aging studies and women's studies. In K. Woodward (Ed.), *Figuring age: Women, bodies, generations* (pp. 112-127). Bloomington and Indianapolis: Indiana University Press.

Katz, S. (2000a). Reflections on the gerontological handbook. In T. R. Cole & R. E. Ray (Eds.), *Handbook of the humanities and aging* (2nd ed., pp. 405-418). New York: Springer.

Katz, S. (2000b). Busy bodies: Activity, aging and the management of everyday life. *Journal of Aging Studies, 14*(2), 135-152.

Kenyon, G. M., Birren, J. E., & Schroots, J. F. (Eds.). (1991). *Metaphors of aging in science and the humanities.* New York: Springer.

Laws, G. (1995). Understanding ageism: Lessons from feminism and postmodernism. *The Gerontologist, 35*(1), 112-118.

Lynott, R. J., & Lynott, P. P. (1996). Tracing the course of theoretical development in the sociology of aging. *The Gerontologist, 36*(6), 749-760.

Lyotard, J-F. (1984). *The postmodern condition: A report on knowledge* (G. Bennington & B. Massumi, Trans.). Minneapolis: University of Minnesota Press.

Marshall, B. (2001). Much ado about gender: A conceptual travelogue. *Advances in Gender Research* (Special Issue, An International Feminist Challenge to Theory), *5,* 97-117.

Marshall, V. (1978). Notes for a radical gerontology. *International Journal of Aging and Human Development, 9*(2), 163-175.

Marshall, V. (1999a). Analyzing social theories of aging. In V. L. Bengtson & K. W. Schaie (Eds.), *Handbook of theories of aging* (pp. 434-455). New York: Springer.

Marshall, V. (1999b). Reasoning with case studies: Issues of an aging workforce. *Journal of Aging Studies, 13*(4), 377-389.

Minkler, M. (1996). Critical perspectives on ageing: New challenges for gerontology. *Ageing and Society, 16*(4), 467-487.

Minkler, M. (1999). Introduction. In M. Minkler & C. L. Estes (Eds.), *Critical gerontology: Perspectives from political and moral economy* (pp. 1-13). Amityville, NY: Baywood.

Minkler, M., & C. L. Estes (Eds.). (1984). *Readings in the political economy of aging.* Amityville, NY: Baywood.

Minkler, M., & C. L. Estes (Eds.). (1991). *Critical perspectives on aging: The political and moral economy of growing old.* Amityville, NY: Baywood.

Minkler, M., & C. L. Estes (Eds.) (1999). *Critical gerontology: Perspectives from political and moral economy.* Amityville, NY: Baywood.

Moody, H. R. (1988a). *Abundance of life: Human development policies for an aging society.* New York: Columbia University Press.

Moody, H. R. (1988b). Toward a critical gerontology: The contribution of the humanities to theories of aging. In J. Birren & V. L. Bengtson (Eds.), *Emergent theories of aging* (pp. 19-40). New York: Springer.

Moody, H. R. (1993). Overview: What is critical gerontology and why is it important? In T. R. Cole, W. A. Achenbaum, P. L. Jakobi, & R. Kastenbaum (Eds.), *Voices and visions of aging: Toward a critical gerontology* (pp. xv-xli). New York: Springer.

Myles, J. (1984). *Old age in the welfare state.* Boston: Little, Brown.

Neugarten, B. L. (1988). The aging society and my academic life. In M. W. Riley (Ed.), *Sociological lives* (pp. 91-106). Newbury Park: Sage.

Ogburn, W. F. (1957). Cultural lag as theory. *Sociology and Social Research, 41,* 167-174.

Olson, L. K. (1982). *The political economy of aging: The state, private power and social welfare.* New York: Columbia University Press.

Parsons, T. [1937] (1968). *The structure of social action.* New York: Free Press.

Patton, P. (2000). *Deleuze and the political.* London & New York: Routledge.

Phillipson, C. (1982). *Capitalism and the construction of old age.* London and Basingstoke: Macmillan.

Phillipson, C. (1998). *Reconstructing old age: New agendas in social theory and practice.* London: Sage.

Phillipson, C., & Walker, A. (1987). The case for a critical gerontology. In S. Di Gregorio (Ed.), *Social gerontology: New directions* (pp. 1-15). London: Croom Helm.

Rabinow, P. (1989). *French modern: Norms of forms of the social environment.* Cambridge, MA: The MIT Press.

Rabinow, P. (1996). *Making PCR: A story of biotechnology.* Chicago: University of Chicago Press.

Ray, R. E. (1996). A postmodern perspective on feminist gerontology. *The Gerontologist, 36*(5), 674-680.

Ray, R. E. (1999). Researching to transgress: The need for critical feminism in gerontology. *Journal of Women & Aging, 11*(2/3), 171-184.

Riley, M. W. (1994). *Structural lag: society's failure to provide meaningful opportunities, in work, family and leisure.* New York: John Wiley.

Russell, C., Hill, B., & Basser, M. (1996). Identifying needs among "at risk" older people: Does anyone here speak health promotion? In V. Minichiello, N. Chappell, H. Kendig, & A. Walker (Eds.), *Sociology of aging: International perspectives* (pp. 378-393). Melbourne: Thoth.

Scaff, L. (1998). The "cool objectivity of sociation": Max Weber and Marianne Weber in America. *History of the Human Sciences, 11*(2), 61-82.

Scambler, G. (Ed.). (2001). *Habermas, critical theory and health.* London & New York: Routledge.

Squier, S. M. (1995). Reproducing the posthuman body: Ectogenic fetus, surrogate mother, pregnant man. In J. Halberstam & I. Livingston (Eds.), *Posthuman bodies* (pp. 113-132). Bloomington and Indianapolis: Indiana University Press.

Twigg, J. (2000). *Bathing—The body and community care.* London & New York: Routledge.

Walker, A. (1981). Towards a political economy of old age. *Ageing and Society 1*(1):73-94.

Weiland, S. (2000). Social science toward the humanities: Speaking of lives in the study of aging. In T. R. Cole & R. E. Ray (Eds.), *Handbook of the Humanities and Aging* (2nd ed., pp. 235-257). New York: Springer.

Woodward, K. (1991). *Aging and its discontents: Freud and other fictions.* Bloomington and Indianapolis: Indiana University Press.

Woodward, K. (Ed.). (1999). *Figuring age: Women, bodies, generations.* Bloomington and Indianapolis: Indiana University Press.

# CHAPTER 2

# The Perils and Possibilities of Theory

## Ruth E. Ray

A 1972 cartoon by Jules Feiffer, reprinted in Warren Farrell's *The Liberated Man* (1974), characterizes the perils and possibilities of theory during the second wave of the American feminist movement. In a series of frames, Feiffer tells this version of feminism: in the beginning was oppression, which led to analysis and consciousness-raising, which led to rage, which led to rebellion, which led to theorizing, which produced "hokum," which led, in the end, back to oppression. The irony, of course, is that feminist "liberation" led only to more oppression. Feiffer's dark humor resonates even more at the turn of the twenty-first century. As the feminist activism of the 1960s and 1970s gave way to the postmodern intellectualizing of the 1980s and 1990s, the goal of social change receded. There are important lessons in this story for gerontologists, feminist and otherwise, looking to "theory" for the development of social gerontology. In this chapter, I tell another story of feminism that ends on a more positive, revisionist note, one that will be instructive for gerontologists looking to critical theory for new ways of researching and teaching.

As background to this story, we must first distinguish between "theory" and "critical theory." When James Birren made the statement that gerontology was "data rich and theory poor," (1999) he was referring primarily to theory with a capital T—an overarching system of thought that seeks to explain the meaning of discrete occurrences and observations (data). Although gerontology was built on a foundation of Theories—disengagement theory, activity theory, life-span development theory—Birren was reacting to what he perceived as an over-emphasis on scientific data gathering to the exclusion of interpretation and meaning-making across data sets. He saw the intellectual work in gerontology as primarily additive, as opposed to integrative, and argued that gerontology needs a

33

better balance between scholars who amass "findings" and those who connect and explain the significance of those findings. Birren is surely right in his assessment, but he didn't go far enough; gerontology also needs research that questions the findings *and* the integrative gestures, in other words, critical theory. Lynott and Lynott define critical theory as a critique of "the so-called 'facts' of aging themselves, focusing on the socially constructive and ideological features of age conceptualizations . . ." (1996, p. 749). Critical theory, then, is "not so much the recognition of theory as a reflection of that recognition itself, being metatheoretical" (p. 749). Critical theories (feminism, Marxism, etc.) stand in opposition to established ways of knowing and making knowledge, focusing on what is missing, ignored, and denied in them. Gerontology needs theory to construct meanings, but it also needs critical theory to remind us that all theories are partial, that other meanings are always possible, that meaning-making itself is an exercise in power and authority, and that we promote some meanings at the expense of others. Without critical theory, we become complacent (or even worse, arrogant) in terms of our findings, explanations, and methods of inquiry; we lose perspective on the world outside our belief systems.

But there are limits to critical theory. The sobering lesson in Feiffer's characterization is that critical theory itself is potentially oppressive. It can be a means of discovery and empowerment or another dominating belief system. It can be a way of thinking and talking that encourages open-mindedness and inclusiveness, or it can intimidate and exclude. It can clarify or obfuscate. Unfortunately, obfuscating discourse ("hokum") is what critical theorists in academe often produce. This is because they have lost sight of the proper "ends" of theory, namely critical awareness and social change.

My purpose in this chapter is to work against this grain, suggesting how critical theory, starting with feminist criticism, might be used in the service of empowerment and transformation in gerontology.

## THEORY AS DISCOURSE

My story begins with the premise, established fairly convincingly by Foucault and other postmodern thinkers, that all theories, critical or otherwise, are discourses. As sociolinguist James Paul Gee describes them, discourses are "ways of being in the world; they are forms of life which integrate words, acts, values, beliefs, attitudes and social identities as well as gestures, glances, body postures and clothes. Whole systems of thought and behavior are embedded in the linguistic aspects of Discourses" (2000, p. 538). Gee refers to discourses as "identity kits" because they come complete with "instructions on how to act, talk and often write, so as to take on a particular role that others will recognize" (p. 526).

Gee asserts that discourse is liberating, by which he means powerful and change-oriented, when it is "used as a 'metalanguage' (a set of meta-words, meta-values, meta-beliefs) for the critique of other [discourses] and the way they constitute us as persons and situate us in society" (p. 529). Liberating discourses "reconstitute us and resituate us." Feminist criticism has had this powerful effect on me personally and professionally, and for this reason I teach it to my students and use it to advance the agenda of critical gerontology (Ray, 1996, 1999, 2000).

It is important to note, however, that any critical theory, feminism included, is *potentially,* not *inherently,* liberating. Sometimes critical theorists, in pursuit of intellectual dominance and academic status, neglect to turn the critique onto themselves. They come to assume the superiority of their own discourse—the problem that Feiffer identified in the American feminist movement. The story of feminist arrogance is instructive for gerontologists at this juncture when critical gerontology is in the midst of developing its identity as a site of research and teaching.

## FEMINIST CRITICISM AS CAUTIONARY TALE

In a recent book entitled *Critical Condition,* literary scholar Susan Gubar (2002) surveys feminism at the turn of the twenty-first century and concludes that "feminist criticism has always been in the process of reinventing itself, and now we must reinvent it for the 21st century" (p. 8). This "reinventing" is necessary because, in its 35-year journey from social activism to scholarly enterprise, feminist criticism has become increasingly exclusionary and less relevant outside the academy. In short, "feminism as a political movement appears to be imperiled [at least by accounts in the popular American press] while the social problems it addresses remain intact" (p. 17). Within academe, the main issue for today's students and faculty is "how to gain the niche once monopolized by the Good Old Boys, but without turning into Old Boys . . ." (p. 107). In other words, we must learn to assume positions of power and authority without becoming oppressors ourselves. This speaks to the issue that Feiffer was raising 30 years ago.

In a chapter called "What Ails Feminist Criticism?" Gubar chronicles four periods in feminist literary criticism, three of which coincide with the development of critical gerontology. The first period, which began in the 1960s and was motivated by anger and a sense of injustice, is characterized by vigorous critique. Feminist writings functioned to undercut the universality of meaning, interpretation and knowledge-making and to introduce alternative scholarship and non-canonical texts into the curriculum. A similar period of critical gerontology began in the late 1970s and is characterized by the same kind of questions that dominated feminist criticism, only with "age" substituted for "gender": "(1) What is the nature of age and how can it be described; and (2) whose interests are served by thinking of age in particular ways . . . ?" (Lynott & Lynott, 1996, p. 749). The second period of feminist criticism, which began in the early 1970s, is characterized by the recovery of female literary traditions and the uncovering of gender-related standards of publication and reception. During this period, many new journals, book series, and presses were established to disseminate work in women's studies. Critical gerontologists have just entered this period of establishing their own venues for publication, including the *Journal of Critical Gerontology*. Although there is no *Journal of Feminist Gerontology*, there have been special issues of existing journals devoted to the subject (see, for example, vol. 7 of the *Journal of Aging Studies* and vol. 11 of the *Journal of Women and Aging*). The third period of feminist literary criticism, beginning in the 1980s, brought gender to bear on other categories of difference and emphasized overlapping oppressions—race, class, ethnicity, able-bodiedness—in the production and interpretation of texts. A few feminists have initiated a similar agenda in gerontology. Eleanor Stoller and Rose Gibson (1994), Collette Browne (1998) and Toni Calasanti (1999) have examined the overlapping oppressions of age, race, class, and gender and proposed research, policy, and practice agendas that start from the premise of social inequity. The fourth period of feminist literary criticism, in full flourish throughout the 1990s, was a time of metacritical dissension, marked by divisiveness and fragmentation within the movement itself. In their efforts to specialize and "gain the niche," feminist critics turned against each other and engaged in a sometimes viscious infighting. Gubar (2000) describes this turn as "churlish or cultish, stifling rather than nurturing, theoretically correct rather than liberating" (p. 130). In moving into this last period, many feminists lost sight of their common enterprise—to fight that which is dismissive or hostile toward the welfare of women and minorities—and instead fought discursive wars among themselves, co-opted by the very oppressive forces (exclusionary intellectualism, elitism, privileging, status-seeking, hierarchy-making) that feminists originally resisted in the name of liberation. Critical gerontologists have not yet moved into this period, and they need not, if they begin now to develop a common enterprise and keep the proper ends of theory in sight.

## THE ROLE OF CRITICAL GERONTOLOGY

What *is* the common agenda of critical gerontologists? What distinguishes us from other gerontologists? In an early formation, Harry R. Moody (1988, 1993) defines critical gerontology in terms of the oppositional stance of researchers, suggesting that critical gerontologists oppose the domination of conventional positivism and empiricism; oppose the domination of research, practice and policy by bureaucracy and the marketplace; cast suspicion on "the cozy idea that interest-group politics and value-free science promote well-being and progress for all" (1988, p. 295); uncover systems of domination and oppression; critique ideology and hidden interests; critique efforts to explain the natural and social world in order to control it; and rethink and revise, continually, their own critical foundations, as well as the foundations of mainstream gerontology (1988, p. 295).

Thomas R. Cole (1993), in his preface to *Voices and Visions of Aging*, the first edited collection on critical gerontology, characterizes critical gerontologists as possessed of two essential tendencies that work in tandem: critical thinking and a sense of social responsibility. He further sees critical gerontologists as role models for a kind of humanistic thinking that values uncertainty and instability over prediction and control:

> the "stock-in-trade" of the humanities—self-knowledge, historical understanding, imaginative communication, and critical appraisal of assumptions and values—can promote a more intellectually rigorous gerontology in several ways: *heuristically*, by offering new hypotheses for empirical inquiry; *critically*, by revealing values and power relations often concealed in existing methods and findings of empirical research; and *practically*, by offering reflection on the intentions and values realized by human actors in particular cultural settings. (1993, pp. vii-viii)

Both Moody, a philosopher, and Cole, a cultural historian, argue that critical gerontologists demonstrate wide-ranging thought and communication across historical periods, theories and disciplines, as well as a questioning, critical stance toward knowledge-making within gerontology as a field. This way of thinking and communicating is a central aspect of our common identity and our shared enterprise.

These behaviors and values are certainly shared by most feminists in gerontology (Bernard, Phillips, Machin, & Davies, 2000; Browne, 1998; Calasanti, 1999; Estes & Minkler, 1999; Gullette, 2000; Hooyman, 1999; Laws, 1995). I would take Cole's agenda further, however, and argue for a "values in action" approach to critical inquiry, where social change is the desired end to critical theorizing. From my perspective, the primary task of critical gerontologists is the search for emancipation from oppressive forces, in and out of academe, which dictate how we should think, research, write about, teach, and otherwise construct knowledge regarding age, aging, and age relations. By "emancipation" I mean freedom to use critical discourse on behalf of oppressed groups or "cultures of silence" (Freire, 1998), including the very young and the very old, the marginalized, the disenfranchised, and the dispossessed. By "emancipation," I also mean the pursuit of knowledge for empancipatory purposes. In a 1988 article, Moody draws on the Frankfurt school of critical theory to articulate a role for gerontologists that resonates with this feminist goal of emancipation:

> Theories cannot be constructed with moral indifference toward the practical horizon of their validation and application in human affairs. Put differently, any theory of aging that settles for less than a form of emancipatory knowledge runs the risk that knowledge gained . . . will be used for purposes that lead not to freedom but to new dominations, perhaps a domination exercised ever more skillfully by professionals, bureaucrats or policy makers. (1988, p. 26)

Moody provides a theoretical rationale for an emancipatory agenda in gerontology, but he does not go on to develop or pursue that agenda. I see the pursuit of emancipation as the primary role of feminists and other critical gerontologists in the next decade.

For me, the empancipatory agenda must entail the integration of feminism and other forms of critical thought, not just in research but in teaching the next generation of gerontologists. In my own search for integration, I have been inspired by the Brazilian educator Paulo Freire, who, in turn, was informed by numerous other critics and visionaries, including "Sarte and Mournier, Eric Fromm and Louis Althusser, Ortega y Gassett and Mao, Martin Luther King and Che Guevara, Unamuno and Marcuse" (Shaull, 1998, p. 13). I see Freire's theory of liberatory pedagogy, in conjunction with feminist critiques of knowledge-making and dissemination, as a means of advancing critical gerontology in the direction of social, as well as intellectual change (i.e., "emancipation" of thought and knowledge-making). I am thus calling for a fourth period in critical gerontology, one marked by theory-in-action, as the "right end" to theory.

Another word for theory-in-action is "praxis." Freire argued that, in all forms of social change, there must be a dialectical relationship between subjectivity (perception, feeling, response) and objectivity (objects of analysis), which produces "knowledge in solidarity with action, and vise versa." He defined "praxis" as "intellectual activism" or "active reflection." For Freire, any practice requires theory to illuminate it, but this theoretical reflection occurs *simultaneously with* action, not prior to it. Related to praxis is Freire's concept of the "authentic word." Authentic words are those which are converted to action; inauthentic words are "hokum," having no function beyond mere verbalism. They are stripped of action, unable to effect any change in the world. For Freire, "there is no true word that is not at the same time a praxis"; thus, "to speak a true word is to transform the world" (1998, p. 68).

If we agree with the characteristics assigned to critical gerotologists by Moody and Cole, and if we agree that a common goal for critical gerontology is emancipation, then we must conclude that the common enterprise for critical gerontologists is to transform the status quo. Such transformation must occur outside of academe, in the form of social policies and practices, as well as inside academe, in the form of teaching, research, and service. I focus in my final section on teaching, because it has been so under theorized in gerontology and is therefore ripe for a feminist Freirian revision.

## TOWARD AN EMANCIPATORY PEDAGOGY IN GERONTOLOGY

Teaching, like theorizing, either promotes conformity to the status quo or critical examination and transformation. Gerontologists with an emancipatory agenda would think of teaching, like research, as a form of resistance. How might we better structure our pedagogy along these lines? Freire and feminist critic bell hooks offer useful insights.

For Paulo Freire, the purpose of education at every level is at once existential and political: the vocation of humankind is to name, act upon, and transform the world, thereby moving toward a richer and fuller life individually and collectively. Every human being must be taught to "read the word and the world" critically and to interact dialogically. Such interaction is based on dialogue in egalitarian relationships conducted in order to name the world and to change it. Freire spent much of his life teaching Brazilian illiterates to "read" the social, economic, and political contradictions in their lives and to take action against the forces that oppressed them, not the least of which was illiteracy itself. Freire noted, however, that most educators are antidialogical: their teaching is based on the imposition of objectivism and the conquest of pre-formed knowledge. In contrast, he identified himself as a "radical" educator working against the "sectarian" educators who use propaganda—leftist or rightist—to dominate and silence students. Freire also contrasted "humanistic pedagogy," which liberates individuals and communities by promoting critical reflection and self-examination, with "humanitarian pedagogy," which, under the guise of good intention, is actually "false charity" because it encourages passivity and alienation and thereby embodies and sustains oppression (however unconsciously).

Freire's humanistic or emancipatory pedagogy follows a problem-posing method, where students "develop their power to perceive critically the way they exist in the world with which and in which they find themselves; they come to see the world not as a static reality, but as a reality in process, in transformation" (1998, p. 64). A problem-posing approach affirms that students, like all social and intellectual systems, are "in the process of becoming." As such, students work to develop their critical and historical consciousness, learning to see individual and local problems in their totality, as part of larger oppressive systems that operate in the world. The study of any subject, then, (including age and age relations) involves becoming conscious of one's place in the world and one's ability to intervene. The educator's role is to enter into dialogue with students and to offer ideas and thinking strategies which students then continue to use to teach themselves. Freire contrasts humanistic pedagogy with what he calls the "banking" method, which dominates nearly all schools and universities world-wide. This method is based on the premise that teachers "own" knowledge, which they "deposit" in students and expect later to "withdraw" in the form of examinations. "Instead of communicating, the teacher issues communiqués and makes deposits which the students patiently receive, memorize and repeat. . . . They do, it is true, have the opportunity to become collectors and catalogers of the things they store. But in the last analysis, it is the people themselves who are filed away through the lack of creativity, transformation and knowledge. . . ." (1998, p. 53). In sum, the banking method serves the status quo, while the problem-posing method works to challenge and change it.

Critical theorist Bell Hooks has integrated feminist criticism and Freire's problem-posing method, arguing that all teaching should be both critical *and* change-oriented. She models her own teaching on the strategies she learned in the Southern black schools of her childhood, where "our devotion to learning, to a life of the mind, was a counter-hegemonic act, a fundamental way to resist every strategy of white racist colonization" (1994, p. 2). In her teaching, Hooks tries to establish "education as the practice of freedom," by interrogating the racism in feminism itself and assisting students in developing a consciousness of overlapping oppressions. She argues, too, that emancipatory pedagogy must be "embodied" as well as intellectualized, reminding us that excitement is generated not only by critical thinking about ideas, but also by a keen interest in each other's lives and in improving the human condition outside the classroom. Combining Freire's dialogic method with a feminist emphasis on personal validation and community building, Hooks concludes that "there must be an ongoing recognition that everyone influences the classroom dynamic, that everyone contributes . . . [that] excitement is generated through collective effort" (1994, p. 8).

Our teaching of critical gerontology, following these examples, would itself be a critical gesture. It would invite students to collaborate with others of "difference"—especially older adults who experience overlapping oppressions—to examine problems of concern across generations and to propose solutions to those problems, worked out dialogically. More specifically, a critical or emancipatory pedagogy informed by both feminism and Freirean ideology would entail:

1. critical reading and writing of the word, the world, and one's own place in the world, especially in regards to age and age relations;
2. a problem-posing approach to learning;
3. an orientation toward both personal (existential) and social (political) transformation;
4. sustained efforts at raising students' consciousness about overlapping oppressions and their individual and social consequences;
5. an integration of experiential and scholarly ways of knowing; and
6. a focus on human connection, community, and dialogic interaction.

What might such a class look like? And how would it serve the common enterprise of critical gerontology?

For several years I have been developing my own emancipatory pedagogy, testing its limits and potential with undergraduate and graduate students. As an English professor, I do not teach gerontology as an academic subject, but I do teach many aspects of critical gerontology. In all of my classes, through readings, discussions, and writing assignments, students are called upon: to question the age ideologies and age identities that popular culture promotes; to engage in interactive dialogue with different "others," including older adults; to confront and, hopefully, learn to value alternative ways of thinking, knowing and behaving; to consider how age, race, class, ethnicity, and gender interact to affect our identities and social positions; and to become an integral part of a community of learners engaged in collective action (as opposed to the common classroom scenario in which a group of individuals pursue their own private agendas). This kind of pedagogy is potentially "emancipatory" for all concerned—students, teacher, and community partners.

An undergraduate writing class that I taught recently illustrates the basics of my pedagogy-in-progress. English 3010–Multimedia Writing met at a senior center near the university during the Fall, 2001 semester. Students and seniors worked together in teams to research and write scripts for Web cast and broadcast on a local radio program called SeniorVoice (see http://www.seniorvoice.org). The stated purpose of SeniorVoice, broadcast from the basement of an urban senior center dedicated to giving "voice" to minority elders, is to provide "opportunities for older Americans to express their concerns and interests by creating written, audio and visual messages for transmission through various media." Nine staff members from SeniorVoice, ranging in age from 55 to 85, participated in the class, including five African American women, three African American men, and one Caucasian woman. Their personal agendas were overtly activist; they wanted to help change students' attitudes toward age, as well as race and class, and to improve intergenerational relations. The 13 college students enrolled in the class represented the diversity of the student body at my university: they included one white female; three white males; one male, ethnicity unknown, but a practicing Sikh; three Arab women; one Arab man; three African American women; and one African American man. Students ranged in age from 19 to 22. I co-taught the class with the producer of SeniorVoice, a white male who is himself a senior citizen. I am a white female in mid-life (age 47). Together, we modeled a critical and collaborative pedagogy and assisted the 22 students in forming a learning community dedicated to producing change-oriented public radio.

My purpose here is merely to show how a feminist, Freirean critical pedagogy puts diverse people together, gives them problems to solve, and assists them in negotiating the conflicts that inevitably arise in the process. Take, for example, the case of one group from the class, consisting of two Arab students and two African American seniors, all female. Their final writing task was to research and produce (in the aftermath of the September 11 terrorist attacks on the World Trade Center in New York) a mini documentary on the subject of U.S. foreign policy in the Middle East. Besides their social, religious, political, and generational differences, the group also had to negotiate variations in writing and speaking ability, as well as considerable difference in the ways they "experienced" and processed conflicts in the Middle East (one of the students had fled to the United States with her family to escape the Israeli bombing of Beirut). These four women managed to produce an exemplary radio script which integrated solid academic research and personal experience; which drew on live interviews with local community members, as well as internet sources and historical data; which took audience and purpose into account, appealing to listeners across generations; and which drew on each team member's particular strengths. The learning process was transformative for the group members, each of whom developed a better sense of her own agency, and for all other class members, who learned from their example of dialogue and collaboration. Students gave this group a standing ovation upon hearing their final production, recognizing the amount of effort and attention that went into overcoming individual differences to generate a change-oriented documentary for public broadcast.

A feminist Freirean course in critical gerontology might include interactive, problem-solving activities of a similar kind, while introducing theories of aging along with feminist and other critiques of those theories. Critical reading and writing would figure prominently, with students encouraged to question and challenge the "word" about aging and age relations in their textbooks and the world at large (family interactions, media representations, institutional policies, etc.). A central task of this course would be to empower students with a sense of their own abilities to identify age-related social problems and to contribute to solving them. The existential component would also be addressed; students would be required to reflect on their own positions in the world, to examine the extent to which they currently feel empowered to change their own social positions, and to address their responsibilities for the empowerment of others. The latter issue—an individual's civic responsibility to contribute to the betterment of the community—is often difficult for American students to grasp and internalize. The words of feminist rhetorician Donna Qualley (1997) help me explain to my students why they must examine their own lives and motivations in order to engage dialogically with others:

> It is difficult to be open and receptive toward others without a strong sense of our own agency. If we have too little sense of agency, we can be disempowered, subsumed by the other; with too much sense of our own agency, we may overpower or oppress the other. We also need to have enough autonomy, self-trust and self-esteem to withstand our own rigorous self-scrutiny. (1997, p. 144)

These are not only important lessons for students, but also for the older adults with whom they interact and for faculty, as well. As Qualley suggests, emancipatory pedagogy requires, necessarily, a rigorous self-analysis on the part of all involved. Her words speak, as well, to critical gerontologists wishing to interact dialogically with one another in the academic world and with researchers and practitioners who do not share our common enterprise. If we collectively engage in a discourse which is overly abstract, removed from experience, nondialogic, and self-serving, our critical theory will be oppressive and restrictive. If, however, we engage in authentic discourse in the full Freirean sense of the term, our critical theory can be liberatory and transformative.

## REFERENCES

Bernard, M., Phillips, J., Machin, L., & Davies, V. H. (2000). *Women ageing: Changing identities, challenging myths.* London: Routledge.

Birren, J. (1999). Theories of aging: A personal perspective. In V. L. Bengtson & K. W. Schaie (Eds.), *Handbook of theories of aging.* New York: Springer.

Browne, C. (1998). *Women, feminism and aging.* New York: Springer.

Calasanti, T. (1999). Feminism and gerontology: Not just for women. *Hallym International Journal of Aging, 1,* 44-55.

Cole, T. R. (1993). Preface. In T. R. Cole, W. A. Achenbaum, P. L. Jakobi, & R. Kastenbaum (Eds.), *Voices and visions of aging: Toward a critical gerontology.* New York: Springer.

Estes, C., & Minkler, M. (Eds.). (1999). *Critical gerontology: Perspectives from political and moral economy.* Amityville, NY: Baywood.

Farrell, W. (1974). *The liberated man.* New York: Basic Books.

Freire, P. (1998). *Pedagogy of the oppressed.* Revised, 20th anniversary ed. New York: Continuum.

Gee, J. P. (2000). Literacy, discourse and linguistics: Introduction and what is literacy? In E. Cushman, E. Kintgen, B. Kroll, & M. Rose (Eds.), *Literacy: A critical source book.* Boston: Bedford/St. Martin's.

Gubar, S. (2000). *Critical condition: American feminism at the turn of the century.* New York: Columbia University Press.

Gullette, M. (2000). Age studies as cultural studies. In T. R. Cole, R. Kastenbaum, & R. Ray (Eds.), *Handbook of the humanities and aging* (2nd ed.). New York: Springer.

Hooks, B. (1994). *Teaching to transgress: Education as the practice of freedom.* New York: Routledge.

Hooyman, N. (1999). Research on older women: Where is feminism? *The Gerontologist, 39,* 115-118.

Jamieson, A., & Victor, C. (1997). Theory and concepts in social gerontology. In A. Jamieson, S. Harper, & C. Victor (Eds.), *Critical approaches to ageing and later life.* Buckingham: Open University Press.

Laws, G. (1995). Understanding ageism: Lessons from feminism and postmodernnism. *The Gerontologist, 35,* 112-116.

Lynott, R. J., & Lynott, P. P. (1996). Tracing the course of theoretical development in the sociology of aging. *The Gerontologist, 36,* 749-760.

Moody, H. R. (1988). Toward a critical gerontology: The contribution of the humanities to theories of aging. In J. E. Birren & V. L. Bengtson (Eds.), *Emergent theories of aging.* New York: Springer.

Moody, H. R. (1993). Overview: What is critical gerontology and why is it important? In T. R. Cole, W. A. Achenbaum, P. L. Jakobi, & R. Kastenbaum (Eds.), *Voices and visions of aging: Toward a critical gerontology.* New York: Springer.

Qualley, D. (1997). *Turns of thought: Teaching composition as reflexive inquiry.* Portsmouth, NH: Boynton/Cook.

Ray, R. (1996). A postmodern perspective on feminist gerontology. *The Gerontologist, 36,* 674-680.

Ray, R. (1999). Researching to transgress: The need for critical feminism in gerontology. In J. Garner (Ed.), *Fundamentals of feminist gerontology.* New York: Haworth.

Ray, R. (2000). *Beyond nostalgia: Aging and life story writing.* Charlottesville, VA: University Press of Virginia.

Shaull, R. (1998). Introduction. *Pedagogy of the oppressed* (Revised, 20th anniversary ed.). New York: Continuum.

Stoller, E. P., & Gibson, R. C. (1994). *Worlds of difference: Inequality in the aging experience.* Thousand Oaks, CA: Sage.

## CHAPTER 3

# The Legacy of Social Constructionism for Social Gerontology

### *Hans-Joachim von Kondratowitz*

Social constructionism has attracted wide but not unchallenged attention in the social sciences in general. It can thus now be justifiably considered a well-established albeit controversial approach to theoretical reasoning and research design in social gerontology, as well.

This chapter undertakes the following tasks: it will first try to distinguish the main lines of theoretical reflection in social constructionism and explore some of the perspectives this approach offers in the field of gerontology. In a second paragraph one dominant sociological orientation for analysis (development and diffusion of knowledge) will be chosen to guide gerontological research questions, and to present historical-sociological evidence for the relevance of a constructionist framework for gerontology. It will then thirdly try to defend some of the premises of social constructionism against critical objections, and will advance a wide array of contemporary empirical evidence from the field of the utilization of gerontological knowledge for the innovativeness of such an approach to gerontological analysis. And finally it will offer certain recommendations concerning the processing and diffusion of knowledge based on empirical observation and trends.

First of all, however, a brief explication is needed of the theoretical and epistemological dimensions of constructionism as it is understood in this chapter.

## THE HERITAGE OF DIFFERENT APPROACHES IN "SOCIAL CONSTRUCTIONISM"

The term "social constructionism" now generally applies to an intellectual position that explores and questions attitudes to "social reality." And this exploration centers on the constructive processes by which an understanding of reality is accessed. Today social constructionism derives from a wide range of intellectual traditions which may be grouped in at least four lines of reasoning whose relevance for gerontology differs considerably:

1. The most common stance in social sciences is one associated with the comprehensive heritage of philosophical *phenomenology* and its different research strategies, such as *objective hermeneutics, symbolic interactionism,* and *ethnomethodology.* Gubrium and Holstein (1995) have recently recapitulated the main analytic assumptions and key concepts. They consider the principal difference from empirical-analytically oriented research to be that all these different constructionist approaches

> are *not conceived as causal explanations* of the social world but instead focus attention on problems of *meaning in everyday life.* As *analytical perspectives, not theories,* they provide broadly sensitizing orientations to the socially constructed features of experience, including aging. Empirically, this results in analytical descriptions of how the social categories and forms of age enter into everyday life how they are managed and how they are socially organized. (Gubrium & Holstein, 1999, p. 287, italics added)

And they conclude: "If 'theory' must be the necessary term of reference for the perspectives, it would direct research toward the broad question of *how,* not *why* ordinary persons themselves 'theorize' their worlds." A number of empirical studies have focused on this reconstruction of life worlds, mostly in the fields of institutional settings, care giving, behavioral development of professions, etc., and its main impact has found further expression and elaboration in gerontological research in these areas.

2. The consideration of subjective orientation, meaning, and context as key perspectives of social constructionism in the *phenomenological* vein has undoubtedly enriched gerontological knowledge. But there are other scientific agendas that take an equally constructionist stance and which have less apparent potential implications for the gerontological enterprise. In the seventies, French social psychology research introduced the concept of "*social representation*" as a system of values, ideas and patterns of activity. This term is highly relevant for the cultural and historical analysis of aging processes, as well. In its double function of giving individual actors an ordering scheme for orientation in the material and social world and to facilitate communication among members of a community by offering codes for social exchange and classification of the social world (cf. Gergen, 1985, 1994, 2001; Moscovici, 1973), this concept has helped to identify the cultural distinctions of health and illness (Herzlich & Pierret, 1984) and of the aging body (Personne, 1994). But it has also become increasingly important for the cultural history of aging from a comparative viewpoint (Conrad & von Kondratowitz, 1993), and provides an intellectual interface to the cultural studies perspective.

3. Another approach to social constructionism derives from the important work done by J. Piaget and B. Inhelder (1955/1977)—who predominantly interpret the perception of the child's surrounding world and the development of accountable knowledge about this world as forming social constructions to accompany and shape this developmental stage. This way of relating knowledge formation to the construction of images, which allows no direct relationship with reality, has had a particularly strong impact on the European social constructionism debate, and has favored the development of a deliberately radical version of constructionism (Luhmann, 1997; Schmidt, 1987, 1998; von Glasersfeld, 1996).

In a separate but related discourse, social constructionism has also been increasingly influential in a field of utmost importance for gerontology, the *history and sociology of (social) sciences* and the utilization of social science knowledge in practical contexts of action. The central concern is how different social, practical, historical etc. factors affect the production and evaluation of scientific knowledge in such a way that scientific facts are perceived and treated as social constructions (e.g., Beck & Bonß, 1989).

4. Finally, the constructionist agenda ought to include the more recent *cultural studies* approach, which seeks to analyze cultural processes as embedded in power relations, to determine the influence these relations have on cultural praxis. As a multidisciplinary research program, this approach allows the incorporation of elements of knowledge relevant to gerontological research. They are often contrasted, compared, and linked in the context of *discourse analysis.* The elements in question are culled from historical sociology, societal analysis, and gerontology. The aim is to reconstruct the fluctuating societal status and meaning of "old age." Research thus addresses macro-level "longue durée" phenomena (to use the French historian Fernand Braudel's term), concentrating on the sequencing, simultaneity or historical overlap of competing or additive conceptions of old age and their interdependence. In such a perspective, "discourse" comprises contexts of public recognition, socializing agencies, and collective public actors. What is meant by "public" is, of course, variable and changes over historical time. It identifies no stable relationship between actors but rather demonstrates a highly indeterminate or even discontinuous sphere of mutual definitions. Unquestionably, the work of Michel Foucault is still the most prominent example for such a perspective in discourse analysis resp. analysis of "discursive formations."

A number of social science traditions have treated the discourse as a central element in societal negotiation. One, predominantly associated with the inter-actionist approach (as outlined above by Gubrium & Holstein, 1999), is the analysis of how societies define "social problems." Within this analytical tradition there is a central link relating macro developments and emerging micropolitical definitory processes. The "appearance" or "manifestation" of a "social problem" is defined by a whole range of activities: selecting, emphasizing, and empirically describing certain societal modes of behavior; identifying certain groups as affected by these behaviors; presenting the construct of *possible societal threats* associated with certain groups; and proposing ways to balance or to regulate the situation through compensations and new entitlements. This creates a certain public awareness of the potential and of the groups involved. The creation of such awareness serves to counter the assumption that there are automatic reactions to the pressure exerted by problems, and that all that is needed to "solve" a particular problem is to obey functional prerequisites and constraints—which, in effect, means nothing more than different ways of "dealing with" the social problem in question. Attention is focused on how group members and participants in the public debate select and actively construct this "handling" of social developments perceived as "social problems." In the social history of Germany, individual aging and the aging of German society have been societal topics that early became examples for the definition of social problems in this respect. The material presented in Table 1 provides ample evidence for such an observation.

## GERONTOLOGICAL KNOWLEDGE AND SOCIAL REPRESENTATIONS OF OLD AGE

In the following paragraphs *several layers of empirical evidence* for a social constructionist perspective in gerontological research are presented. All *four approaches distinguished above* as different research programs within this social constructionist paradigm are shown to produce theoretically relevant statements and conjectures and to offer a range of empirical support for central hypotheses. Nevertheless, the aim is also to confront this evidence of social constructionist research with critical questions and objections from different research traditions, and this chapter seeks to encourage the taking into account of diverse research perspectives and to demonstrate that this will enhance the quality of gerontological research. The necessary empirical evidence has been collected in the context of an highly important but still substantially underresearched field: the *development and diffusion of gerontological knowledge over time,* and this subject will be the core element of all the following considerations.

For our purposes, this essential subject can be operationalized as the use, the incorporation, and distribution of single terms bearing gerontological meaning, of a comprehensive gerontological terminology, and of complex concepts with gerontological connotations in specific discipline-oriented as well as everyday language, and the conversion of scientifically legitimized terms and concepts into everyday conceptions about the structuring of the course of human life. If the influence of gerontology is to be taken as a central point of reference, the *formation of gerontological knowledge* must first be examined as a distinctly historical process of developing and structuring the central components of this knowledge, in Stephen Katz' terms (Katz, 1996), the "disciplining of old age." At this "longue durée" level, everyday conceptions are shaped by *historical*

Table 1. Social Representation of Old Age in Modern Society

| Dichotomizations of old age (social representations) | Essential content of the dichotomously organized social constructions | Dominance of the dichotomous models over time |
|---|---|---|
| 1. "High of Age" vs. "Worn Out Age" ("Hohes Alter" vs. "Abgelebtes Alter") | Discourse of "veneration" as a reflection of an age-related power structure—Gradual disappearance of "vital force" over the life time | 18th century to the first half of 20th century |
| 2. "Still hale and hearty age" vs. "Infirm/Decrepit Age" ("Rüstiges Alter" vs. "Gebrechliches Alter") | Remaining ability to show cooperative societal achievements—Body images accentuate signs of weakening capabilities (by using the metaphor of fragile bones) | Turn of 19th/20th century to mid-century |
| 3. "Normal Age" vs. "Pathological Age" ("Normales Alter" vs. "Pathologisches Alter") | "Majority" definitions of social adequacy of old age developments—"Minority" definitions of old age as "unproductive" (Quetelet) or as a social burden | Late 19th century into the fifties of 20th century |
| 4. "Age in Need" vs. "Frail Age" ("Bedürftiges Alter" vs. "Hinfälliges Alter") | Old age as increasingly exposing material and emotional needs—Old age as being dominated by the need to take care (by using the metaphor of the fall syndrome) | Late forties to the early seventies |
| 5. "Active Age" vs. "Age in Need of Care" ("Aktives Alter" vs. "Pflegebedürftiges Alter") | Construction of old age as participating in offers of local social policy and as increasing competence—Health impaired older people as potential clients of the service sector | In the seventies |
| 6. "Young Old" vs. "Old Old" ("Junge Alte" vs. "Alte Alte") | Adopting the Anglo-American distinction between two different need constellations | In the eighties |
| 7. "Third Age" vs. "Fourth Age" ("Drittes Lebensalter" vs. "Viertes Lebensalter") | Adopting the Anglo-American/French distinction between two complex and highly differentiated life situations in old age (explicitly "value neutral") | In the late eighties and early nineties |
| 8. "Autonomous Age" vs. "Dependent Age" ("Autonomes Alter" vs. "Abhängiges Alter") | Emphasis on the degree of freedom to organize life in old age as a self-determined process—Emphasis on the increasing necessity to negotiate service packages according to the relative status of health | In the early nineties |

*processes of expert dominance and administrative regulation* in the process of determining and shaping the "risk of old age" in modern society.

The empirical basis for this reconstruction is provided by three sources of written material:

- a comparison of articles concerned with aging and life cycles in widely distributed and popular encyclopedias from the eighteenth century to the beginning of the twentieth century;
- a comparison of entries on the same subject matter in specialized medical encyclopedias from the eighteenth century to the beginning of the twentieth century (Kondratowitz, 1991);
- an evaluation of written material dealing with questions of societal aging and its consequences. The material comes from a wide range of experts and administrative personnel involved in social and medical reform in Germany from the end of eighteenth century to present times (Kondratowitz, 2000).

Table 1 shows how these typologies of old age or types of social construction are organized, processed, and negotiated at the societal level in Germany and how they change over historical time. Indeed, with such a broad background they can be regarded as "*social representations of old age*" in their own right. As far as the differences in content between developmental stages are concerned, the explanatory remarks in the middle section of Table 1 (under the heading of "dichotomously organized social constructions") make some reference to the formation of age categorizations and their variability—they are to be found in much greater detail in the publications mentioned above.

The following remarks focus not so much on the content of the two representations as on shifts in weighting over historical time. Table 1 shows a clear dividing line between—to use Anthony Glascock's (and also Leo Simmons) terminology (Glascock, 1981)—"intact age" as opposed to "increpit age." In its various representations, this dichotomization table emphasizes the presence or absence of *orientation* toward *societal achievement* in the course of the phase of life termed "old age," while the associated need constellations (as representations of the developing and expanding welfare state) figure as the central elements in ascribing *societal inclusion* or *exclusion.*

While the empirical material offered by various studies demonstrates this impressive kind of long-term continuity, there is also considerable change over time, and the closer one comes to the present, the *shorter* becomes the *span of time* involved. More and more emphasis is placed on the "healthy side," bringing an imbalance in the weighting of the two representations and putting more pressure on the "increpit side"—with a tendency almost to eliminate this less comforting part of old age. Indeed, one might ask whether more recent and powerful concepts like "successful aging" still have any valid counterpart on the "infirm side" at all.

A process of *societal acceleration* is also apparent. Together with the extension of the healthy side and contraction of the infirm side, models and concepts succeed at an *ever faster pace* sometimes in competition and with more and more overlap as we approach the present situation. German old age policy design and implementation at the local authority level has been more than ever characterized by competition and interaction between the differing concepts of old age implemented at the central and local welfare state levels (cf. Kondratowitz, 2000). The emphasis is nevertheless clearly on the healthy aspect of age. And even the concepts for long-term care—with their explicit concentration on rehabilitation and prevention—which on the surface appear to differentiate the "infirm age," are in fact intensively committed to the vision of prolonged activity patterns even under less favorable bodily conditions. "Intact age" now extends even into the highest age groups, for which the medical science discourse used to apply the term "incurable" and which is now endowed with the new connotation of being "chronically ill."

## CRITICISM OF THE
## SOCIAL CONSTRUCTIONIST LEGACY

The groundwork of historical-sociological analysis and the historically variable dynamic of boundary-setting between the social representations of old age have proved a decisive frame of reference for determining the value of discourse analysis in the gerontological research presented here. However, skepticism has been voiced at the epistemological radicalism of social constructionism and the implications resulting from such a perspective. It has been directed with particular emphasis at the research logic of discourse analysis (cf. Hacking, 1999). Considering the opposition that such work still attracts in the scientific arena, the inclusion of discourse analysis would even intensify criticism not only by historians of science development but also by gerontologists and welfare state researchers. All these critical objections could be summed up as addressing the *methodological comprehensibility* and *sequencing* of the different analytical steps in the course of the research undertaken.

The undeniable fact that social constructionism does not subscribe to the idea of a outer reality as a controlling factor of acquiring knowledge has been a key point of criticism for some observers. This is made apparent in the use of the term "creation" and its accompanying implications. Using such a term, it has been said, generally introduces an unlimited *arbitrariness* to the defining situation. "Creations" or "inventions" claim to be generated independently of the respective framing factors, of social structural constraints and social situations. In support of this criticism, comparative welfare state research has pointed out that modern welfare states seem to prefer and develop quite similar or sometimes even identical sociopolitical strategies despite quite diverse histories of definition setting (e.g., designing retirement systems, health care, etc.). This appears to support the idea of the dominance of "reality" as taking into account situations of pressure to design sociopolitical instruments and strategies regardless of definitional competition between group settings. But these critical remarks underestimate the specific quality of a position that centers on "creations": the objective of explaining how and why a specific understanding of reality consists of quite diverse and possibly unrelated components of knowledge and which seems to be self-evident today is possible and can become dominant only under certain institutional and cultural conditions and in specific constellations of actors that shape the perceptions of their environment by advocating a certain "reading" of reality.

Another reservation relates directly to the first point. Criticism has been leveled in both the societal and sociopolitical arenas at the *opacity* of the *criteria for choice making* in considering old age. For instance, in analyzing change in medical definitions of old age, a common frame of reference, a background of the intellectual order of scientific objects is needed. Here again, there are two aspects: while the epistemologically radical outlook of discourse analysis allows the conscious fragmentation of knowledge elements if it serves to isolate certain developments and argumentation, the other critical aspect might be considered valid. The principles of rational communication must be insisted upon, even if the researcher chooses a strategy of fragmentation to deliberately emphasize a certain discourse. Nevertheless, the grounds for and ambient intellectual tradition of this fragmentation should be made visible and comprehensible to the observer (in the intellectual tradition of Habermas' theory of communicative action). This would be a clear plea for transparency in communicating these surrounding factors to a wider scientific and lay public.

A number of critics have questioned the *representativity* of findings and interpretations in discourse analysis. The term "representativity" is not meant in the sense of empirical-analytical research but refers more to *relational dimensions,* e.g., how a certain discourse about old age in the developing life sciences of the early nineteenth century reflects the mainstream in medicine or biology, in which this discourse has generally been embedded. Adequate knowledge about the history of science in its different aspects is therefore needed and must be pivotal to evaluation of discourse analysis. However, the decisive critique is directed at the *transparency* of the conditions for discourse analysis. While discourse analysis obviously needs to evidence its scientific prerequisites—methods, epistemological basis, essential techniques, etc., it has often proved difficult to place such analysis in a broader multidisciplinary context and relate it to contrasting experience in other research agendas.

In reviewing the quality of objections to the use of discourse analysis, the key criticism seems to be a *lack of transparency* on the part of researchers. It therefore seems essential to design a strategy open enough to satisfy the need for accompanying and competing discourses that would help to guide analysis, but which is also epistemologically sound enough to hold its own as an entity in its own right. A *praxeology* model for discourse analysis may be proposed for the systematic organization of comparison between different types of knowledge, which is responsive enough to facilitate an interchange of research ideas and a creative confrontation of research perspectives. This model will be elaborated at the end of the chapter.

## ORGANIZING TYPES OF KNOWLEDGE AND AMBIVALENCES IN UTILIZATION

The broad frame of reference which has been discussed in the preceding sections shows how comprehensive the field of normative structures is in which everyday perceptions of old age are formed, and that there are experts and specialists who serve as "gate-keepers of meaning." Indeed, this points to a research program in a long-term perspective. For there are clear indications that the current competing concepts of aging mentioned and their verbal expressions and connotations are slowly entering a wider public domain, and are now even accepted as legitimizing models by self-help groups and social movements among the aged. If we therefore address the subject of how and to what extent they will be integrated at the everyday level, certain important questions—which can be no more than raised at this point—will have to be answered.

From a sociological point of view, we are dealing with the much broader problem of how scientific (or, modestly formulated, systematically organized) knowledge is adopted and integrated into everyday life. According to a well known thesis, any completely successful integration of such structured knowledge would consistently but paradoxically further its invisibility and might cause its oblivion. The utilization of knowledge ought therefore to be considered a process of reinterpretation in given contexts of action and praxis. Elements of knowledge collected and contemplated, free from the pressure of specific action, are now confronted by constraints, perceptions, and situational factors that tend to divest this knowledge of its scientific roots, transforming and translating it into modes of everyday conversation and rules of action. Such transformation would also markedly *increase* the *autonomy* of those using the transformed knowledge. "Split utilization" of knowledge in terms of user definition is conceivable, which means the knowledge in question could be rejected in one context and accepted in another, giving the framing of the context a decisive function. Some authors, including Ulrich Beck, have characterized this process as a *trivialization* in that knowledge loses its theoretical refinement and its sensitivity for situational variations in the process of utilization (cf. Beck & Bonß, 1989). However, they have been criticized for tacitly assuming a hierarchy in which a still identifiable "scientific knowledge" it attributed a higher quality standing from the outset, and therefore confronts and even competes with "lower level knowledge" in everyday life.

This point of criticism alone makes it clear that the theoretical perspective just elaborated raises several controversial issues. Is or should "everyday consciousness" be the objective of scientific investigation at all? Is social science knowledge really so exclusively enriched by interpretations as these observers claim? Is there not a wide range of sociological information that could be qualified as technical, data-specific or at least relational in quality? And are contexts of utilization not rather confronted by existing institutional structures, by "systems of utilization" (in the words of Niklas Luhmann), rather than by individuals pursuing different strategies for gaining possession of scientific knowledge? These ineluctable questions impose scrutiny of these implicit "hierarchizations" of knowledge and their societal perception.

## EMPIRICAL INVENTORY OF THE USE OF GERONTOLOGICAL KNOWLEDGE

Clearly the notion of a hierarchy of knowledge that renders the development of "trivial transformations" necessary leaves several questions unanswered. The inability to conceptualize sociological knowledge in a non-essential manner is one of the main reasons why interactionist approaches, which constitute one of the approaches of social constructionism, are now attracting more attention than before. The issue is how users of sociological knowledge define this type of knowledge for themselves. Whether such a perspective can reflect long-term societal influences as described above rather than merely mirroring what users attribute to organizational sources as "knowledge" remains to be seen, and makes further empirical investigation imperative. After looking at macro-level changes in the preceding chapters we now to introduce a "meso"-level in order to trace negotiations on the implementation of sociological expertise about old age. While this level should mirror the increasing autonomization of users and a consequent increase in *user-dominated contexts,* it should also reflect the existence of institutional contexts that shape the use of knowledge if it is to be able to describe these new contexts of user-domination more appropriately.

In order to analyze this for the case of gerontological knowledge, a three-city comparative study (Berlin, Munich, Wiesbaden) dealing with discourses and negotiations relating to the development of projects on supportive counseling for home care delivery in Germany was undertaken (von Kondratowitz, 1993). The research centered on interviews held during the restructuring of national policy on care in Germany, which began with the 1989 Health Reform Act and ended with implementation of the new Long Term Care Insurance in 1995/1996. The field of research was thus strongly influenced by the discussions and turbulences arising from these radical changes in service delivery and the accompanying changes in language and perceptions, while it proved to be highly dynamic, flexible, and open for contrasting experiences. Besides a thorough socio-political analysis of welfare strategies for the aged within the "local welfare state," two consecutive rounds of qualitative interviews about these problems were conducted in the three municipal settings with different groups of knowledge users from different levels of expertise. There were *four main groups* of interviewees: members of *public administration* in the *local welfare state* and at various levels of the hierarchy and with differing qualifications; members of *local welfare associations* equally distributed in qualification; *employees of local care* and *counseling initiatives;* members of *self-help groups* and *care initiatives.* An ethnomethodological approach was chosen in that I tried to relate the routine practices of everyday men and women to the knowledge production which was justified scientifically in order to let them share a common construction of reality.

The approach to "practical gerontological knowledge" has three aspects. A first assumption is that such knowledge is formed by rules, propositions, and specialized terms that reveal a certain familiarity with the discipline-specific findings of social science-oriented research on aging, but which are nevertheless translated into a different language and flexibly adapted to the given situation (e.g., critique of the "deficit model of aging," the role of "independent living," "active aging"). A second aspect is concerned with patterns of interpretation at the everyday level as expressed in proverbs, governing principles of aging, recipe-type recommendations, etc., which tend to be independent of scientific knowledge but most of which relate to "body images" of age as shown in Table 1 and are of early modern descent. The third perspective could be summed up as looking at the process of "dealing with knowledge," as pointing to a more self-reflexive and critical way of handling information, depending on the given situation and needs. The interview material yielded five new and differing types of gerontological knowledge, made useful by attribution to and processing in different settings, referred to as "contexts of utilization." Table 2 tries to categorize them by presence and degree of intensity. It should be stressed that these contexts are to be considered as prearranging and framing conditions for visualizing knowledge for the user.

While different loadings are apparent, and a concentration of certain types across most contexts (knowledge of production; knowledge of negotiation), it is clear that Table 2 cannot adequately reflect change in following the implementation of home care programs and the gerontological knowledge types used. In a next phase of research it would be important to know whether there are "coalitions" between different contexts—the concentration referred to above seems to point in this direction. Change over time is also not adequately reflected. Certainly the picture would be different now that the German Long Term Care Insurance Law has been fully implemented and specific networks of new initiatives and of constraints to renegotiate benefits have developed, as we are now aware six years after the legislation came into effect.

This section can be concluded with Table 3 showing the presence or absence of the three perspectives on gerontological knowledge in the five types of knowledge identified in the context of practical, local home-care programs.

It is clear that the increasing incorporation of gerontological knowledge and the consequent self-evidence of its role in practical work is only slowly gaining ground in the different contexts of utilization. The administrative domination of

Table 2. Gerontological Knowledge and Utilization Contexts

| Contexts of utilization | Types of knowledge | | | | |
|---|---|---|---|---|---|
| | Gerontological knowledge of justification and legitimation | Gerontological knowledge of (nonjuridical) competence | Gerontological knowledge of production | Gerontological knowledge of negotiation | Gerontological knowledge of everyday experience |
| Administrative action and activities | Dominant | Strong | Balanced | Dominant | Weak |
| Professional cultures | Moderate | Weak | Balanced | Strong | Balanced |
| Public domain | Moderate | Weak | Balanced | Strong | Balanced |
| Organized interests | Moderate | Balanced | Dominant | Strong | Moderate |
| Micropolitical processes | Balanced | Weak | Moderate | Balanced | Strong |

Table 3. Presence of Types of Gerontological Knowledge

| Type of knowledge | Perspectives | | |
|---|---|---|---|
| | First perspective: Reinterpreted adaptations of science; concepts; terms | Second perspective: Everyday life patterns of interpretation; recipe-type knowledge | Third perspective: "Dealing with" knowledge; self-reflexive modes |
| Gerontological knowledge of justification and legitimation | Present | Not present | Not present |
| Gerontological knowledge of (nonjuridical) competence | Present | Present | Not present |
| Gerontological knowledge of production | Present | Present | Present |
| Gerontological knowledge of negotiation | Not present | Present | Present |
| Gerontological knowledge of everyday experience | Not present | Present | Present |

the implementation of gerontological knowledge is still strong although there is already a shift toward a more reflexive mode of action and a trend toward making the persisting boundaries between scientifically and practically grounded gerontological work more permeable. Nevertheless, the heritage of the highly differentiated German welfare state with its corporatist negotiatory structures seems to make the implementation of more "fluid" ways of organizing services and using gerontological knowledge quite arduous.

## THE COMPLEXITY OF KNOWLEDGE AUTONOMIZATION

The increasing autonomization of demand vis-à-vis the offerings of social-science knowledge is not specific to social gerontology, as we have seen in the preceding sections. In fact, the common basis for the discourse summed up above is not a particular knowledge type but social-science knowledge and its transformation rules in general. But it is obvious that a scientific endeavor like gerontology with weak theoretical ties and intellectual traditions is subject to particular pressure. Here the long deplored poor theoretical base of gerontological reasoning produces ambivalent results. On the one hand, the existing dominance of practical contexts, which the insistence on more theoretical work was intended to offset, is now even stronger and potentially more difficult to counterbalance. On the other hand—and this complicates the situation even more—a clear pattern of increasing diversification in gerontological research is apparent beyond the already implicit autonomization of knowledge production in the social sciences, due to important changes in the welfare regimes, at least in Germany.

While this diversification proceeded at a slower pace in the early nineties, it received marked impetus from the introduction of new provisions on care (LTCI) and the considerable changes they brought. They included an enormous increase in new organizational units for home care (e.g., private and non-profit care service organizations) as well as institutional care. The old image of Germany presented by comparative welfare state research as typically low on social services and high on informal family work in the area of care for the aged began to crumble and cautiously change. At the same time the boundaries between institutional and home care have become more and more flexible, now allowing the design and implementation of a multiplicity of new care arrangements between "home" and "institution" at the local level. This differentiation has in turn produced a greater need for coordination and cooperation and for accompanying scientific expertise among care providers and their support structures at several older and more recent levels. The trend is toward more user-dominated research contexts, and the resulting short- and long-term consequences for research strategies are now the subject of debate. In any case, the research outlook seems more than ever to be governed by the requirements of practical contexts rather than the discourses of theoretically refined gerontological reasoning. It remains to be seen whether this is necessarily detrimental to the attempts of critical gerontologists to urge the theoretical reassessment of gerontology in general, but such a development cannot be disregarded and may make the project even more difficult. The strong trend toward more practical and user-dominated gerontological research contexts may therefore prove a two-edged blessing with unbidden consequences.

Another clear trend in the development of gerontological research is somewhat related to the topics just mentioned. The now acute awareness of the social consequences of aging societies has engendered a strong desire to take over "best practices" from other countries as functioning examples of policy-driven solutions. This is fostered by the growing sense of interconnectedness among national societies, with particular urgency in a united Europe where a wide range of long-term adaptations and structural changes have to be adopted by parliaments and Commission. In the face of this pressure, the perspective of *comparing* welfare states and their achievements has been an increasingly important topic for gerontological research. The debate goes far beyond the classical procedure of comparing organizational arrangements or service networks. The attention of gerontological research is focusing more and more on the *embedded cultural prerequisites and normative foundations of welfare states* (e.g., as manifested in family cultures and care cultures). Recent British publications offer excellent examples of work being done in this direction. *User domination* as an expression of the ongoing *autonomization* of social science, together with this *gerontological* outlook on *comparative work* on the changing normative foundations of our welfare delivery, seem to constitute one important line of research in a gerontology of the future, in which cultural foundations may play a much more important role than before.

## TOWARD A "PRAXEOLOGY" OF THE SOCIAL CONSTRUCTIONIST AGENDA

The term "praxeology" was coined in Polish scientific philosophy and sociology in the early twenties of the last century, being further developed and elaborated by Kazimierz Twardowski, Tadeusz Kotarbinski, Jan Zieleniewski, and others (cf. Kotarbinski, 1965). "Praxeology" means the structuring and defining of a set of rules in order to implement a science of systematic and efficient action. By reinterpreting this concept for the negotiating process of social constructionist analyses under gerontological conditions, it is useful to relate it to the process of interlinking and balancing both complementary and contradictory modes of scientific reasoning. "Praxeology" can then be understood as an expression of processing and acting on *self-reflexive grounds,* giving both stimulus and direction to the elaboration of *research programs.* Discourse analysis is seen as such a developing research program which needs praxeological procedures to become widely established. Such a praxeology would guarantee greater transparency on the part of research actors and research critics. But, most of all, it could serve as a collaborative effort to group "scientific" and "practical" research contexts not only on a casual but on a continuous level. Addressing the topic of praxeology conceptualizes discourse analysis in general and by preference as a *joint venture* between disciplines, in which the clarifying of respective epistemological and methodological boundaries is a necessary planning process for the a "side-by-side" examination of different discourses on old age that does not require adoption of one approach to the exclusion of others. Several procedures can help this venture to flourish, particularly when operating under the conditions of a *multidisciplinary team* and by deliberately incorporating contexts of practical gerontology:

- *Consultations* with well-informed researchers as well as users of gerontological knowledge in the public sphere on a regular and systematic or casual basis in order to test and sharpen a certain perspective within a discourse context and type.
- *Counterreading,* which means the systematic development of perspective a in clear contrast or opposition to the one elaborated in a discourse analysis or in another piece of constructionist research. This would provide an opportunity to systematically mobilize opposing evaluations from which to derive quite different research and practical consequences. Here the importance of such a strategy for the public use of gerontological knowledge is particularly striking and is an adequate expression of the impact of user-dominated contexts in gerontology.
- *Contrasting* as a juxtaposition of contradicting and/or fragmented results and evaluations thus giving the outside observer a chance to play out different options within discourse analysis.
- *Accompanying* or *context protocols* as means of making public a self-reflexive process of observing one's own research by deliberately opening up a level of distance to the gerontological research process. These protocols may then serve as documents for demonstrating the stages and pitfalls of the research process itself. Again, such texts may also be an incentive for a more intensive exchange between the public use of gerontology and social science.
- *Elaborating competing consequences* of discourse analysis thus allowing the consultation of different disciplines and different fields of gerontological research and practice.

All these different procedures have been already used—at least to some degree—in qualitative research work grounded in a social constructionist approach and mostly concerned with the micro-political level. But it is also possible to organize such a procedural framework at the meso or macro levels by constituting systematic forums for researchers, all the more so today in view of the new means of communication available. It is important to realize that any such procedure should not be misunderstood as the organized "falsification" of a perspective in the line of analytical philosophy of science. It should instead be possible to maintain a radical perspective in discourse analysis by confronting research efforts and results and allowing this confrontation to develop its own logic of comparison, judgment, and evaluation, and in the negotiation of evaluation. Again, what is important is the transparency of the research process in its different stages, particularly for outside observers or researchers less familiar with the topics under discussion. This branch of gerontological research thus needs not only theory but also an awareness of the conditions under which theories interact.

## REFERENCES

Beck, U., Bonß, W. (Eds.) (1989). Weder Sozialtechnologie noch Aufklärung? Analysen zur Verwendung sozialwissenschaftlichen Wissens [Neither social technology nor enlightenment? Analyses on utilization of social science knowledge]. Frankfurt a.M.: Suhrkamp.

Conrad, C., & von Kondratowitz, H. J. (1993). Zur Kulturgeschichte des Alterns [Toward a cultural history of aging] (German-English ed.). Berlin: DZA.

Gergen, K. (1985). The social constructionist movement in modern psychology. *American Psychologist, 40,* 266-275.

Gergen, K. (1994). *Realities and relationships. Soundings in social construction.* Cambridge MA: Harvard University Press.

Gergen, K. (2001). *Social construction in context.* London: Sage.

Glascock. A. (1981). Social asset or social burden: An analysis of the treatment of the aged in non-industrial societies. In C. Fry (Ed.), *Dimensions: Aging, culture and health* (pp. 34-47). New York: J. F. Bergin.

Gubrium, J. F., & Hollstein, J. A. (1999). Constructionist perspectives on aging. In V. Bengtson & K. W. Schaie (Eds.), *Handbook of theories of aging* (pp. 287-305). New York: Springer.

Hacking, I. (1999). Was heißt Soziale Konstruktion? Zur Konjunktur einer Kampfvokabel in den Wissenschaften [What is social construction?]. Frankfurt a.M.: Fischer.

Herzlich, C., & Pierret, J. (1984). Malades d'hier, malades d'aujourd'hui. Paris: Editions Payot.

Katz, S. (1996). *Disciplining old age.* Ithaca: Cornell University Press.

Kotarbinski, T. (1965). *Praxeology. An introduction to the science of efficient action.* Oxford: Pergamon Press.

Luhmann, N. (1997). Die Gesellschaft der Gesellschaft [The society of society]. Frankfurt a.M.: Suhrkamp.

Moscovici, S. (1973). The phenomenon of social representations. In R. M. Farr & S. Moscovici (Eds.), *Social representations* (pp. 3-69). Cambridge: Cambridge University Press.

Personne, M. (1994). Le corps du malade âgé. Pathologie de la vieillesse et relation de soins. Paris: Dunod.

Piaget, J., & Inhelder, B. (1955/1977). *Von der Logik des Kindes zur Logik des Heranwachsenden. Essay über die Ausformung der formalen operativen Strukturen.* Olten (1997).

Schmidt, S. J. (Ed.) (1987). Der Diskurs des radikalen Konstruktivismus [The discourse of radical constructionism]. Frankfurt a.M.: Suhrkamp.

Schmidt, S. J. (1998). Die Zähmung des Blicks. Konstruktivismus–Empirie–Wissenschaft [The taming of glance. Constructionism–empirical world–problems]. Frankfurt a.M.: Suhrkamp.

von Glasersfeld, E. (1996). Radikaler Konstruktivismus: Ideen, Ergebnisse, Probleme [Radical constructionism]. Frankfurt a.M.: Suhrkamp.

von Kondratowitz, H. J. (1991). Medicalisation of old age. Continuity and change in Germany from the late 18th to early 20th century. In M. Pelling, R. Smith (Eds.), *Life, death and the elderly. Historical perspectives* (pp. 134-164). London and New York: Routledge.

von Kondratowitz, H. J. (1993). Verwendung gerontologischen Wissens in der Kommune [Utilization of gerontological knowledge in the local community]. Berlin: DZA.

von Kondratowitz, H. J. (2000). Konjunkturen des Alters. Die Ausdifferenzierung der Konstruktion des "höheren Lebensalters" zu einem sozialpolitischen Problem [Cyclical conceptions of age. Differentiation of the construction of "old age" as a sociopolitical problem]. Regensburg: Transfer-Verlag.

# CHAPTER 4

# Structure and Identity—
# Mind the Gap: Toward a Personal
# Resource Model of Successful Aging

*Jon Hendricks*

## I. INTRODUCTION

### A. Shaping the Self

Linking structural issues and individual experiences is a vexing conundrum for social gerontology. Despite reminders and admonitions, gerontological investigation has made uneven headway in mapping conceptual connections between subjective experience and contextual grounding (Chappel & Penning, 2001; Diehl, 1999; George, 1993; Lawton, 1985; Maddox, 2001; Settersten, 1999). The disjuncture is not unexpected given long-standing propensities in the West to see individuals as sole authors of their every action. In light of this emphasis on autonomy, it is not surprising that a primary precept in the explanatory armamentarium for examining how people age has been a focus on individual attributes. Even so, there is no gainsaying the fact that throughout life actors belong to an assortment of social categories and can never stand free of their sway.

In recent years social gerontologists have also been striving to redress previous assumptions of homogeneity among older actors. People do not become more alike with age; in fact, the opposite may well be the case (Dannefer, 1996). Their heterogeneity is entrenched in disparate master status characteristics, including membership groups and social-economic circumstances, race and ethnicity, gender, subcultural, or structural conditions on the one hand, and personal attributes on the other. A synthesis bringing personal and contextual dimensions into a concatenated framework may yield insight into the variability found among older actors as well as an appreciation of the malleability of the life course. It may also offer a framework for integrating individual and social factors affecting the experience of aging. This synergistic interaction influencing a great many facets of the life course has been labeled a "self-structure dialectic" (Hendricks & Leedham, 1992). The goal of this chapter is to pursue a conceptual union between individual-level factors and contextual considerations as they play out in life course change and personal agency.

In order to craft a conceptual blending of individual and social attributes, I outline what will be labeled a personal resource model. Concepts of human and social capital will be incorporated to help explicate micro- and macro-level connections as manifested through fiduciary, psychological-physiological, and social-familial resources. These three dimensions are generally seen as vital for maintaining mastery, agency, sense of self, health, resilience, and adaptative reactions to social-environmental change. They also underpin subjective feelings of integrity and well-being in the face of life's vicissitudes. Maddox is representative of those calling for conceptual bridge building. He was clear, "Causal agents and events must always be placed in environmental context and the actors are assumed to be active agents as they create as well as respond to their environments" (Maddox, 2001, p. 112). Early in the twentieth century Cooley (1902) made a similar declaration apropos the present discussion. He was resolute; to understand sense of self, actors must be considered as outcomes of the social orders in which they are grounded.

Phillipson and Biggs (1998, p. 18) posit much the same point, "asking questions about the status of selfhood in late life is fundamental to any understanding of the problems facing older persons." Accordingly, this discussion explores how changes in sense of self are linked to issues arising with age, especially age-related shifts in person-contextual bonds. To anticipate my own conclusions: personal resources anchored in structural and social circumstances circumscribe parameters of identity and transitional phases of life's trajectory, imposing important boundary conditions delimiting person-contextual connections.

## B. Agency, Roles, and Social Context

I will not delve into comparative perspectives, historical moments, or their effects on how the self is formulated; suffice it to say agency, self, identity, and meaningfulness are culturally relative constructs rooted in the reach of historical time and place (Elder, 1974; Gecas, 1991; Gecas & Burke, 1995; Logan, 1987; Markus & Kitayama, 1991; Neisser & Jopling, 1997). Under alternate conditions, questions of sovereign selfhood simply may not arise. To illustrate: ideology and language promoting individualized identity are prevalent in the West, rare in the East, and virtually non-existent in certain cultures (Neisser & Jopling, 1997). Without a configuration of cultural precepts supporting notions of autonomy or personal volition, the individualism frequently taken-for-granted, may be atypical.

Even though notions of identity, autonomy, and meaning are historically and culturally contingent, being able to conceive of the self as both knower and as known drives to the heart of the human condition (Mead, 1934).

Four themes characterize contemporary accounts of self and identity. Sense of self is frequently portrayed from a "multilevel life course" perspective incorporating: 1) situated interactions; 2) structural aspects of social roles and group life; 3) personal experience in time and place; and 4) intrapersonal processes linked to biological and psychological processes of an ontogenetic or corporeal nature (Gecas & Burke, 1995, p. 42; Hatch, 2000). Implicit in such a schematic is a belief that the path through life is contingent on personal resources playing out in various contexts. That is to say, experience, perception, and interpretation are mediated by one's social life space with its coupled norms, commitments, and entitlements. The relativity of personal experience, expectations, and self-concept is circumscribed by public constructs built-in to shared experiences affecting interaction, education, health, work, and retirement—to name but a few.

There is another facet of the interplay of actor and context that should be kept in mind. Actors are never merely reactive; they are also proactive and volitional. Agency is one of the things that unites structure and self—in carrying out an agenda, actors define themselves and their world *via* behavior and interpretative practice. In so doing, they may modify the ways in which social structure is conceived, exerting themselves in such a way that seemingly rigid social arrangements may become malleable. Within the constraints of social capital, actors author their own development–creating and corroborating interpretation through action (Diehl, 1999, p. 156; Rosenberg, 1981; Turner, 1994). At the same time, sense of self is anchored in memory-endowed sequencing pertaining to past experience, but concomitantly reaching ahead in time to affect how events unfold. That is to say, past and future supply syndetic constructs, in the form of remembrances of things past as well as purposive anticipated scripts actors envision as they formulate their lives (Hazelrigg, 1997, p. 118; Hendricks & Peters, 1986). As actors move through life, the meanings attached to experience reflect past and future trans-temporal, self-referential interpretations (Dittmann-Kohli & Westerhof, 2000; Hendricks, 1999; Markus & Nurius, 1987).

In melding temporal perspectives, actors draw upon generative memories and proleptic imagery of plausible futures to steer a desired course, to plot their own destinies (Hendricks, 2001a). Their autobiographical worldviews arise from historically situated, normative life transitions, alloyed by anticipated scripts, and lead to an assertion that social framing furnishes the blueprint by which life is conceived (Hagestad, 1991; Heckhausen & Lang, 1996; Hendricks, 1984; Mayer & Muller, 1986). Successive social statuses mete out order for an age-segmented life course by bringing together institutionally determined opportunities for action with personal resources. As status passages occur, redefinitions of selfhood incorporate normative guides providing cognitive maps utilized by actors to chart their path. It is reasonable to assert that the social organization of temporality, via sequencing of opportunities, obligations, and processes, all maintained with reasonable synchronicity, provides benchmarks and boundaries actors use to gauge their progress (Hazelrigg, 1997, p. 122; Hendricks, 1984). These norms and social resources are historically situated and simultaneously presage variations in the experience of life-course transitions (Hogan, 1985). What gerontology may need is a conceptual focus on the sequelae of passage, reformulation, and reestablishment of stability that distinguish phases of life.

It is through the actions of situated actors that structures are fashioned, then reproduced (Giddens, 1993, p. 134). In fact, Giddens declared that social categories are realized by dint of actors' transactions. He is of the opinion that; "structural properties . . . exist only insofar as forms of social conduct are reproduced chronically across time and space" (Giddens, 1984, p. xxi). The relationship is thought to be reciprocal; actors are fashioned through structural considerations and, in turn, the collective action of successive cohorts is the impetus for structural transformation (Giddens, 1993; Hess, 1988). It seems straightforward, yet as Chappel and Penning (2001) point out, considerable ambiguity remains in explaining why structure is not thoroughly deterministic of experience. Even Giddens appears to vacillate on questions of degrees of freedom (Archer, 1995). One possibility posed by this chapter is that although interpretative practices are necessarily consensual and normatively defined, personifying, if you will, structural grounding, they also have a highly personal or self-verifying aspect. In acting on their intentions, actors create meanings that are personally focused, reflecting current and trans-temporal self-referential intentionality (Hendricks, 1999).

Social roles are affirmational conduits between structural conditions and individual lives (Park, 1926), and they are also constitutive of consciousness. In all instances, an actor's roles are configured *via* their master status with its accompanying norms and priorities, and in terms of their own project-based, self-referential agenda. In either case, social feedback mechanisms and personal meaning systems, alloyed by reflected appraisals emanating from everyday interaction, intertwine to circumscribe what experience means and how actors are perceived. These spatial or social frames are actual or virtual arenas in which behavior occurs. It is important to bear in mind that these arenas are never merely places, however; they are emphatically relational—defined through dealings (Heckhausen & Lang, 1996; Kohli & Meyer, 1986; Marshall, 1995).

The recursive sweep of social roles, rituals, norms, and expectations are cradle not only of opportunity, or stress, but knowledge, attitudes, and preferences nurturing personal initiative and interpretative premises. Roles are the origin of situated identity, habits of the mind, natural attitudes, or worldviews. It should come as no surprise that differences in interpretation and understanding follow disparate role performances. An actor's interpretative framework and life style reflect clusters of practices and knowledge emerging from roles assumed within given contexts. In fact, it is fair to say, personal experience and meaning systems cannot be context neutral but are, in effect, ecological constructs emerging from differential practices. These social contexts provide the fabric of our lives, they convey interpretative procedures, mindsets, and access to opportunities actors assume as their own in formulating life's script (Bronfenbrenner, 1979; Gecas & Burke, 1995; Hendricks, 1984; Yardley, 1987).

This person-context linkage has been described as situated development, or as a contextual-dialectical process (Riegel, 1979), sometimes labeled "the ecology of human development" (Bronfenbrenner, 1979), or as "situationalism." Regardless of terminology, the point is that life is nuanced by the array of consequences, constraints, and prescriptions contained in contexts in which actors find themselves (Hazan & Raz, 1997, p. 261). As far as aging is concerned, participation carries with it cohort norms and timing sequences, as well as mechanisms maintaining synchronicity among members by providing flexible temporal prospects and normative expectations defining generation, age, or other temporally derived designations (Hardy & Waite, 1997; Neugarten & Hagestad, 1976).

## II. DIMENSIONS OF CAPITAL

With growing recognition of the lifelong interchange between actors and macro-level influences, termed the self-structure dialectic above (Hendricks & Leedham, 1992), has come increased attention to the nesting of human and social capital resources having a bearing on ". . . how people anticipate, offset, or deal effectively with stressful events" (Taylor & Aspinwall, 1996, p. 71). In their daily lives, actors call upon their stock of human capital—their talents, aptitudes, skills, and capabilities. Simultaneously, they utilize the social capital at their disposal—their relationships, roles, and place in the world—those concomitants of their being that impart an ineffaceable, socially constructed master status mitigating how events unfold. Social capital is embedded in socioeconomic status, ethnicity, gender, occupation, modes of production, informal or formal networks, policy, and social processes characteristic of all social locations. These structural characteristics entail inclusive or exclusive frameworks for evaluation of personal attributes and access to opportunity, as well as utile ideological and political trappings justifying distinctions. Such schema spawn matrices of precedential norms, values, roles, and relationships inflecting lifestyle and experience. The challenge is to meld human and social capital, personal, and contextual circumstances into a unified conceptual lens. Though the two dimensions of capital are discussed in turn, a key claim of this chapter is that they are more analytically distinct than discrete phenomena. They intertwine, divisions meandering and inexact, reciprocally influencing one another. Taken together, they comprise the array of personal resources upon which actors draw in sorting-out lifestyle and negotiating life chances.

## Human Capital

Human capital encompasses personal attributes, traits, and skills enabling actors to act as their own agents, seeking their own ends—it is the more proximal of the two forms. Human capital is an amalgamation of personality, talents, training, competencies, physical, and/or psychological capabilities (Coleman, 1988). Human capital variables underpin the way many researchers conceive of status attainment and it is widely held that such variables are fundamental to systems of social stratification (cf. Davis & Moore, 1945). The contention is that those whose investment in human capital make them best prepared to contribute to societal well-being should be rewarded the most, with rewards predicated on the conditional value of their human capital. In practice, both evaluation of attributes and assignment of rewards fall disproportionately to those already occupying advantaged positions. Consequently, an exclusionary rationale rationalizes distribution of claims and opportunities based on possession of socially valued qualities, capabilities, or achievements. These human capital characteristics are customarily labeled "objective," measurable by standardized criteria. Interestingly, many of these same factors are believed to display age-related decrements and a great many social roles or entitlements are allocated on the basis of putative age-related declines.

It is possible to think of functionality, physical or mental, abilities appropriate for participation in informational exchanges, and other individual attributes or skills that ensure performance and ability to manipulate the environment as forms of human capital and, simultaneously, as the rationale underpinning social assignments and rewards. Some investigators are of the opinion that even genetic endowments, the ultimate form of human capital, affect such things as social networks and coping behavior (Taylor & Aspinwall, 1996).

## Social Capital

The concept of social capital has long been part of the stock in trade of sociology, though current interpretations derive from Bourdieu's (1986) contention that relationships are the fundamental unit of analysis for examining human affairs. Social capital is comprised of those resources actors access by means of participation in socially relevant categories and through interpersonal ties. Social capital is the more distal and intangible of the two forms, embedded in social relations, yet available to actors via affinity, attachment, and association (Coleman, 1988). Social locale is said to affect the likelihood of certain returns—instrumental and expressive—and influences life chances across diverse dimensions. Social capital is also highly fungible, underpinning differential achievement, experience, health, perceived mastery, resilience, social control, and life satisfaction, to name but a few consequences (Coleman, 1988; Lin, 2000; Rowe & Kahn, 1998). In addition to being an asset accessible to actors, social capital is a composite that is characteristic of collectivities, employed to further their interests and define communal distinctiveness (Portes, 1998). It is important to note that such assets are not distributed randomly or equally across social groups, and to underscore that there is consensus that advantageous rankings are synonymous with better access to and use of societal resources by virtue of social location, the social capital ingrained in that location, and accompanying relationships (Lin, 2000).

Membership in any collectivity establishes boundaries for entrée and opportunity, not to mention providing public constructs and interaction integral to self-perception and social identity. In the course of interaction an enduring moral order is fashioned that creates codes for interpretation, representation, performance, convictions, and networks of exchange. Continuing interaction and shared outlooks ensure the dissemination of cultural scripts among consociates and are the source of the "we-ness" by which groups define themselves and others (Cerulo, 1997). Consequently, membership is both prologue and provenance of the unfolding of duration dependent sequelae comprising the life course. It is not a matter of binding rules, but of non-equivocal beliefs and relative privilege adhering to groups that undergird actions and experience. Because of differential patterns of association, whether by design, default, or interaction preference, people interact primarily in affinity groups more like themselves than dissimilar (Lin, 2000). The shared perspectives gained through sociability assure "naturalness," or what might be termed effective communication, certainly communication that feels comfortable and easy. It would not be an overstatement to assert that interaction creates enclaves of identity, major anchorages for self-validation, and personal meaning. In characterizing the role of structure and its appurtenances, Callero (1991, p. 51) was succinct; structural relations are enabling resources facilitating or impeding particular outcomes and worldviews. Structural grounding guides the nature of experience, provides archetypes for interpretation, and is source of both misery and advantage. Hierarchical or differential status groupings, based on ascribed or intrinsic characteristics, such as the socioeconomic status into which one is born, or other dimensions of master status, including gender, race, religion, or age, augur disparate access to resources and opportunities.

In this view, actors are conceived as consequences of social relationships and allied institutional practices grounded in the social order (Meyer, 1988; Stryker, 1980, 1987). These social or environmental contingencies are sources of the "stuff" actors utilize as they negotiate their way. Whether *via* access to opportunity or information, differential locales provide differential resources—thus sustaining broad-reaching social heterogeneity and pluralism. The social capital derived from interpersonal interaction and structural conditions provides frames of reference integral to all manner of differential outcomes.

The relevance of master status characteristics, including social class and other distinctive components, is that they are resources affecting diverse domains through a causal chain of direct or indirect effects (Diehl, 1999; Han & Moen,

1999; Pillemer, Moen, Wethington, & Glasgow, 2000; Rowe & Kahn, 1998; Thoits, 1982, 1995). It is *via* an amalgamation of human and social capital that institutionalized pathways through life unfold. In addition to furnishing a template for experience, these moorings provide assumptive, taken-for-granted propositions thought of as indisputably warranted: their persistence taken as proof positive of their applicability. The presumption is that though social capital may be independent of individuals, it is not peripheral as it is available to them, central to how experience unfurls, and accounts for a plurality of outcomes (Bourdieu, 1989).

Rowe and Kahn (1998) contribute considerable evidence that concomitants of lifestyle serve to differentiate usual from successful aging. Seemingly, many undesirable effects encountered in life vary as a consequence of social location, through exposure or differential vulnerability traceable to forms of social capital (Aneshensel, 1992; Dohrenwend & Dohrenwend, 1969; Hayward, Crimmins, Miles, & Yang, 2000; Ryff, 1999). In commenting on "extraordinary rates of premature aging," including "truncated lives and extended periods of life with disabling conditions" among middle-aged African Americans, Hayward and colleagues (2000, p. 926) recognized essential social circumstances, including social environment and workplace experience as causally implicated. The linkage, often discussed under the rubric of a social causation hypothesis, reflects structural contexts and communal conditions (Pearlin, 1989; Thoits, 1982; Turner, Wheaton, & Lloyd, 1995). Blane (1995), among others, has pointed out the "striking consistency" between socioeconomic status and health outcomes. In summarizing the connection, he observed that factors typically construed as social capital variables have profound effects on life experiences so that relative advantage or disadvantage clusters cross-sectionally and accumulates longitudinally (Blane, 1995).

A remark by Heinz (1991) is apropos for condensing the consequences of social capital: the course of life reproduces the distribution of resources. He contended that life's transitions are "dependent on developments in the labor market, (and) individuals are experiencing rather new conflicts and risks that may lead to a variety of innovative, compensatory or irregular status passages that combine traditional norms, self-centered values and extended options" (Heinz, 1991, p. 13). The point is that for much of the twentieth century the organization of work was central to the institutionalization of the life course, not to mention various turning points segmenting its divisions. Work frequently conferred the predominant blueprint for anticipated scripts, even for those not necessarily involved in the labor market. Imagine how life might unfold if employment and retirement cease to emulate career trajectories of the last century. What if work approximates "spot markets," with episodic employment rather than career ladders? If traditional labor market-mediated constraints or opportunities are no longer normative, will it augur sweeping changes in the organization of the life course (Cutler & Hendricks, 2001; Han & Moen, 1999; Henretta, 1994)?

## III. PERSONAL RESOURCES AND THE EXPERIENCING OF AGING

The dynamic interleaving of fiduciary, psychological-physiological, and social-familial resources circumscribe life course, life space, and life chances. Their combined effects reflect personal resources and I assert that these resources affect all aspects of experience from normative trajectories to critical life events. Next, I allude to ways in which self and adaptation are relative concepts, grounded in these same resources. My intent is to shift consideration of self and adaptation from the realm of human capital and autonomous particularized attributes of individuals, to a concatenated framework attentive to the nesting of human and social capital combined with the filtering effects of self-referential processing. In order to do so, it is necessary to provide insight into personal resources, as an amalgamation of human and social capital, and suggest how these resources are central to personological outcomes, be they sense of efficacy or experience of stress (Pearlin, 1989).

A personal resource model emphasizes the contexts of life. A compliment of personal resources is essential for people to remain engaged and in control even though resources are inevitably defined in situationally relevant terms. Concurrently, actors seek reasonable congruence between their abilities and expectations prevailing in particular contexts. The prospect of maintaining positive relationships infuses life with a "sense and semblance of order" (Marshall, 1980). Fiduciary, psychological-physiological, and social-familial resources are hypothesized to maximize satisfaction, promote viability as creative agents, and affect interpersonal negotiations. These three dimensions are shown graphically in Figure 1. I refer briefly to each in turn but it may also be constructive to consider how the constitutive elements distinguish the social life space in which people operate.

For purposes of depicting social life space, the volume of the cube (Figure 1) may be viewed ecologically. Caution must be exercised, however; it is a mistake to conclude that social life space is only a physical place. Still, the volume of the cube may be thought of as representing life space—as a generative transaction zone wherein tacit conventions affect relative adaptation. At the same time, the volume of the cube can symbolize adjustment and adaptation. An optimum array of resources, high ratings on all three dimensions, would place an actor in the front, upper-right quadrant while low ratings would result in placement in the diagonally opposite, rear corner. Not only does Figure 1 provide a helpful portrayal for conceptualizing relative resources found among older people, but placement in the cube may evoke appropriate intervention strategies, provided the dimensions are anchored in contextually meaningful standards of measurement.

### Fiduciary Resources

Money matters affect how experience unfolds. In simple terms, assets make it feasible to negotiate using locally meaningful coin of the realm. The transactional

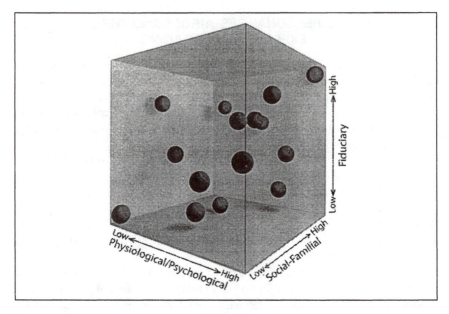

Figure 1. Personal resource dimensions of social life space.

worth of pecuniary resources is evident—legal tender being only the most familiar illustration given value by virtue of public trust and credit. But currencies come in many guises, each imbued with emblematic exchange value reflecting communal meanings. There are, for example, countless "created currencies," ranging from money orders, postal currencies, bank certificates, and savings bonds to negotiable instruments, promissory notes, vouchers, or checks. The contrived soft currencies of families and households, token coinages of total institutions, and instances of in-kind transfers ubiquitous in social economies are other illustrations. Each of these currencies represents meanings above and beyond their simple transactional significance. They serve as social markers, create cognitive maps, reflect assessments of worth, sustain social relations, and are indicative of circles of confidence radiating around particular actors or contexts (Simmel, 1978; Zelizer, 2000).

The fiduciary dimension encompasses any medium of exchange within a cluster of social relations used by actors as they negotiate with other actors. Although money is conventional, complementary commodities, goods, or services such as information and other items of trade or privilege may also be bartered and serve as a resource. Any socially accepted article of trade or symbolic possession could become an instrument of exchange transactions. Special purpose monetary-like currencies of one denomination or another, used in various arenas of life, have always been integral to social relations. Their value is not determined only by abstract links to production or consumption, but signals trust, confidence, communal definitions, networks of exchange and circulation. Furthermore, their relevance extends to non-economic realms pertinent to the organization of social relations (Zelizer, 1989).

## Psychological-Physiological Resources

Psychological and physiological competences are seminal factors shaping life. Acquiring and responding to information or sensory input is basic to bodily and psychological performance, to development, and to aging. Barred by health or impairment from embracing the unfolding of events, actors find it arduous if not nigh impossible to sustain meaningful participation. Hearing, vision, information processing, kinesthetic sense and motor performance affect sensory thresholds, levels of functionality, and other physical or psychological capabilities conditioning an actor's ability to maintain autonomy. Each aspect affects management of environments, and/or ability to be an exchange partner in interpersonal relations. In cases of extreme illness, sensory or psychological incapacity, opportunities for action may be greatly curtailed. Of course, there are also lesser limitations revolving around reduced physiological resilience or competency, sensory impairment, and increased susceptibility to disability that have far reaching effects in interpersonal interaction and environmental usage (Rowe & Kahn, 1998; Whitbourne, 1999). If cues are not perceived, responses are not possible. Put simply, an option is not an option if an actor is unable to take action, exercise choice, or perceive subtle changes in the ebb and flow of events. In addition to perceptual, sensory, and sensorimotor changes, other psychological dysfunctions, including central nervous system problems, cognitive deficits, depression, and dementia, may also constrain opportunity.

What are widely described as normative age-related physiological changes are principal facets of the psychological-physiological dimension of personal resources. Such factors as cardiovascular capacity, organ function, pulmonary reserve, musculature, and so on change over time but may be debilitated by pathology as well. Any physical or psychological decrement that impedes activities of daily living inevitably leads to management issues. Some changes are organ or system specific; others have to do with maintaining homeostasis, and still others have to do with chronic or acute diseases. The point is that physiological and psychological changes interact with the situations actors inhabit. These capacities serve not only as markers of aging, but provide the wherewithal for dealing with internal or external contingencies. Many researchers concede that basic health and physiological capabilities as well as psychological status are linked to social circumstances and accompanying lifestyles insofar as such factors as socioeconomic status are known to be associated with the epidemiology of a wide range of conditions (Rowe & Kahn, 1998). Because psychological and physiological functioning can be influenced by circumstantial factors, the two cannot really be separated and ought to be considered in an articulated framework.

## Social-Familial Resources

Social networks and interpersonal ties are vital to the formulation of experience, constitutive of life, and predictive of well-being (Lin, 2000). Among other things, they are the forums where reflexive redefinitions of self are tested and validated and they provide essential buffers against whatever travails arise. The social-familial dimension refers to interdependent networks of partners that are sources of social capital and furnish instrumental aid and/or expressive corroboration. Such family, affinity groups, proximate or intermediary group-level contacts, are described by Marshall (1995) as meso-structures providing bonds between individuals and broad reaching social relationships.

One impetus for the current conceptualization of relational resources traces to Simmel's contention that individuals are corollaries of the intersection of the various social circles to which they belong, beginning with family groupings. In the 1930s, Lewin characterized an actor's social life space as the total of their social relations within an interaction context. For Simmel, Lewin, and their followers, social networks are vital resources supplying direction, attachments, and anchorages by which life is experienced (Scott & Wenger, 1995). A dearth of close ties portends not only the prospect of isolation, but implies a paucity of primary resources and normative guidance.

Many gerontologists maintain that interpersonal relationships are meaningful even if they treat them atheoretically. The literature is replete with references to the palliative effect of friends, family and spouses, and their value for cushioning negative experience (Pillemer et al., 2000). At the same time, these interpersonal contacts bestow comparative, affirmative, and reflective appraisals relevant to sense of self, providing invaluable normative formulations actors take as their own. A necessary caveat is that relationships can be caustic as well as palliative, with strong as well as weak ties. For example, divorce, family dysfunction, or death may portend considerable adaptative issues and have implications for access to social resources. In either case, the bottom line is that if patterns of differential association are coupled to the distribution of social capital as spread among status groupings, then differential consequences will accrue (Lin, 2000).

Social support is a slippery concept and thinking through how it fits with other resources is a complex issue. The consensus is that it is important to have connections and a retinue of people upon whom one can call for instrumental and expressive assistance and as sounding boards. Although highly variable, with differential valences, ties to family and other forms of association, as well as formal networks of support, are critical for pragmatic as well as subjective outcomes. Those who are bereft of a referential entourage encounter greater stress not only via exposure to risk, but through an absence of buffering (Miner &

Montero-Rodriguez, 1999). Seemingly, growing old in the company of a convoy of consociates mediates much of the negativity encountered along the way by ensuring a well-defined social identity, better self-concept, more effective coping strategies, and a stronger sense of internal control (Antonucci, 1990; Marsden, 2000). Whether analyzed via exchange or socioemotional selectivity theory, interpersonal bonds afford three transactional functions: affirmation, instrumental exchange, and emotional comfort. The universality of the salience of interpersonal networks may be demonstrated anecdotally by the fact that even homeless people develop interpersonal ties and a means of keeping track of associates, offering mutual assistance as possible (Cohen & Sokolovsky, 1989). Part of the significance of social relations lies in their abetting adaptation and affirming sense of self. Given a choice, actors select companions and interact with others based on this affirmational promise (Carstensen & Lang, 1997). In general, interaction patterns reflect exchange parameters operating in the present, as well as the cumulative consequences of a lifetime's decision-making and structural constraints beyond individual control (Heckhausen & Lang, 1996; Hendricks, 2001b).

## IV. DELINEATING THE SELF—CREATING MEANING

How do people create meaning? The proposition propounded here involves a fusion of personal resources, roles, master status, self-referential interpretation, and social contexts. Even the information actors rely on to make decisions is a type of resource derived from social grounding. The confluence of these factors creates not only meaning, but also selves and social differentiation. Furthermore, each is transactional, bringing together public constructs and personal accounts and yielding differential interpretations, serving as a touchstone for moral certainty. Individual meaning systems inevitably represent a combination of social and human capital operating as personal resources, and past performances shaping worldviews grounded in affirmation, or deprecation, and self-referential perception (Hendricks, 1999).

### Self-Boundary Bonding

Association and involvement do more than inform identity. As pointed out above, neither self nor adaptation occurs in isolation; each is unambiguously transactional and always *in situ*. Self-concept and meaning are outcomes of relational bonding and opportunity structures emerging from engagements with social orders operating within particular contexts. In fact, the concepts may be threadbare if divorced from social and situational milieu. Heidegger employed the term *dasein*, or "there-being," to convey his belief that actors—including all dimensions of subjectivity—are ecologically grounded, standing as embodiments of interpersonal and environmental transactions. He also spoke of "instancy" to emphasize emergent links between consciousness and context. In short, situational and interactional arenas contain accouterments that enable or constrain, serving as fundamental framing mechanisms, constitutive of outcomes, personal meaning, and action. Turner and Billings (1991, p. 103) characterized the imminent bond thus: "A key orienting hypothesis in the study of self-processes should be that self-discovery, self-recognition, and self-presentation take place in identifiable social contexts" (see Figure 2).

## Self-Referential Interpretation

The sense actors make is not a passive reflection of experience but is purposive, predicated on reflexive self-referential perception. A handy definition of reflexivity is an ability to be both subject and object; to be consciously aware and continually reframe experience as it unfolds (Gecas & Burke, 1995; Giddens, 1991; Rosenberg, 1991, p. 123). The relationship is central to what Harre (1984) termed "identity projects," wherein actors endeavor to manage change, and create domains of meaning filtered through ongoing concerns and by plying a self-referential agenda. To put it another way, an actor's reflexive sense of self influences what he/she perceives, the meanings created, and how he/she adapts to

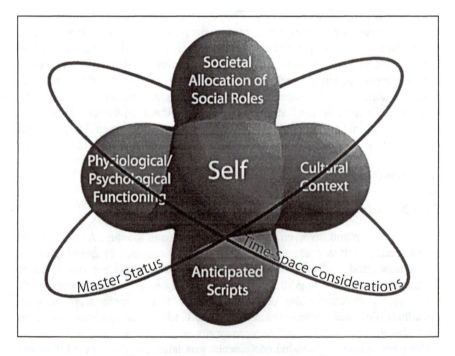

Figure 2. Contingent nature of the self.

contingencies as they come along. Markus and Nurius (1986, p. 159) described the practice as a self-schema that is foundational to all self-defining mechanisms, reflecting personal concerns of enduring salience. The generative prospects of idealized or prototypical self-concepts are temporally fluid in that actors derive constructs from past experience and from mentally reaching ahead in time, bringing future prospects into an intentional present (Hendricks, 1984, 1999; Markus & Nurius, 1986). The question is: how does the process work?

I am of the opinion that sense of self is intentional, expressive, dynamic. In the course of daily life, self-referential processes exert primacy over other factors inflecting perception and interpretation. In this way it is possible to say people "participate in the construction of their own personhood, their own conditions of life, and their own social world" (Dannefer & Perlmutter, 1990, p. 116). Without trying to put too fine an edge to it, sense of self and perception by others are filtering lenses for interpreting life's contingencies. The two dimensions are reciprocal, providing pragmatic principles, powerful pattern-maintenance mechanisms channeling experience, understanding, and adaptation. Of course the task is to cast process and intentionality holistically, in a self-in-situation framework (Hendricks & Leedham, 1992).

As has been pointed out, actors are not passive in the face of what they encounter. They express agency *via* efforts to manage their milieus, the results having wide-ranging ramifications for all aspects of subjectivity. Actors generate their own development, in an effort to maintain competence as they age (Diehl, 1999). A crucial aspect of Riegel's (1979) notion of dialectical change is that it is through managing events that "development" occurs. However, if the demands of a situation tax adaptative capacity, stress or dysfunction rather than development may occur (Burke, 1991, p. 836; Hendricks, 1997). Dowd (1990, p. 149) was prophetic in pointing out that environments are concurrently mediums in which development takes place, as well as opportunity structures with differential distributions of resources. Because there is variability, there will be disparate outcomes and differential success in maintaining mastery, meaning, and purpose across successive phases of the life course.

The roles available to actors are vital to their self-concept. Building on notions of self-efficacy (Bandura, 1977; Gecas, 1982; Zusman, 1966) and the long-standing tradition of the "looking glass self" (Cooley, 1902), Kuypers and Bengtson (1973) referred to "social breakdown" and "social reconstruction" processes, wherein context and accessible roles connect with personal competencies to affect sense of self as well as perceptions by others. Depending on feedback, affirmational or deleterious messages are returned to actors and ultimately internalized. Once a negative cycle is initiated it reinforces unfavorable assessments of competency, leading to further encounters leading to learned helplessness (Zusman, 1966). Whatever the message, with internalization, a self-fulfilling prophecy is initiated. As Turner and Billings (1991, p. 119) avow, regardless of the nature of the feedback, self-boundary exchanges are endemic to the human condition and unavoidably intermingle. Nurius (1991) referred to working self-concepts as emergent from situations and reconfigured sequentially in terms of self-relevant environmental or interpersonal cues. None of this is to say there are not significant elements of self-concept that are not transcendent, nor is it to imply that people may not react to negative situations with a determination to succeed. It is only to contend that the facet turned to the audience, and simultaneously to actors' consciousness, evolves according to priming originating from specific contexts and/or interactions (Nurius, 1991, p. 240).

## V. MEANING AND CHANGE IN OLD AGE

Much of what older actors encounter in their lives results from the way societies organize. With age as a systematizing principle, age-related changes may symbolize social transformations, perhaps even invidious distinctions that undermine the basis of self-concept and magnify lifelong disparities (Calasanti & Slevin, 2001; Estes, Swan, & Gerard, 1982; Foner, 1988; Hendricks & Leedham, 1992; Irwin, 1996, 1999). As Estes, Swan, and Gerard (1982, p. 155) recognized, ". . . the status and resources of the elderly, and even the trajectory of the aging process itself, are conditioned by one's location in the social structure and the economic and political forces that affect it." Differential access to resources, opportunities to use or develop capacities, and exposure to stress that accompanies social order play out in the daily lives of aging actors. Changes that perturb homeostasis or necessitate adjustment to new states may be harbingers of stress-ful outcomes—regardless of positive or negative loadings. Whether socially created or reflecting physiological change, demands embedded in ambient conditions are more complex than meets the eye (Hendricks, 1997; Lawton & Nahemow, 1973; Turner & Billings, 1991). Changing norms and altered access to opportunity may not only marginalize older actors, but place them at risk for self-doubt and loss of perceived efficacy. A dearth of fiduciary, psychological-physiological, or social-familial resources may mesh to erode an actor's self-concept, exacerbate existing inequalities, and lead to corrosive outcomes (Pavalko, 1997; Rowe & Kahn, 1998; Whitbourne, 1999).

What changes accompany age? Does social status and thereby bargaining position change? Do feelings of efficacy reflect issues of mastery? The consensus is that feelings of efficacy underpin subjective appraisals of worth and well-being (Gecas, 1982, p. 26; George 1998; Mortimer, Schuman, & French, 1981). What is often overlooked is how each is grounded in ecological niches wherein development takes place (Hendricks, 1999; Settersten, 1999). Are there physical or social characteristics foreshadowing alterations or inconsistencies? How do meaning and self-worth fare in the face of variable facility? These are more than idle questions. If separation from long-standing referential communities accompanies age, it may herald self-doubt, attenuation and/or negative feedback (Markus, Crane, Berstein, & Siladi, 1982). In many social groups, age—either chronological or social—is a primary criterion by which master status is defined. Thus it may be that aging portends not only somatic change, but an accompanying reflexive cast that alters consciousness and others' perceptions of an actor (Hazelrigg, 1997, p. 105; Kupyers & Bengtson, 1973). Insofar as age carries with it relational meanings that commingle with other relational categorizations of people and places, age will augur change. And, as Bandura and Jourden (1991, p. 942) assert, once beset with doubt, regardless of source, sweeping reformulations of self-concept may accrete, leading to accumulating adverse consequences.

Obviously the issue is one of whether with age an actor's perception and interpretation of events and interactions shift as competencies and facility for managing situations wane (Kuypers & Bengtson, 1973; Smith-Lovin, 1991). Phillipson and Biggs (1998) characterized the too frequent consequence of aging as a type of marginalization that, in effect, generates "zones of indeterminacy" wherein "fit" becomes problematic and identity is eroded. If there is no forum to demonstrate competence, there will be no demonstration of competence. If social accommodations lag behind life expectancy, older actors may find themselves faced with circumstances that effectively exclude them to an extent that their anticipated scripts are breached (Hendricks, 1984; Riley, Kahn, & Foner, 1994). Absent meaning sustaining relational frames, customary practices and experiences may be altered to the point that horizons narrow and boundaries blur, resulting in pernicious challenges to personhood and identity (Phillipson & Biggs, 1998, p. 19; Taylor, 1989). It is as though presumptions that previously fashioned experience dwindle away (Lipka & Brinthaupt, 1991; Rosenburg, 1979).

Though explicit attention to person-contextual transactions predates Lewin's (1935) field theory and its contention that behavior is a function of personality played out within ecological niches, it came much later to social gerontology. Lawton and Nahemow (1973), following Lewin's legacy, coined the phrase "environmental press" to conceptualize experience and adaptation in situ. They sought to bridge personal capabilities as decontextualized phenomena, and competence as it reflects resources and demands within a given life space. They recognized, too, that competencies are themselves dynamic rather than constant across all situations. When people are resource deprived, thereby challenged in negotiating their environmental situations or adapting to critical life events, a kind of "press," disquietude, or stress results.

A personal resource model might generate the following trajectory for those experiencing impaired functioning within their particular niche: 1) Formerly automatic behavior becomes a matter of apprehension and concentration, demanding vigilance and close monitoring. With initially slight effort, mastery may be maintained or restored without major compromises to sense of self as actors experience acceptable levels of proficiency. 2) Continued management may be feasible but entails the expense of delimiting other foci, accompanied by nagging second thoughts, self-doubt, and challenges to competency as increased attention is directed to perceived discrepancies. 3) Behavioral modifications and weakened milieu management abilities further undermine sense of competence, foreshadowing diminished leverage in interpersonal negotiations and simultaneously serving as reminders that previous levels of functioning have been diminished. 4) Expectations are altered and abeyances sought as routines wane. In effect, exemptions, based on current functioning become normative. For example, neither patient nor others expect hospitalized individuals to leap tall buildings; personal care, compliance, and reasonable hygiene are sufficient and interaction partners accommodate. None of these steps, or modifications to them should be construed as saying people with limitations cannot find meaning. It is only to say that challenges increase as personal resources diminish and meaning systems inevitably evolve to reflect new realities.

## VI. CONCLUSIONS

A common and widely accepted perspective in social science has been that individual-level factors are generally responsible for adaptive ability as well as subjective states experienced by older persons. However widespread this perspective has been, it proffers scant insight into life's realities. One of the aims of this chapter is to recommend a more inclusive template for looking at how actors and contexts fuse. Personal experience and agency are inevitably conditioned by the ambit of social circumstances and by being bound to other lives. The personal resource model draws attention to the ways in which social and human capital are nested together and mediate how lives unfold. Their influence crops up in all dimensions of a person's life, including personal agendas and interpretative processes. Regardless of their individual attributes, actors never navigate life entirely of their own volition. Even so, there is not a deterministic correlation between categorical memberships and individual behavior but rather a probabilistic relationship incorporating an actor's intentional consciousness. The need to explain deviations continues to stalk structural explanations of human events. Perhaps the apparent indeterminacy can be resolved by inclusion of self-referential perception and interpretation wherein agency and agenda steer apprehension.

Most actors go thorough life with human and social capital resources in reasonable correspondence. Human capital can be conceived as those personal skills, talents, and competencies an actor carries around and claim as their own. At the same time, actors also enjoin social capital—resources derived from categorical memberships, master status, and interpersonal relations. As some social scientists assert, interpersonal dyads may be the smallest meaningful unit of analysis, representing one type of social capital. Neither self-consciousness nor other dimensions of subjectivity are arrived at *ex cathedra*; they are rooted in relationships upon which individuals draw and are mediated by self-referential perception. The experiences people have and their comprehension of their situations reflect the relative availability and configuration of resources blended through capacities and personal agenda. As an actor's social or physical circumstances evolve, so, too, do mechanisms by which sense of self, personal meaning systems, and feelings of control are exercised–it is an on-going, dynamic process.

Recent research has accentuated the generative nature of age-related changes but with a significant shift. Current formulations address considerable attention to questions of power, control, and context as key factors defining the life world of the elderly. Among advocates of a more dynamic model, the interaction of people with contexts is parsed as a transactional process. With every transition across the life course, and with every recognized status passage, whether physical or social, an actor's bargaining position is reconfigured. Insofar as personal identity is grounded in a confluence of social relations, that is, in social roles, role transitions, proximate circumstances, and changing status positions, mechanisms to maintain feelings of purpose, control, efficacy, and mastery are essential if morale and life-satisfaction are to be preserved.

There is great variability in social-ecological models being propounded to explain the situated nature of adaptation and adjustment. Yet, nearly all represent a shift away from social gerontology's early preoccupation with the psychology of adaptation and adjustment wherein individuals were thought to be primarily reactive agents. Investigators are looking instead at effects of structural considerations, an actor's ability to deal with emergent situations, and their interpersonal linkages. One addition this chapter provides is that personal agenda and interpretative practices are put forward as important mediators interrelated with structural locale. As personal resources available to actors change, so, too, will the ability to manage and respond to environments, whether those be physical or social. At the same time, each such change brings forth a type of renewed marginalization prompting actors to reformulate their "theory of the self." Perhaps what is called for is a new theory of the self explaining how adjustment and reintegration are maintained as successive life transitions occur.

## REFERENCES

Aneshensel, C. (1992). Social stress: Theory and research. *Annual Review of Sociology, 18*, 15-38.

Antonucci, T. (1990). Social supports and social relationships. In R. H. Binstock & L. K. George (Eds.), *Handbook of aging and the social sciences* (pp. 205-226). San Diego, CA: Academic Press.

Archer, S. (1995). *Realist social theory: The morphogenesis approach.* Cambridge: Cambridge University Press.

Bandura, A. (1977). Self-efficacy: Toward a unifying theory of behavior change. *Psychological Review, 84*, 191-215.

Bandura, A., & Jourden, F. J. (1991). Self regulatory mechanisms governing the impact of social comparison on complex decision making. *Journal of Personality and Social Psychology, 60*, 941-951.

Blane, D. (1995). Editorial: Social determinants of health—socioeconomic status, social class, and ethnicity. *American Journal of Public Health, 85,* 903-905.

Bourdieu, P. (1986). The forms of capital. In J. Richardson (Ed.), *Handbook of theory and research for the sociology of education* (pp. 241-258). Westwood, CT: Greenwood.

Bourdieu, P. (1989). Social space and symbolic power. *Sociological Theory, 7,* 14-25.

Bronfenbrenner, U. (1979). *The ecology of human development.* Cambridge: Cambridge University Press.

Burke, P. J. (1991). Identity processes and social stress. *American Sociological Review, 56,* 836-849.

Calasanti, T., & Slevin, K. (2001). *Gender, social inequalities, and aging.* Walnut Creek, CA: Altamira.

Callero, P. (1991). Toward a sociology of cognition. In J. A. Howard & P. L. Callero (Eds.), *The self-society dynamic: Cognition, emotion, and action* (pp. 43-54). Cambridge: Cambridge University Press.

Carstensen, L., & Lang, F. (1997). Social relationships in context and as context: Comments on social support and the maintenance of competence in old age. In S. Willis, K. W. Schaie, & M. D. Hayward (Eds.), *Societal mechanisms for maintaining competence in old age* (pp. 207-222). New York: Springer.

Cerulo, K. A. (1997). Identity construction: New issues, new directions. *Annual Review of Sociology, 23,* 385-409.

Chappel, N. L., & Penning, M. J. (2001). Sociology of aging in Canada: Issues for the millennium. *Canadian Journal on Aging, 20*(1), 82-110.

Cohen, C. I., & Sokolovsky, J. (1989). *Old men of the bowery: Strategies for survival among the homeless.* New York: Guilford Press.

Coleman, J. (1988). Social capital in the creation of human capital. *American Journal of Sociology, 94,* S95-S121.

Cooley, C. H. (1902). *Human nature and the social order.* New York: Charles Scribner.

Cutler, S. J., & Hendricks, J. (2001). Emerging social trends. In R. Binstock & L. K. George (Eds.), *Handbook of aging and the social sciences* (pp. 462-480). San Diego, CA: Academic Press.

Dannefer, D. (1996). The social organization of diversity, and the normative organization of age" *The Gerontologist, 36,* 174-177.

Dannefer, D., & Perlmutter, M. (1990). Development as a multidimensional process: Individual and social constituents. *Human Development, 33,* 108-137.

Davis, K., & Moore, W. (1945). Some principles of stratification. *American Sociological Review, 10,* 242-249.

Diehl, M. (1999). Self-development in adulthood and aging: The role of critical life events. In C. D. Ryff & V. W. Marshall (Eds.), *The self and society in aging processes* (pp. 150-183). New York: Springer.

Dittmann-Kohli, F., & Westerhof, G. J. (2000). The personal meaning system in a life span perspective. In G. Reker & K. Chamberlain (Eds.), *Exploring existential meaning: Optimizing human development across the life span* (pp. 107-123). Thousand Oaks, CA: Sage.

Dohrenwend, B., & Dohrenwend, B. (1969). *Social status and psychological disorder: A causal inquiry.* New York: John Wiley.

Dowd, J. J. (1980). *Stratification among the aged.* Monterey, CA: Brooks/Cole.

Dowd, J. J. (1990). Ever since Durkheim: The socialization of human development. *Human Development, 33,* 138-159.

Elder, G. H. Jr. (1974). *Children of the great depression.* Chicago: University of Chicago Press.

Estes, C. L., Swan, J. H., & Gerard, L. E. (1982). Dominant and competing paradigms in gerontology: Towards a political economy of ageing. *Ageing and Society, 2,* 151-164.

Foner, A. (1988). Age inequalities: Are they epiphenomena of the class system? In M. W. Riley, B. J. Huber, & B. B. Hess (Eds.), *Social change and the life course: Social structures and human lives* (pp. 176-191). Thousand Oaks: Sage.

Gecas, V. (1982). The self-concept. *Annual Review of Sociology, 8,* 1-33.

Gecas, V. (1991). The self-concept as a basis for a theory of motivation. In J. A. Howard & P. L. Callero (Eds.), *The self-society dynamic: Cognition, emotion, and action* (pp. 171-187). Cambridge: Cambridge University Press.

Gecas, V., & Burke, P. J. (1995). Self and identity. In K. S. Cook, G. A. Fine, & J. S. House (Eds.), *Sociological perspectives on social psychology* (pp. 41-67). Boston: Allyn & Bacon.

George, L. K. (1993). Sociological perspectives on life transitions. *Annual Review of Sociology,19,* 353-373.

George, L. K. (1998). Self and identity in later life: Protecting and enhancing the self. *Journal of Aging and Identity, 3,* 133-152.

Giddens, A., (1984). *The constitution of society: Outline of a theory of structuration.* Berkeley, CA: University of California Press.

Giddens, A. (1991). *Modernity and self-identity: Self and society in the late modern age.* Stanford, CA: Stanford University Press.

Giddens, A. (1993). *New rules of sociological method.* Stanford: Stanford University.

Hagestad, G. O. (1991). Trends and dilemmas in life course research: An international perspective. In W. R. Heinz (Ed.), *Theoretical advances in life course research* (pp. 23-57). Weinheim: Deutscher Studien Verlag.

Han, S-K., & Moen, P. (1999). Clocking out: Temporal patterning of retirement. *American Journal of Sociology, 105,* 191-236.

Hardy, M., & Waite, L. (1997). Doing time: Reconciling biography with history in the study of change. In M. Hardy (Ed.), *Studying aging and social change: Conceptual and methodological issues* (pp. 1-21). Thousand Oaks: Sage

Harre, R. (1984). *Personal being: A theory for individual psychology.* Cambridge, MA: Harvard University Press.

Hatch, L. R. (2000). *Beyond gender differences: Adaptation to aging in life course perspective.* Amityville, NY: Baywood.

Haywood, M. D., Crimmins, E. M., Miles, T. P,. & Yang, Y. (2000). The significance of socioeconomic status in explaining the racial gap in chronic health conditions. *American Sociological Review, 65,* 910-930.

Hazan, H., & Raz, A. E. (1997). The authorized self: How middle age defines old age in the postmodern. *Semiotica, 113,* 257-276.

Hazelrigg, L. (1997). On the importance of age. In M. Hardy (Ed.), *Studying aging and social change: Conceptual and methodological issues* (pp. 93-128). Thousand Oaks, CA: Sage.

Heckhausen, J., & Lang. F. R. (1996). Social construction and old age: Normative conceptions and interpersonal processes. In G. R. Semin & K. Fiedler (Eds.), *Applied social psychology* (pp. 374-398). Thousand Oaks, CA: Sage.

Heinz. W. R. (1991). Status passages, social risks and the life course: A conceptual framework. In W. R. Heinz (Ed.), *Theoretical advances in life course research* (pp. 9-22). Weinheim: Deutscher Studien Verlag.

Hendricks, J. (1984). Lifecourse and structure: The fate of the art. *Ageing and Society, 4,* 93-98.

Hendricks, J. (1992). Learning to act old: Heroes, villains or old fools. *Journal of Aging Studies, 6,* 1-11.

Hendricks, J. (1997). Bridging contested terrain: Chaos or prelude to a theory. *Canadian Journal on Aging, 16,* 197-217.

Hendricks, J. (1999). Practical consciousness, social class, and self-concept: A view from sociology. In C. Ryff & V. Marshall (Eds.), *The self and society in aging processes* (pp. 187-222). New York: Springer.

Hendricks, J. (2001a). Its about time. In S. McFadden & R. Atchley (Eds.), *Aging and the meaning of time* (pp. 21-50). New York: Springer.

Hendricks, J. (2001b) "Exchange theory in aging." In Maddox, G. L. (Ed.), *The encyclopedia of aging, 3/e* (pp. 367-369). New York: Springer.

Hendricks, J., & Leedham, C. A. (1992). Toward a moral and political economy of aging: An alternative perspective. *International Journal of Health Services, 22,* 125-138.

Hendricks, J., & Peters, C. B. (1986). The times of our lives: An integrative framework. *American Behavioral Scientist, 29,* 662-676.

Henretta, J. (1994). Social structure and age-based career. In M. W. Riley, R. L. Kahn, & A. Foner (Eds.), *Age and structural lag* (pp. 57-79). New York: Wiley.

Hess, B. B. (1988). Social structure and human lives: A sociological theme. In M. W. Riley (Ed.), *Social structures & human lives* (pp. 16-23). Newbury Park, CA: Sage.

Hogan, D. P. (1985). The demography of life-span transitions: Temporal and gender comparisons. In A. Rossi (Ed.), *Gender and the life course* (pp. 65-78). New York: Aldine.

Irwin, S. (1996). Age related distributive justice and claims on resources. *British Journal of Sociology, 47,* 68-92.

Irwin, S. (1999). Later life, inequality and sociological theory. *Ageing and Society, 19,* 691-715.

Kohli, M., & Meyer, J. (1986). Social structure and the social construction of the life stages. *Human Development, 29,* 145-156.

Kuypers, J. A., & Bengtson, V. L. (1973). Social breakdown and competence: A model of normal aging. *Human Development 16,* 181-201.

Lawton, M. P. (1985). The elderly in context: Perspectives from environmental psychology and gerontology. *Environment and Behavior, 17,* 501-519.

Lawton, M. P., & Nahemow, L. (1973). Ecology and the aging process. In C. Eisdorfer & M. P. Lawton (Eds.), *Psychology of adult development and aging* (pp. 619-674). Washington, DC: American Psychological Association.

Lewin, K. (1935). *A dynamic theory of personality.* New York: McGraw-Hill.

Lin, N. (2000). Inequality in social capital. *Contemporary Sociology, 29,* 785-795.

Lipka, R. P., & Brinthaupt, T. M. (1991). *Self-perspectives across the life span.* Albany: SUNY Press.

Logan, R. D. (1987). Historical change in prevailing sense of self. In K. Yardley & T. Honess (Eds.), *Self and identity: Psychosocial perspective* (pp. 13-26). Chichester: John Wiley & Sons.

Maddox, G. L. (2001). Commentary: Sociological issues for the millennium. *Canadian Journal on Aging, 20*(1), 111-117.

Markus, H., Crane, M., Berstein, S., & Siladi, M. (1982). Self-schemas and gender. *Journal of Personality and Social Psychology, 35,* 63-78.

Markus, H., & Kitayama, S. (1991). Culture and the self: Implications for cognition, emotion, and motivation. *Psychological Review, 98,* 224-253.

Markus, H., & Nurius, P. (1986). Possible selves. *American Psychologists, 41,* 954-969.

Markus, H., & Nurius, P. (1987). Possible selves: The interface between motivation and the self-concept. In K. Yardley & T. Honess (Eds.), *Self and identity: Psychosocial perspectives* (pp. 157-172) Chichester: John Wiley & Sons.

Marsden, P. V. (2000). Social networks. In E. F. Borgatta & R. J. V. Montgomery (Eds.), *Encyclopedia of sociology* (pp. 2727-2735). New York: Macmillan.

Marshall, V. (1980). No exit: A symbolic interactionist perspective on aging. In J. Hendricks (Ed.), *Being and becoming old* (pp. 20-32). Amityville, NY: Baywood.

Marshall, V. (1995). The micro-macro link in the sociology of aging. In C. Hummel & C. J. L. D'Epiny (Eds.), *Images of aging in western societies* (pp. 337-371). Geneva: Center for Interdisciplinary Gerontology, University of Geneva.

Mayer, K., & Muller, W. (1986). The state and the structure of the life course. In A. B. Sorensen, F. E. Weinert, & L. R. Sherrod (Eds.), *Human development and the life course: Multidisciplinary perspectives* (pp. 217-245). Hillsdale, NJ: Lawrence Erlbaum.

Mead, G. H. (1934). *Mind, self and society.* Chicago: University of Chicago Press.

Meyer, J. W. (1988). Levels of analysis: The life course as a cultural construction. In M. W. Riley (Ed.), *Social structures and human lives* (pp. 49-62). Newbury Park, CA: Sage.

Miner, S., & Montero-Rodrigeuz, J. (1999). Intersections of society, family, and self among Hispanics in middle and later life. In C. Ryff & V. Marshall (Eds.), *The self and society in aging processes* (pp. 423-452). New York: Springer.

Mortimer, J. L., Schuman, L., & French. L. (1981). Epidemiology of dementing illness. In J. A. Mortimer & L. Schuman (Eds.), *The epidemiology of dementia* (pp. 3-23). New York: Oxford University Press.

Neisser, U., & Jopling, D. A. (Eds.) (1997). *The conceptual self in context: Culture, experience, self understanding.* Cambridge: Cambridge University Press.

Neugarten, B., & Hagestad, G. O. (1976). Age and the life course. In R. H. Binstock & E. Shanas (Eds.), *Handbook of aging and the social sciences* (pp. 35-55). New York: van Nostrand Reinhold Co.

Nurius, P. (1991). Possible selves and social support: Social cognitive resources for coping and striving. In J. A. Howard & P. L. Callero (Eds.), *The self-society dynamic: Cognition, emotion, and action* (pp. 239-258). Cambridge: Cambridge University Press.

Park, R. E. (1926). Behind our masks. *Survey, 56,* 135-139.

Pavalko, E. K. (1997). Beyond trajectories: Multiple concepts for analyzing long-term process. In M. Hardy (Ed.), *Studying aging and social change: Conceptual and methodological issues* (pp. 129-147). Thousand Oaks: Sage.

Pearlin, L. (1989). The sociological study of stress. *Journal of Health and Social Behavior, 30,* 241-256.

Pillemer, K., Moen, P., Wethington, E., & Glasgow, N. (Eds.) (2000). *Social integration in the second half of life.* Baltimore, MD: Johns Hopkins University Press.

Phillipson, C., & Biggs, S. (1998). Modernity and identity: Themes and perspectives in the study of older adults. *Journal of Aging and Identity 3,* 11-23.

Portes, A. (1998). Social capital: Its origins and applications in modern sociology. *Annual Review of Sociology, 24,* 1-24.

Riegel, K. (1979). *Foundations of a dialectical psychology.* New York: Academic Press.

Riley, M. W., Kahn, R., & Foner, A. (1994). *Age and structural lag.* New York: Wiley.

Rosenberg, M. (1979). *Conceiving the self.* New York: Basic Books.

Rosenberg, M. (1981). The self-concept: Social product and social force. In M. Rosenberg & R. Turner (Eds.), *Social psychology: Sociological perspectives* (pp. 593-624). New York: Basic Books.

Rowe, J., & Kahn, R. (1998). *Successful aging.* New York: Pantheon.

Ryff, C. D. (1999). *The self and society in aging processes.* New York: Springer.

Scott, A., & Wenger, G. C. (1995). Gender and social support networks in later life. In S. Arber & J. Ginn (Eds.), *Connecting gender and ageing* (pp. 158-172). Buckingham, UK: Open University Press.

Settersten, R. (1999). *Lives in time and place: The problems and promises of developmental science.* Amityville, NY: Baywood.

Simmel, G. (1978/1900). *The philosophy of money.* London: Routledge and Kegan Paul.

Smith-Lovin, L. (1991). An affect control view of cognition and emotion. In J. A. Howard & P. L. Callero (Eds.), *The self-society dynamic: Cognition, emotion, and action.* (pp. 143-169). Cambridge: Cambridge University Press.

Stoller, E., & Gibson, R. (2000). *Worlds of difference.* Thousand Oaks, CA: Pine Forge.

Stryker, S. (1980). *Symbolic interactionism: A social structural version.* Menlo Park: Benjamin Cummings.

Stryker, S. (1987). Identity theory: Developments and extensions. In K. Yardley & T. Honess (Eds.), *Self and identity: Psychosocial perspectives* (pp. 89-103). Chichester: John Wiley & Sons.

Taylor, C. (1989). *Sources of the self.* Cambridge: Cambridge University Press.

Taylor, S. E., & Aspinwall, L. G. (1996). Mediating and moderating processes in psychosocial stress. In H. B. Kaplan (Ed.), *Psychosocial stress: Perspectives on structure, theory, life-course, and methods* (pp. 71-110). San Diego: Academic Press.

Thoits, P. (1982). Life stress, social support and psychological vulnerability: Epidemiological considerations. *Journal of Community Psychology, 10,* 341-362.

Thoits, P. (1995). Stress, coping, and social support processes: Where are we? What next? *Journal of Health and Social Behavior, Special Issue,* 53-79.

Turner, R. (1978). The role and the person. *American Journal of Sociology, 84,* 1-23.

Turner, S. (1994). *The social theory of practices: Tradition, tacit knowledge, and presuppositions.* Chicago: University of Chicago Press.

Turner, R., & Billings, V. (1991). The social contexts of self-feeling. In J. Howard & P. L. Callero (Eds.), *The self-society dynamic: Cognition, emotion, and action* (pp. 103-122). Cambridge: Cambridge University Press.

Turner, R. J., Wheaton, B., & Lloyd, D. A. (1995). The epidemiology of social stress. *American Sociological Review, 60,* 104-125.

Whitbourne, S. (1999). Identity and adaptation to the aging process. In C. Ryff & V. Marshall (Eds.), *The self and society in aging processes* (pp. 122-149). New York: Springer.

Yardley, K. (1987). What do you mean "Who am I?": Exploring the implications of a self-concept measurement with subjects. In K. Yardley & T. Honess (Eds.), *Self and identity: Psychosocial perspectives* (pp. 211-230). Chichester: John Wiley & Sons.

Zelizer, V. (1989). Social meaning of money. *American Journal of Sociology, 95,* 342-377.

Zelizer, V. (2000). Money. In E. Borgatta & R. Montgomery (Eds.), *Encyclopedia of sociology, 2/e* (pp.1888-1894). New York: Macmillan Reference USA.

Zusman, J. (1966). Some explanations of the changing appearance of psychotic patients: Antecedents of the social breakdown syndrome concept. *Milbank Memorial Fund Quarterly, LXIV,* 63-84.

# SECTION TWO

# Theorizing Micro Relations

# CHAPTER 5

# Sense and Structure:
# Toward a Sociology of Old Bodies

## *Emmanuelle Tulle*

Bodies have always occupied an ambiguous position in the social sciences, but this applies particularly to social gerontology. In an oft quoted argument made by Öberg (1996), old bodies have largely been absent from the purview of empirical and theoretical investigations in social gerontology but also in sociology. Previously (Tulle-Winton, 2000) I have explored how older bodies have been deployed in the social gerontological literature. I made suggestions for an approach to old bodies which combined an awareness of the discourse in which they are understood and experienced (informed in large part by biomedicine and welfare), with the search for alternative ways of imagining bodies which did not necessarily rely on their disappearance through the pursuit of agelessness or their relegation in institutions. The need to capture the intimate sensations and the mundane strategies people engage in to respond to the changes, bodily and otherwise, involved in the process of becoming older was identified as a way of broadening our understanding of the later year. I posited that it was also perhaps in these micro strategies that we might find the key to resistance to what Gullette (1997) called the "narrative of decline." But perhaps we need to broaden our remit further and I would now like to propose that we need to develop a sociology of old bodies, that is develop linkages between the physicality of aging and the social positioning of older people.

First, I will look at recent debates in the sociology of the body and tease out some of the main issues to have emerged. Second, I will examine how we might extend the lessons learned in sociology to social gerontology, in effect making a case for a sociology of old bodies. Thus I will engage in a selected review of the current state of the old body in the literature. Third, I will propose that empirical and theoretical developments should seek to combine an understanding of how the lived experience of the body reflects or perhaps challenges the status of older people. I will argue that conceiving of older bodies as physical capital yielding particular forms of social capital allows us to take account of a multiplicity of bodies, not just those of the fittest.

Paradoxically, in order to do this, I will draw upon fit bodies, namely the bodies of Veteran or Masters elite runners (subsequently referred to as Masters runners) whose involvement in the sport has spanned several decades from early or mid-adulthood to the present or to semi-retirement in the recent past.

## THE BODIES OF SOCIOLOGY

Twenty years ago, Berthelot (1983) explained why the body should be a central aspect of sociological inquiry. He remarked that all social practices bring the body into play, either as a "tool" or as the target of meaning, which in the process produce the body as concrete and real, caught up in a grid of meanings and dualisms, one of the most tenacious being that which opposes the social to the biological, or the mind to the body. In echo of Foucault (1984), it can be said that the social can be read off bodily practices. But it can also be read off what we choose not to say about the body. Thus abandoning bodily functioning to disciplines outside the social sciences is itself a reflection of dominant discursive practices which construct a clear separation between the social and the biological. And yet, Berthelot notes that emergent cultural developments in high modernity, such as sport cultures (crystalized in the emergence and consolidation of the Olympic movement), reflect the emergence of a new cultural context oriented toward the development of bodily practices which demand that social actors engage intimately with bodily functioning in order to situate themselves. Turner (1996) has shown that health and health-related behaviour is another arena in which work on the body is key to social recognition. Shilling (1996) makes the point that the biological boundaries of the body have been relaxed in ways hitherto unseen, with advances in medicine and genetics opening the potential for manipulations of whole or parts of bodies which fundamentally alter their functioning or their appearance. But in a less spectacular way, cosmetic surgery and programs of physical exercise to transform bodily appearance reflect the increasing belief in the "malleability" of the body, although aging and death are still seen as the ultimate obstacles to the complete overturning of our finitude.

Already, what is emerging here is the recognition that the body as a socio-logical concept needs to be disaggregated. Berthelot identifies three facets of corporeality upon which sociological investigations may be designed: 1) body "marking" or the control of bodily appearance through clothing and adornment for instance; 2) acts of bodily maintenance which produce social value, ranging from dietary prescriptions, cleaning regimes to programs of exercise or at any rate physical regimens deemed valuable for society; 3) the impact of the social on the body: this relates to the inscription on the body of particular forms of social action.

The body is brought into play in a range of spaces, in the home, at work, but also on the outside, in the streets, in shops, etc., the emphasis being on the achievement of "modal bodies," that is, socially and culturally valued, or modal, bodies. There is little room here for an understanding of corporeality as resistance to the normative management of bodies.

Shilling (1996) identifies different theoretical frameworks in which the body has been captured. He evaluates and finds wanting theoretical approaches which lurch too much toward social constructionism or too much toward biologism. He finds more satisfactory approaches which explore the ways in which bodies are shaped by structural forces but are also accorded a role in shaping broader social and structural forces. He is particularly attracted to theoretical contributions which incorporate regulation, bodily dispositions, self-identity, agency, and an awareness of finitude into a set of broader structural forces.

## CORPOREALITY AND LATER LIFE

Later life is an embodied experience. The status of the body, as has already been stated, has not been explicitly or systematically explored in social geron-tology, although that is changing. This is reflected in the greater attention paid to the impact of bodily aging on self-identity (Hepworth, 2000), emanating from the belief that self-identity is a key marker of our sociality. In addition, in line with the sociology of the body, it also seems essential to explore the relationship between the older body and social structure, on the one hand, and culture, on the other, and what bodies emerge from these relationships.

So far, social gerontology has made sense of the body in mainly two ways: as a biomedical event and as the something which threatens well-being and identity. These have been implicated in particular constructions of later life.

In a critique of the place of the body in social gerontology, Powell and Longino (2002) argue that the body only appears in relation to the disaggregation of the aging experience into consecutive age categories, almost opposing the young old, or the midlifers, to the old-old or the "frail elderly," to support the identification of different categories of need. They also explore the continued role of biomedicine in the pervasive association between old age and deterioration and decay, thus lending legitimacy to the cultural devaluation of old bodies but also passing itself as the only source of support in the management of old age and of its decrements. Within this framework no attention is given, by health and social service providers, to lived bodies in practice beyond the management of illness and disability. The denial of alternative ways of imagining older bodies constitutes the main mechanism by which they are controlled and regulated.

Elsewhere postmodernity and consumption have been offered as a way out of the medical discourse. It has become a commonplace to assert that postmodernity and consumption have transformed the aging experience. The claim that aging presents difficulties for a satisfactory sense of self in a context which favors aesthetic and controlled bodies is the crux of such analyses. Aging assaults both the body and the self. On the other hand however, it is argued, the new cultural context presents opportunities for resistance to aging. Featherstone and Hepworth (1989) have argued that in recent years traditional, linear, age-bound life course patterns had been under assault and their replacement by postmodern life patterns have given older people the opportunity to have aspirations not necessarily associated with their age. This therefore allows people to lead ageless rather than age-bound lifestyles. Featherstone, Hepworth, and Turner (1991) have noted that people themselves conceive of their aging body as a "mask" betraying the ageless self that lies beneath. Gilleard and Higgs (1998) argue that consumption may act as a way of resisting the mask of age, by making available forms of bodily modification or alternative lifestyles, or cultures of aging.

However real living, sensate bodies and their deployment in their broader structural context do not feature in these approaches, which tend to homogenize older bodies, in some ways, seeking their salvation from deterioration and medicalization in the denial of the body as a key component of the aging experience (Tulle-Winton, 2000).

## Mapping the Discourse of Old Age

I would argue that current theoretical approaches need to differentiate between different bodies, rather than point us in the way of ageless or invisible bodies. Thus we need to consider gender, class, cohort, and ethnicity when mapping out an appropriate way of accounting for the body in later life. However, there may also be other lines of demarcation, which cut across these differences. There are different bodies out there and they need to be brought to life.

This claim is supported by an emergent critique of the techniques of resistance to aging outlined above. Andrews (1999) shows that resisting aging through agelessness amounts to the rejection of what she calls "agefulness," or the devaluation of experience and maturity. This is particularly relevant for very old people (Gilleard & Higgs, 1998) whose bodies are no longer amenable to modification and whose finitude is more acutely real. Elsewhere we find that it is the spaces in which people become older which differentiates them, not only from other older people but also from the rest of the population. For instance, the reality or simply the anticipation of physical disability may encourage affluent older people to move house and in this way fulfil their obligation to take responsibility for their own care in an ideological context which favors the individual, privatized management, over the collective bearing of risks (Tulle & Mooney, 2002). Gubrium (1999) and Hazan (1994) have explored the ways in which bodies are deployed but also interpreted in institutional contexts. The boundary between different bodies is reflected in the boundaries drawn between the institution and the outside. In these examples age or disease are used as ways of differentiating between bodies.

Gender is also an obvious organizing principle. Powell and Longino (2002) explore the contribution of feminism to uncovering the gendering of the corporeal experience, both as a personal issue and as a cultural feature of Western societies.

However the focus tends to be on the bodies of older women and their impact on identity, well-being and the management of everyday life (see for instance, Hurd, 1999), rather than on the gendering of corporeal ability and experience. Nevertheless these contributions are crucial to an understanding of how older women are not only regulated by the discourse of agelessness but how they themselves make use of it to retain their presence in the world. But we need to find out more about older men's bodies too.

Thus the literature is beginning to identify a multiplicity of bodies. It is also engaging with the wider cultural context in which these bodies are apprehended. I would argue that this context is changing and broadening.

## Widening the Discursive Grid

The identification of changes in life course trajectories and consumption, the emergence of agelessness as a way out of social obsolescence are, I would argue, part of the contemporary discourse of later life. By this I mean that they create a field of possibilities within which particular choices about the conduct of everyday life can be negotiated. It seems however that the discursive grid in which old age can be imagined and experienced is much broader.

For instance, the empirical evidence for agelessness as a way of papering over the gaps between bodily deterioration and the self is ambiguous and much more research needs to be carried out to explore, first, how people engage with the dominant discourse of old age/agelessness and, second, how different groups of people negotiate this hiatus but also what its value as a social act is.

This is crucial as in other ways older bodies continue to be understood within what I would call a framework of "enfeeblement."

Vertinsky (1998) argues that physical exercise is encouraged in later life but within very tight constraints. Older bodies, those of post-menopausal women in particular, are seen to be at particular risk of wearing down if engaged in physical activity deemed to be too strenuous. She places blame for this overcautious attitude on medical professionals who, she argues, are more likely to recommend rest or, at best, gentle exercise, than more physically challenging activities.

Recent evidence from biomedical research is conflicting (Tulle, 2003) however. On the one hand some of the literature suggests that older bodies, including very old bodies, can be exercised strenuously and that performance in sporting activity can be improved considerably through strength and aerobic training. This data is derived from studies among Masters sportsmen and women, typically distance runners, track athletes, and swimmers aged upwards of 50. Age boundaries can also be unsettled. One study in particular showed that a small sample of people in their 90s who had been asked to follow a strength training program had all improved stability and mobility in their hips and lower limbs, a few regaining the ability to walk with a stick as a result of the program (Benyo, 1998). Overall then, strenuous exercise is not only possible, it also has a positive impact on both physiological function and musculo-skeletal strength, irrespective of gender or age. There is also a group of publications which is addressed specifically at Masters athletes and which is aimed at maximizing performance, at levels which most people, irrespective of age, would not dream of achieving!

On the other hand the literature is also replete with examples to back up Vertinsky's claims that exercise is recommended as beneficial but in moderation. Widely cited manuals dealing with exercise in later life contain large sections describing physiological, musculo-skeletal, and cognitive aging, i.e., deterioration. Exercise then is viewed primarily through the lens of restricted abilities and reduced accomplishments and disability prevention (Shephard, 1997; Spirduso, 1995). It is also advocated in the context of maintaining an active lifestyle into the later years.

## Accessing the Sensate Body

The study on which the rest of my argument is based was, in part, an experiment into how both the intimate and public processes associated with becoming older could be accessed. Why would this be important? We do not understand well how people come to know that their bodies are aging. We know that illness or disability may be a trigger for the realization of age. We also know that when they are not ill, people like to claim that they are not old, and that whatever negative processes of change they may be experiencing, will be rationalized as an act of betrayal. Hurd (1999) found that women attending a day care center concealed illness from other attendees to avoid being labeled as old by their contemporaries. So in fact the sensations are there and some people will manage them through a set of strategies of concealment, by denying their existence and diverting the gaze of others toward their activities and the "ageless" self.

Thus, paradoxically, aging is conceived primarily as a biomedical event which normalizes the relationship between aging and disease and masks the minute, mundane processes to which the body is subjected as it ages and which may nonetheless signal aging and trigger reflections about age and perhaps even encourage particular strategies of resistance to or acceptance of aging. So, in order to understand later life outside an illness and disability framework, we also need to explore "healthy" bodies, like those of physically competent people.

The advantage of focusing on serious runners is that they subject their bodies to forms and levels of exertion which would not be possible without an intimate knowledge of their bodies. They are also conversant with bodily processes, especially when they train, race or when they become injured: over time athletes, of necessity, develop an intimate knowledge of their bodies and are often very articulate about them. Thus the passage of time alters the dialogue with the body.

Empirically we can investigate how people deploy their bodies in the pursuit of their sport and in the realization that they are aging. For instance we can elicit accounts about the changes to their performance but also to their ability to sustain high levels of physical exertion that have taken place over time, what linkages people make to interpret these changes, whether for instance change was perceived as attrition in performance and explained by aging, how they respond to this process of attrition but also how they experience the more "mundane" aspects of looking and feeling older.

What I would also like to do, in light of the empirical evidence presented below, is move the debate toward the search for a theoretical framework which explains how people in their later years experience and manage their bodies, and how these experiences locate them as social actors.

## DEPLOYING THE BODY

### Running and Everyday Life

Being a runner is timebound in a multiplicity of ways. Masters athletes are either recent entrants into their sport or continue what is a lifelong engagement. Some runners start running at school. Most continue into their senior and Masters years, although women are less likely to persist beyond school. For them marriage and childrearing would have interrupted participation or even delayed first entry till their late 20s or even mid-30s. Most of the variation in participation and the intensity of participation in the later years is displayed in the extent of commitment as seniors. For those who start very early, there appears to be a tail-off in their late 20s and early 30s. Serious injuries or illness would be the main reasons for not picking up again as veterans. What binds all Masters athletes is the presence of structures which allow them to do sports in their later years. Two structures are worth mentioning: first the formal, official structure provided by the athletics community and second the individual management of everyday life. Gender plays a key role here. Women have been affected by their exclusion from long distance running until the early 80s when they were allowed to compete in marathons. Family commitments and marriage also affect women, as they do men. However, it appears that men are better able to override these constraints.

People who retire from running because of illness or injury often continue to be involved in other ways, usually as coaches and in sport administration. What is however striking among those involved in Masters athletics, either as competitors or as officials, is the centrality of athletics in their lives. It structures their entire lives in various ways: daily and weekly (when and how many times to run), according to the racing season (dividing the year into competition, training up to competitions and resting). It affects how and where they spend their holidays. It may even affect their jobs. Working part-time or turning down a job offer away from one's running club reflect Masters athletes' commitment.

Running also affects the lives of partners and children. Runners rely, if not on active support, at any rate on their tacit acceptance of the demands of participation in sports. Strategies to facilitate this process vary, ranging from coopting the partner into the sport either as a participant or as a supporter to simply imposing these demands. While women are able to coopt their spouses into their own activities—and here the support appears to be willingly given and part of a wider encouragement to do well—it is among the wives of male runners that the most passive acceptance at best, and hostility at worst, is encountered (Barrell, Chamberlain, Evans, Holt, & MacKean, 1989).

This level of commitment enables the runners themselves to make a distinction between two types of runners: *recreational* runners or joggers and *serious* runners, or simply runners. The jogger merely runs a few times a week to keep fit, rather than to improve performance. The impact on his/her life is minimal. In contrast the *serious* runner submits him/herself to the rigors of training and competing, is prepared to make sacrifices in the pursuit of achievement and let as few demands as possible interfere with running. This typology retains its relevance after retirement from the sport, particularly for those who were forced to retire through illness or injury.

## Disciplining the Body

Above we looked at the ways in which lives were disciplined by running. Bodies are also disciplined and the body work involved remains intensive until late in life.

The weekly mileage can range from 35 to 100 miles, is typically spread over six or even seven days and sometimes includes two runs per day. A handful run every day of the week. They race at least once every four weeks. In summer, they tend to compete more often. There was attrition in this work rate as one moved beyond 70 years of age.

This intensification of training is a relatively recent occurrence and coincided with the introduction of new training methods in the 1970s and 80s when this cohort of runners became Masters (at age 35 for women and 40 for men). These transformed performance for all age-groups, but in counter-intuitive ways, for those reaching their Masters years often achieved their personal bests in their later years rather than as juniors or senior runners.

A typical training session is spread out over the week. Runners combine club sessions with individual sessions. Variations around this model were encountered: time constraints, injuries, how easily accessible the club house is from home and work and even age affect the extent to which runners follow this pattern. Usually however, this is followed by runners at the peak of their athletic performance, usually in their late 30s, throughout their 40s, and even perhaps into their 50s. Older athletes tend to jettison club-based training sessions and concentrate more on endurance rather than speed (Weir, Kerr, Hodges, McKay, & Starker, 2002).

## Injuries

The extent to which informants were affected by injuries varied. Those who were still active in the sport were free from serious injury, which accounts for their continued participation at such high levels (but they were not necessarily free of illness). How they interpreted and responded to them was instructive.

A typology of injuries appeared to be in operation. They differentiate between four types of injuries: those caused by an accident (twisting an ankle, breaking a leg, etc.), those caused by overuse or lack of appropriate stretching (knee pain), those caused by wear and tear or aging (hamstring injury), and finally, those with no known cause. Thus aging is only one possible cause of injury. This typology has the advantage of assisting runners in the development of appropriate strategies for recovery. But interestingly it also allows them to distance themselves from the dominant discourse of age.

Runners respond to injuries through a series of decisions which involve a dialogue with the body. Injuries are often brought to their attention runner by what was described as *a niggle*. This is usually ignored until it has turned into a full blown injury. In more dramatic instances, the injury forces retirement from a race. This is usually followed by a period of enforced rest from running, which athletes usually find very difficult to cope with.

Next the injury has to be identified according to the typology described above. This usually entails individual or multiple visits to a range of professionals such as doctors, physiotherapists, acupuncturists, podiatrists. However a few keep away from professionals as a result of negative experiences (aggravation of the injury, in some cases permanently). Surprisingly those who visit professionals, after an extended period of time seem to conclude that they have to resort to resting while doing other exercises like swimming or cycling to maintain their fitness. Giving in to resting appears to result from failed attempts to speed up recovery, from realizing that they have exhausted all available strategies without any visible return on their efforts.

The return to running must be negotiated. In other words, runners must assess when their body has sufficiently recovered to resume training. However there usually is no discernible point at which one can say recovery is complete and so they have to return to running after a while to monitor their recovery. Therefore they often return to running with some pain, perhaps putting their careers, or their physical capital, at risk.

Bodily sensations fuel the dialogue with their bodies. However it takes a while for this dialogue to be established and in some instances runners misunderstand these sensations. What follows are two examples of this dialogical relationship with the body, the second with serious consequences for the runner's health:

> The first runner, a 50-year-old male, has been experiencing persistent knee pain for several years but has not altered his running schedule, thus

putting his running career at risk. The rationale for his decision is that he has had the pain investigated by his doctor and had X-rays taken of his knee. The X-ray showed no sign of bone or joint damage. He also "felt" that his injury affected soft tissue rather than joints and bones (the latter interpreted as more serious) and therefore was containable. This knowledge appeared to be the product of the results of medical investigation interacting with the sensations given to him by the injury. His present strategy was to combine his running with stretching exercises.

The second runner, a 69-year-old male, had been forced to retire from elite running because of illness. He started experiencing symptoms like shortness of breath which he, and subsequently his doctor, interpreted as asthma, until some years later and quite by chance, an ECG revealed heart disease which led to the fitting of a heart pacemaker. The pacemaker now regulates his heartbeat but also the effort he can generate as it has been set at 70 beats per minute. This means that he now has to combine running and walking.

The second example shows how bodily messages can be misinterpreted. It also shows how the introduction of an external device can reinforce the control which the sensate body exerts over the athlete.

## The Realization of Age

Over time, runners' performance changes and this is manifested in the loss of speed, which is made known to runners by slower times to cover similar distances. There is ambiguity in the extent to which the loss of speed is sensed. Runners typically claim feeling the same as before but then report loss of energy and drive, the need to rest for longer periods between hard training sessions as well as loss of confidence in the abilities of their aging bodies—loss of elasticity in the muscles and tendons, and increased fragility in the body are volunteered.

The organization of Masters athletics is such that an awareness of age and changing times is an inescapable part of athletes' lives. Elite performances are calibrated by age using a calculation procedure in which linear speed loss is assumed and factored in. The results can be organized in tabular form, organized by five-year age-groups. Each cell would display the world record time for a particular age-group. Thus athletes who so choose (and not all of them do) can then compare their race times with those of their contemporaries, but also with those of senior elite athletes. If their performance was of world record caliber in their age-group then it is likely to be of similar caliber for each younger age-group. Thus runners can say that they might have been world class athletes had they trained as intensively as youngsters. What is not in doubt however is the ability of the body at any age to improve its capacities well beyond standard expectations.

## Resisting Age?

Not all athletes produce a higher work-rate as a result of attrition in times, but they have several strategies to respond to change: they may focus more on endurance than speed, or incorporate more rest time between speed training sessions, or they may stop racing altogether to concentrate on training. The point is that neither age nor even illness is accepted as a legitimate barrier to the continuation of a training regime, modest though it might be.

Being able to display the characteristics of the serious runner, subjecting oneself and one's body to the discipline required by the involvement in athletics are essential to the identities of these people. They can also compare themselves favorably with their non-athletic contemporaries for skin tone, fitness, well-being, better health, positive approaches to life, and a youthful appearance. On the other hand, however, their continuing engagement in their sport forces them to confront their own aging.

How can we make sense theoretically of these runners' lives and of the part played by their bodies in their social location as they become older?

## The Body as Capital

We have explored the broadening space in which the bodies of older people can be deployed—it is a space which encompasses both the "narrative of decline" as well as an emergent narrative focused around physical activity, given legitimacy by the natural sciences.

We have used Masters runners as exemplars of these broad cultural shifts and elicited a range of key themes within which their lives are made meaningful. Running emerges as one of the key narratives of their lives.

We could compare these runners to boxers whose training, rather than merely being a way of maintaining physical fitness, is geared toward the transformation of the body, life, and soul of an ordinary young man into that of a fighter (Wacquant, 2000). Thus we can say that runners, just like boxers and other dedicated athletes, are engaged in the "transformation of the self" (Hawee, 2001) and, in the case of older runners, in the maintenance of a sense of self connected with their sport. They achieve this through a range of techniques designed to regulate their behaviors, thus fulfilling a range of social obligations (Foucault, 1984).

What the above shows is that, even in the later years, the body is a resource. I would therefore like to argue that older bodies can be understood as "capital." Bourdieu (1979) has argued that the body is fully implicated in social action. The use we make of our body, its appearance, not just its physical characteristics but also our deportment, the way we adorn it, the choice whether or not to engage in sporting activities, the type of sports we choose, but at a more intimate level, its dispositions—all are structurally situated. That is bodies reflect our structural location. Gender and class are therefore important frames in which bodies are experienced and shaped. Thus our bodies have social value in varying quantity, depending on our social location and the meanings attributed to our bodily characteristics. Bodies which do not match their structural characteristics are transgressive.

In this way, we can see that all bodies have capital. Socially dominant bodies, i.e., the bodies of the dominant social groups, yield more social capital than those of the subordinate social groups and allow them to reproduce themselves and maintain their structural dominance. Bodies are therefore subjected to body work, either to reflect social position or to produce or achieve social or cultural capital.

This does not mean that body work is unchanging. Sports is an interesting "field" in which body work can bring alterations in capital, either to transcend structural boundaries or to instill desirable social and moral values, such as hard work, bodily and self-control, values which are not normally associated with retirement and old bodies.

## Older Bodies as Physical Capital

Class (Vincent, 1999), gender (Arber & Ginn, 1995), and retirement (Phillipson, 1998) continue to be key determinants of material resources and physical fitness in later life. They are particularly robust in accounting for the lives of people who have lost dependence through illness or disability. Furthermore these factors also intersect with the changing discourse of age, particularly the encouragement to plan for retirement and anticipate the risk of disability and, culturally, the drive toward effacing the signs of age. With the general improvements in life expectancy and physical fitness which we have enjoyed in the last 50 years, opportunities to continue life projects into the later years which do not necessarily conform to widely-held assumptions of appropriate behavior have proliferated. So perhaps assumptions about what is achievable are changing. Nevertheless the body continues to play a salient role in the structural situation of older people, given its propensity to lose aesthetic and health capital.

So do fit older people significantly improve their structural position when their bodies deviate from the modal, that is the young, body?

It appears that older runners have successfully managed to maintain physical capital by adopting a range of strategies. For instance, differentiating between four types of injuries allows runners either to restore the body to its former abilities or to a reasonable "state" of biomechanical functioning that will enable them to continue participating in their sport. However as we have seen, this is predicated on an effective dialogue with bodily sensations being established. Miscommunication with the body can have near-fatal consequences. Nevertheless the willingness of runners to continue subjecting their lives and their bodies to a time-consuming, intensive, and sometimes risky, training regime also brings to light their commitment to the preservation of their running identity.

However this would not be possible without a range of structures facilitating this body labor. The development of Masters athletics provides an organization and cultural framework within which aspirations once denied older people become possible and legitimate. It also provides a framework which both mirrors existing gender differences in relation to exercise and sport (Hargreaves, 1994) and encourages women to participate in disciplines from which they would once have been excluded.

## CONCLUSION

Runners' bodies are interesting—they transgress prescriptions of age-appropriate behaviors, while accruing cultural value through the maintenance of youthful appearance and the prevention of immobility traditionally associated with later life.

In this chapter I have argued that social gerontology needs to pay greater attention to the bodies of older people. I have also argued that this can be accomplished through the development of a sociology of old bodies, the aim being to account for the proliferation of bodies and their impact on the social positioning of social actors as they enter their later years. I have hinted that in order to be able to access this relationship we need to develop ways of capturing the intimate aspects of body work and the dialogue that people engage with their bodies to regulate their behavior.

Bourdieu's concept of capital allows us to examine how this relationship operates. This is particularly salient for late life, given the once narrow discourse of age in which the old body was apprenhended within the narrative of biological and cultural decline and which provided the backdrop for the construction of old age as a problem.

Given the widening of the discourse of age, particularly as it relates to bodies, social gerontology needs to reflect the potential for the proliferation of bodies which deviate from what Berthelot's "modal bodies" or bodies rendered invisible through normative techniques of regulation and examine their social and cultural meanings.

## REFERENCES

Andrews, M. (1999). The seductiveness of agelessness. *Ageing and Society, 19,* 301-318.

Arber, S., & Ginn, J. (Eds.) (1995). *Connecting gender and ageing: A sociological approach.* Buckingham: Open University Press.

Barrell, G., Chamberlain, A., Evans, J., Holt, T., & MacKean, J. (1989). Ideology and commitment in family life: A case study of runners. *Leisure Studies, 8,* 249-262.

Benyo, R. (1998). *Running past 50: For fitness and performance through the years.* Champaign, IL: Human Kinetics.

Berthelot, J.-M. (1983). Corps et société: problémes méthodologiques posés par une approche sociologique du corps. *Cahiers Internationaux de Sociologie, LXXIV,* 119-131.

Bourdieu, P. (1979). *La distinction: Critique sociale du jugement.* Paris: Les Editions de Minuit.

Featherstone, M., & Hepworth, M. (1989). Ageing and old age: Reflections on the postmodern life course. In B. Bytheway, T. Keil, & P. Allatt (Eds.), *Becoming and being old: Sociological approaches to later life* (pp. 143-157). London: Sage.

Featherstone, M., Hepworth, M., & Turner, B. S. (Eds.). (1991). *The body: Social process and cultural theory.* London: Sage.

Foucault, M. (1984). *Histoire de la sexualité, Vol III, le souci de soi* [The history of sexuality, Vol. III: The care of the self]. Paris: Tel Gallimard.

Gilleard, C., & Higgs, P. (1998). Ageing and the limiting conditions of the body. *Sociological Research Online, 3.*

Gubrium, J. (1999). The nursing home as a discursive anchor for the ageing body. *Ageing and Society, 19,* 519-538.

Gullette, M. M. (1997). *Declining to decline: Cultural combat and the politics of the midlife.* Charlottesville, VA: University of Virginia Press.

Hargreaves, J. (1994). *Sporting females: Critical issues in the history and sociology of women's sports.* London: Routledge.

Hawee, D. (2001). Emergent flesh: Physiopoiesis and ancient arts of training. *Journal of Sport & Social Issues, 25,* 141-157.

Hazan, H. (1994). *Old age: Constructions and deconstructions.* Cambridge: Cambridge University Press.

Hepworth, M. (2000). *Stories of ageing.* Buckingham: Open University Press.

Hurd, L. C. (1999). We're not old!: Older women's negotiation of aging and oldness. *Journal of Aging Studies, 13,* 419-439.

Öberg, P. (1996). The absent body—A social gerontological paradox. *Ageing and Society, 16,* 701-719.

Phillipson, C. (1998). *Reconstructing old age: New agendas in social theory and practice.* London: Sage.

Powell, J. L., & Longino, C. L. J. (Forthcoming 2002). Embodiment and the study of aging. In V. Berdayes (Ed.), *The body in human inquiry: Interdisciplinary perspectives to embodiment.* New York: Routledge.

Shephard, R. J. (1997). *Aging, physical activity, and health.* Champaign, IL.: Human Kinetics.

Shilling, C. (1996). *The body and social theory.* London: Sage.

Spirduso, W. W. (1995). *Physical dimensions of aging.* Champaign, IL: Human Kinetics.

Tulle, E. (2003). Physical capital, regulation and self: The bodies of veteran elite runners. In C. Faircloth (Ed.), *The aging body: Meanings and perspectives.* Walnut Creek, CA: AltaMira Press.

Tulle, E., & Mooney, E. (2002). Moving to "age-appropriate" housing: Government and self in later life. *Sociology, 36*:3, 683-701.

Tulle-Winton, E. (2000). Old bodies. In P. Hancock, B. Hughes, L. Jagger, K. Paterson, R. Russell, E. Tulle-Winton, and M. Tyler (Eds.), *The body, culture and society: An introduction* (pp. 64-83). Buckingham: Open University Press.

Turner, B. S. (1996). *The body and society.* London: Sage.

Vertinsky, P. (1998). Run, Jane, run: Tensions in the current debate about enhancing women's health through exercise. *Women and Health, 27,* 81-111.

Vincent, J. A. (1999). *Politics, power and old age.* Buckingham: Open University Press.

Wacquant, L. (2000). *Corps et âme: Carnets ethnographiques d'un apprenti boxeur.* Marseille: Agone.

Weir, P. L., Kerr, T., Hodges, N. J., McKay, S. M., & Starker, J. L. (2002). Master swimmers: How are they different from younger elite swimmers? An examination of practice and performance patterns. *Journal of Aging and Physical Activity, 10,* 41-63.

# CHAPTER 6

# Contemporary Later-Life Family Transitions: Revisiting Theoretical Perspectives on Aging and the Family—Toward a Family Identity Framework

*Ariela Lowenstein*

A quiet demographic revolution has altered the age pyramid of modern societies and has ushered in the transition to a new era of the aging family (Treas, 1995). This revolution has stemmed, from the impact of globalization and broad social changes such as migration and shifting welfare policies on family networks and family support structures. Multiple facets of family life have been transformed, as a consequence, along the following lines:

1. A shift from a horizontal to a more vertical family structure has occurred, namely, a larger number of living generations but fewer members in each generation (Keilman, 1987). This phenomenon, which has been described as the beanpole family structure (Bengtson & Harootyan, 1994; Knipscheer, 1988), is typified by the presence not only of grandparents but also great grandparents, and sometimes the family is made up of five living generations. This phenomenon is a result of increased longevity and decreased fertility and impels a re-examination of long-lasting relationships by family members.

2. The extended aging process within these multigenerational families often engenders new life events that many families have not previously experienced (Brubaker, 1990; Mangen & McChesney, 1988). For example, there is an increased probability that family members will spend a longer time span in intergenerational roles (e.g., as grandparents) than in the past. Additionally, the effects of other family members life-course transitions include the assumption

of new primary functions such as the need to maintain harmonious relationships both within and across a wide span of generations (Troll, 1995).

3. The timing of family transitions, especially marriage and parenthood, cannot be predicted with any certainty today. This has resulted in two distinct family formats, based on timing of fertility: age-condensed and age-gapped family structures (Bengtson, Rosenthal, & Burton, 1995). This diversity of family formats creates uncertainty in intergenerational relations and expectations and has specific effects on life-course role transitions.

4. Diverse family structures and family types have evolved in different population groups and cultural contexts. This diversity is related to what Stacey (1990) has labeled the postmodern family, characterized by "structural fragility" and a greater dependence on the voluntary commitment of its members. Examples of alternative family lifestyles include single-parent families, cohabiting families, reconstituted families, and families of lesbian or gay couples. These family formats are characterized by distinctiveness and pluralism, fitting what Rapoport (1989) has aptly called the "diversity model."

In light of these widespread changes, theories of aging and the family are being challenged, and such new concepts are being introduced as "family ambivalence" (Luescher & Pillemer, 1998) and the postmodern family in reference "to signal the contested, ambivalent, and undecided character of contemporary gender and kinship arrangements" (Stacey, 1990, p. 17). This chapter attempts to analyze the trends cited above and their implications for theories of aging and the family.

The couple and family orientation of social life, and the value attached to sociability position the family as a main reference point in the aging process. Aging needs, therefore, are best understood within the context of the family (Bedford & Blieszner, 1997). Notably, the study of intergenerational family relations in later life and late life transitions is based on the integration of knowledge from two disciplines: the sociology of the family and gerontology. This integration, however, is inherently problematic, for several reasons. First, a gap exists between the knowledge bases, with that of gerontology being much less well-developed. Second, sociological theories focus mainly on the nuclear family rather than on the complex multigenerational family. Third, the emphasis in gerontology is on the personal aging processes, whereas in sociology it is on family development. Last, knowledge in the sociology of the family is based on the "normal" family structure, whereas in gerontology it focuses more on problems in the family, without focusing, though, on minority or international families (Klein & White, 1996).

These difficulties have traditionally influenced the development of theories on families and aging, which essentially fall under the categories of family development or life course perspectives. A critical perspective of these theories is needed in order to gain an understanding of later-life families.

The goal of this chapter, thus, is threefold: 1) to examine the discourse regarding the limitations of family development and life course theories as they apply to different types of late life families; 2) to discuss and analyze changing societal perceptions about life-course transitions in these later-life families that might impact on the development of theory; and 3) to suggest a conceptual framework of family identity that reflects both individual (personal agency) and familial (family groups) levels of analysis and the impact of societal changes on them. This framework attempts to close some of the gaps inherent in the above theories.

## FAMILY DEVELOPMENT AND LIFE-COURSE PERSPECTIVES— A CRITICAL LOOK

### Family Development Theory

The study of changes in the family over time and the evolution of the family development approach was originally linked to policy issues, namely research on poverty. Family development was conceived by E. W. Burgess (1926), who defined the family as "a gestalt of individuals and role relationships over time" (Bengtson & Allen, 1993, p. 474). The notion of changes in family composition was later adopted as a basis for a nine-stage family life cycle paradigm, and the developmental view was posited as a major theory of family behavior and functioning (Duvall, 1971; Duvall & Hill, 1948; Hill & Hansen, 1960).

The most central focal point of family development is family time which relates to the sequence of stages precipitated both by the internal demands of family members and by the larger society. From the beginning, however, family development research has been eclectic and interdisciplinary, with attendant advantages and disadvantages (Mattessich & Hill, 1987). On the negative side, its eclectic tendency may have encompassed too much at the expense of in-depth focus. Its interdisciplinary nature, while contributing to an understanding of the phenomenon from different theoretical perspectives, makes for a multi-level theory concerned with individuals, relationships, the family group, and the family as an institution, without however, clarifying which processes pertain to the individual and which to the family. Moreover, the processes of change at each level—from the individual family member, family relationships, the family group, and the institution of the family—require four levels of analysis, as suggested by Rodgers and White (1993).

Several modifications have been introduced into this perspective in recent decades in light of changing family structures such as single-parent and step-parent families. Stage sequences were defined for single, "female-maintained," and remarried families (Mattessich & Hill, 1987). Some scholars, considered the possibility of cohabitation as evolving into a stage of family development (Gwartney-Gibbs, 1986). Rodgers and White (1993) focused on both household and kinship ties in the identification of important players in the family, i.e., stepparents or former spouses. An additional family format that is becoming more apparent is the truncated family structure, i.e., an increase in the proportion of adults who remain childless. Statistics show, for example, that about 30 percent of the elderly in the United Kingdom were childless in the late 1980s (Chapman, 1989).

Another area of difficulty in defining family events as indicators of stage transitions lies in the use of average ages in identifying the initiation and duration of family events (e.g., spacing and number of children) to establish family sequences. This methodology tends to "wash out" social class and ethnic group variations. For example, many African American families show "age-condensed" family patterns, while Caucasian families increasingly display a pattern of "age-gapped" families as the norm (George & Gold, 1991). Family events are also affected by historical context (Elder, 1985), i.e., scholars point out that it is useful to distinguish invariant developmental features of families across historical periods from those specific to a particular epoch or to particular cohorts.

Essentially, theories of family development tended to:

- Ignore the timing of critical life events and the duration of stages (Mattessich & Hill, 1987, p. 462).
- Blur the identity of individuals as family members because the focus is on the family unit (White, 1991).
- Emphasize family change without specifying the precise type and process of change, thus failing to distinguish between normative developmental changes from other non-normative types of changes occurring in families (Rodgers & White, 1993).

## Life Course Perspectives

By the 1970s, the life-course approach increasingly supplemented and ultimately challenged family development as a means of analyzing systematic family change. The focus shifted to how events and their timing in the lives of individuals affected families in specific historical contexts.

The various life-course perspectives share the following three premises: 1) the life course is a social phenomenon (Hagestad & Neugarten, 1985) that reflects the intersection of social, cultural, and historical factors with personal biography (Elder, 1985; Meyer, 1988); 2) it focuses on age-differentiated sequences of transitions (Rossi, 1980), with transitions and trajectories as key concepts (Hagestad, 1990), and "cultural precepts underlying the life-course system define and locate the meaning of both the individual and the trajectory of the proper life" (Meyer, 1988, p. 62); and 3) life-course research requires a dynamic, longitudinal perspective that is not easily attained (George & Gold, 1991).

The life-course approach has multidisciplinary roots with contributions from life history analysis, life span psychology, age stratification theory, and the concept of age cohort (Elder, 1978; Hareven, 1980, 1995). It links the three metrics of individual lifetime, social (family) time, and historical time. The lifetime metric relates to chronological age and age stratification, and the meanings, behavioral expectations and vulnerabilities associated with particular ages (Riley, Johnson, & Foner, 1972), i.e., whether social clocks are "on time" or "off time" (Hagestad, 1990; Hagestad & Neugarten, 1985; Hill, 1970). The linkage between particular ages and family-event sequences assumes an underlying set of age norms. Lastly, historical circumstances and broad social changes such as migration, wars or economic shifts mold and reshape mutual support within the family (Hareven, 1995).

In summary, life-course concepts are particularly useful in studying issues where the focus is on shifts in the lives of individuals involving their roles in a number of different institutions, of which the family is only one, and relating to institutions such as the educational system or the economy at large. Life-course theorists have linked changed demography with role theory in studying expectable life events, especially across the middle and later years of family life, such as the role of retiree. The theory provides a comprehensive framework for understanding reciprocal relationships between generations, especially within our changing contemporary society. Shortcomings, however, are inherent in the theory, namely, the difficulty of differentiating change and development, and the difficulty in constructing causal theories in light of the diversity of forces, and societal changes that operate on individuals and families.

## Life Course Transitions in Later-Life Families

A primary assumption made by transition theorists is that despite clear differences in the content of major life changes at specific ages—e.g., adolescence or retirement—general principles of transition apply to every phase of the life cycle.

Transitions that are widespread and highly predictable, such as the death of a parent during the offspring's middle age, or voluntary retirement, may still be viewed as life-course markers, while other transitions, such as the timing of first marriage, parenthood, and grandparenthood, are less predictable in modern society. The issue of how individual family members, and families as a whole, adapt to these transitions leads to a consideration of the meaning of transitions, and especially later-life family transitions.

### Transitions

The root of the word transition is derived from the Latin, "to go across." Transition refers to a "passage or change from one place or state or act or set of circumstances to another" (Oxford Dictionary). Van Gennep (1960) in his writings on "the rites of passage" says that "the life of an individual in any society is a series of passages . . . transitions from group to group and from one social situation to the next are looked on as implicit in the very fact of existence, so that a man's life comes to be made up of a succession of stages with similar ends and beginnings . . ." (pp. 2-3).

This premise, however, has never been adequately tested, for several reasons. First, researchers tend to focus on a particular age level, and within that level to investigate a single transition. Second, the use of cross-sectional data in research is prevalent, even if several transitions are examined. The third, problems in the very definition of transition, which is generally equated with change.

Cowan (1991) describes transitions as long-term processes that result in a qualitative reorganization of both inner life and external behavior, or a reorganization of relationships between individuals and their social networks. This definition reflects transition theory, namely, transitional life events are typified by changes in patterns of behavior and roles that may be added, redefined or shifted in salience (Cowan & Hetherington, 1991). Role changes occur during transitions. These changes take place in three ways: 1) roles can be added or eliminated, selected or left behind; 2) the set of expectations and behaviors that determine how the role is to be enacted can be redefined or reconceptualized; or 3) a transitional change may involve marked shifts in the salience of an already existing role. New roles must be integrated and coordinated with old ones. Role losses, whether sudden and unexpected or planned, may stimulate a search for new roles as a replacement. The concept of role, therefore, provides a bridge between a focus on individuals and a focus on their relationships.

The dynamics or mechanisms describing the path followed and the level of adaptation achieved as each individual or family experiences a life transition constitutes the process aspects of the transition model. Implicit in life transitions is what Parke (1988) has described as the individual's assumptive world. Transitions require a qualitative shift in perception of oneself and the world, involving an imbalance that is usually, but not always, followed by a rebalance in emotional equilibrium. Transitions can serve as important turning points, modifying the individual's and the family's life trajectory, i.e., its long-term patterns of stability and change as reflected in the sequence of life events (George, 1993).

### Transitions in Later-Life Families

The average age at which certain transitions traditionally occurred shifted and became less predictable during the twentieth century. Most family transitions in contemporary modern society are less predictable, with the timing of marriage and parenthood in particular exhibiting a much greater heterogeneity (George & Gold, 1991). The timing of transitions in middle and later life also changed. For example, the retirement age has dropped steadily (Tuma & Sandefur, 1988), and widowhood has become more strongly linked to both gender and age, having a much larger percentage of widows in the "old-old" population, from the late nineteenth century onward (Martin-Matthews, 1994).

The feasibility of four- and five-generation families highlights the significance of the study of relationships across multiple adult generations in view of life-course transitions (Bengtson, 2000; Richlin-Klonsky & Bengtson, 1996). Major and universal transitions in middle- and later-life families—retirement, grandparenthood, illness, and caregiving, which cause a renegotiation of roles and relationships with adult children—as well as marital status transitions such as widowhood or remarriage, affect all generations in the family.

Transitions like retirement, grandparenthood, or caregiving, are characteristic of later life even though some, such as grandparenthood in age-condensed families, may occur at earlier points along the life course. All these transitions are accompanied by changes in the lives of elders and their families that are related to the individual life course and familial developmental life stages. For example, changes in an older parent's health or marital status are expected to have consequences for the lives of his/her children, who might have to enter the new role of caregivers. These transitions are also related to broader societal changes that impact on the life course of individuals and families, such as changing retirement and pension benefits that impact on marital relations after retirement (Ekerdt & Vinick, 1991), or assistance provided to caregivers by the state that might alter the components of the caregiving role (Katan & Lowenstein, 1999).

Changes in timing of transitions involve: the impact of late life transitions on different generations in multigenerational families, the importance of addressing the effects of these late life transitions in different family forms and types, and the need to consider broader societal changes in this context. Research on such later-life transitions supports the proposition by Bengtson (2000) that bonds across more than two generations in the family are becoming increasingly important for well-being and support over the life course in a period of accelerated change.

Analyses of the impact of these transitions for individuals and families, however, reveal the shortcomings inherent both in family development and life-course theories. These shortcomings encompass difficulties in relating the variety of transitions experienced by individual family members to a fixed sequence of family stages; difficulties in applying the theories to varied family forms in the era of the post-modern family; over-complexity emanating from the imperative to connect individual, familial, and societal levels of analysis in understanding the impact of late life transitions on individuals within the family context; and methodological problems stemming especially from the lack of enough longitudinal studies. Moreover, if the contemporary emphasis is on ontogenetic time regarding transitions, the meaning of life events is not crucial and the theoretical approach needs to be more deductive (Turner, 1988). By contrast, the more traditional sociological life-course perspectives tend to be more inductive, focusing on age-related transitions (Hagestad & Neugarten, 1985). Some of these lacunae can be filled by developing a perspective based on a composite of several theoretical and research domains, i.e., a cross-fertilized perspective, which may enrich the understanding of life transitions in later-life families. For example, a combination of family development, life course, life-span development, and role theory together with an awareness of different cultural norms, could lead to much needed empirical research on the implications of late life transitions for individuals and family life in a time of changing societal directions.

Such a perspective can lead to a new conceptual framework of family identity that views the evolution of family culture and family transitions as dynamic processes affecting individuals and families, influenced by macro-societal currents and structural changes. Families do not evolve in isolation and are not insulated from broader societal trends. This is especially meaningful in modern individualistic societies where the individual and the life course are culturally constructed (Meyer, 1988). The diversity of family structures in different cultural contexts must also be considered, and point to possible future lines of research.

The next part of the chapter presents a conceptually dynamic model based on the notion of family identity. The framework relates to the social meanings attributed to late life transitions, discussed above, and to their impact on both individual family members and the family as a group within the broader social context. The framework comprises three interlocking circles representing the individual, familial, and societal levels, as well as the interfaces between them (individual-familial, individual-societal, and familial-societal). Ongoing reciprocal interactions between these levels, which differ in meanings and perceptions according to the nature of the transitions, are highlighted. The framework might provide an avenue for the study of simultaneous processes of continuity and change during transitions by examining the interplay between different family subsystems (including individual members) and their shifting sense of family identity.

## FAMILY IDENTITY:
## THE "WE" ELEMENT OF FAMILIES

Any assessment of the multidimensional nature of family life, family transitions, and family well-being must be based on the experiences, observations, and narratives of as many individuals within the family system as possible. Broadly, such an evaluation relies on the extent that personal needs are met within the family group, for example, whether caregiving is provided solely by the informal family network or whether during a crisis of divorce or remarriage one relies only on family members. Such an assessment might also predict whether individuals, couples, and the family itself has a greater or lesser sense of a "we" identity (Reiss, 1981).

The model presented in Figure 1 reflects the dynamic interplay between individual, familial, and societal factors as they mold family identity. It is based on attempts by theoreticians in the family field to revisit the traditional split between the psychosocial interior of the family and the family's relationship with the larger

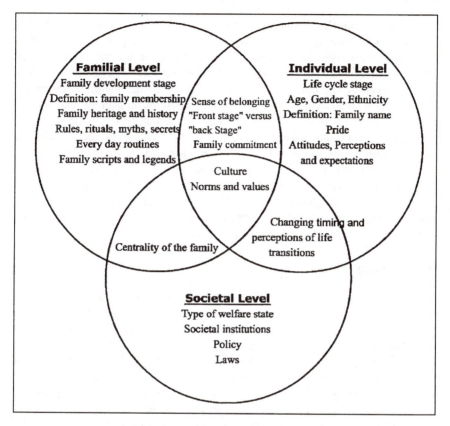

Figure 1. A family identity framework.

society that has underlaid sociological theory for at least the past two decades (Doherty, Boss, LaRossa, Schumm, & Steinmetz, 1993). Inter alia, the three levels influence the impact of transitions in later life on forming and reforming family identity at each level.

According to identity theory, individuals have multiple identities that are relational and hierarchically arranged along a continuum of salience and importance (McCall & Simmons, 1978; Stryker, 1968). A number of investigators have compiled empirical evidence supporting this general view (Burke, 1980; Burke & Reitzes, 1981; Stryker, 1980; Stryker & Serpe, 1982, 1994). The significance of identity salience is that it motivates action in support of a particular identity. The notion of identity salience, also termed psychological centrality, is based on the assumption that identities are hierarchically ordered, i.e., social roles such as parent, spouse, and adult child may be differentially important to the individual.

The proposed family identity framework views the salience of concepts such as family commitment, family membership, sense of belonging, family satisfaction, and family relations as dynamic and as based on the individual-familial interactional context. As such, family identities operate both as causes and as consequences of an individual's family life course, and are in a systematic relationship with other aspects of life interwoven in the broader societal system, such as education or work. If family relationships remain central to the individual throughout the life course, then the quality of family relationships should influence the individual's self-esteem and family identity across all stages of life.

Although the notion of identity has basically evolved as a sociopsychological concept related to the self, groups such as the family also have an identity, as do larger groups such as nations. The concept of family identity can offer additional insights into the complex nature of families and the organization of the life course within a broader societal context.

## Individual Level

A focus on the interaction between family members, especially in the multigenerational families of contemporary society, prompts a consideration of "identity management" and the "dramaturgical perspective" first introduced by Goffman (1963). In defining individual identity, Goffman suggests distinguishing between "felt" identity and the more objective social identity, which consists of the characteristics that the external environment imputes to the individual. "Felt," or personal identity, accordingly, is the image of the individual in the minds of others, and the unique life history that is attached to that individual.

Can family identity be defined in the same terms as individual identity, and if so, what are the worlds of meaning that might form such an identity and how do these worlds facilitate adaptation to late life transitions? Kohli and Meyer (1986) hold that the transition to modernity has been a process of individualization, and that the institutionalization of the individual life course is a key dimension of this process. The life-world perspectives of individuals, therefore, are features of the meaning systems, or culture. Drawing on this premise, the Family Identity Model assumes that the narratives of individual family members are affected both by culture and by more specific attributes such as life stage (age-related), gender, and ethnicity.

The definition by the individual of his/her family identity begins with the delineation of which family he/she is referring to—the family of origin, in which the individual was reared, or the family that he/she formed through marriage or procreation. A small pilot study (Lowenstein, submitted) of Israeli university students (mean age 26) indicated that even though most were married, their first identity designation was their family of origin. When two people marry or live together, both partners must form a new family identity that will integrate their pasts, a process referred to by Berger and Kellner (1974) as an active attempt to "match two individual definitions of reality" (p. 167) or to "combine two family-of-origin experiences within a single marriage." In other words, a young couple just starting their married life must position themselves vis-à-vis their family of origin and define the most salient aspects of their heritage (Wamboldt & Reiss, 1989). In the student study cited above, such an attempt was demonstrated by young women who had difficulty changing their maiden name, or even adding their spouse's last name to their maiden name. The definition of family by its individual members, therefore, is subjective and must be examined through their narratives, noting the articulation of differences.

Definitions of family identity by older family members might be different from those of young married or cohabiting couples: they might, for example, be more connected to their adult children's families and to the broader system of interlocking relationships that is evidenced in multigenerational families (Bedford & Blieszner, 1997; Bengtson, 2000). In cases of grandparenthood in step-families, the issue of relating to a grandchild who does not bear the family name, and is not regarded as part of the family identity, might be problematic. In the case of late life marital transitions such as remarriage, the need to relate to the families both partners had built during their previous marriages might cause difficulties in terms of relations with adult children and with grandchildren, as well as in terms of personal family identity (Connidis, 2001).

The overlapping circles of individual-familial level systems reflects the importance of the particular family heritage, or sense of belonging, and the needs of what Riley and Riley (1993) postulated as a "latent web of continually shifting linkages that provide the potential for activating and intensifying close family relationships" (p. 441). A tentative hypothesis might be posited that highly cohesive families may provide a stronger sense of belonging (Mangen & McChesney, 1988). Such a sense of belonging is also manifested, in Goffman's (1963) terminology, in "front stage" behavior by individual family members that conveys an idealized picture of family life. However, "back-stage" (behind closed doors), family members may attribute less admirable behaviors to the family, or reveal family secrets. For example, couples in later-life remarriages often retain their own original family name, as it defines their individual level of family identity. This might have an impact on their sense of belonging that many times rests with their own adult children and grandchildren. In certain cases it might create stress and even abuse in remarried older couples' relationships (Lowenstein & Ron, 1999, 2000).

Another aspect of the intersecting individual-family circles is the sense of family commitment. The concept of commitment has been applied to gaining an understanding of the link between individuals and their ability to initiate and sustain behavioral acts (Salancik, 1977). Becker (1960), in his theoretical work on commitment, distinguishes between the behavioral act and the mechanisms that produce commitment—mechanisms that ensure stability in a person's behavior. This line of thought suggests a relationship between commitment and identity

(Aryee & Luk, 1996). Family commitment can shift, for example, during the transition to retirement when a sense of stronger "couplehood" might dominate the relationship, especially if both working partners in the couple coordinate the timing of their retirement (Atchley, 1992; Smith & Moen, 1998). This enhanced sense of couplehood helps bridge the individual's changing identity from worker to retiree and his/her perception of his/her changing role in the family structure.

A study by Giarrusso, Feng, Silverstein, and Bengtson (2001) on the self in the context of the family found that family roles appear to be highly salient to individuals at every stage in the life cycle. The relationship between self-perceived improvements in reflected appraisals from family members was associated with improvements in self-esteem across 20 years for grandparents, parents, and adult children. For example, role gain upon entering into marriage was perceived as benefiting the younger generation, a finding that is consistent with other studies (e.g., Elliott, 1996). Similarly, self-perceived success in role performance increased self-esteem (Giarrusso et al., 2001). Moreover, role losses, such as the loss of the child role or the spousal role, did not result in a decrease in self-esteem, whether in the parent or the grandparent generation. Such inherent support might be related to the quality of family relationships and points to the importance of taking role histories into account when making predictions about the outcomes of certain life events (Wheaton, 1990). Social circumstances leading to role transitions, therefore, must be studied. In the context of later-life transitions, role loss should be examined in relation to life events and identity theory in order to understand whether the role in question is salient to the individual's identity. These data might be linked to the shift from the individual to the familial levels of identity.

## Familial Level

Bennett, Wolin, and McAvity (1988) in their seminal work on family identity, discuss some of the components that comprise the familial level, focusing on the subjective sense of the family in terms of its continuity over time and its gestalt qualities. They find this subjective concept to be analogous to the individual-level construct of ego identity in that it is subjective and reflexive and "by definition it must resonate within the family whose identity it is" (p. 212). Like Goffman's (1963) definition of the "felt" identity of the individual, as distinct from the individual's "objective social identity," the family, too, has more than one determinant of its identity. With this, Bennett et al. suggest that family identity goes beyond the notion that family is simply one determinant of individual identity. In their view, family identity is a psychological group phenomenon built on shared systems of beliefs. Similarly, Hess and Handel (1959), in examining "family worlds," presented a view of psychological and social processes as underlying the "whole family" level. However, these "family worlds" might only be inferred by an outside observer at a descriptive level, whereas according to

Bennet et al. (1988), "each expression of family identity is unique" (p. 213) making the construction of a typology quite difficult. This perception is supported by other research on family themes (Handel, 1967), family rules (Ford & Herrick, 1974), family myths (Byng-Hall, 1973; Ferreira, 1966), and family constructs (Reiss, 1981). Themes, rules, and myths are most accurately described as metaphors inferred by an outside observer to account for family behavior patterns.

Reiss (1971), in discussing family constructs, describes how every family creates its own paradigm. Each family identity is expressed uniquely, and there are as many family identities as there are families, making the creation of a typology problematic. However, an attempt to create a typology might help in relating to different types of multigenerational families and different family forms. Handel (1967) describes the "family theme" as "a pattern of feelings, motives, fantasies and conventionalized understanding" that organizes the family's view of reality. It is implicit in the family's notions of "who we are," i.e., who we define as a member of our family, and "what we do about it" (p. 18). Ford and Herrick (1974) describe "family rules" as binding directives for family members regarding how to relate to one another and to the outside world, and which rules serve to transmit family culture from one generation to another. These rules also reflect family heritage, which relates to questions of "where have we come from, and what do we think of those experiences" (Wamboldt & Reiss, 1989). Byng-Hall's (1988) notion of family legends and Ferreira's (1966) notion of family myth, refer to a number of "well-systematized beliefs, shared by all family members, about their mutual roles in the family and the nature of their relationship" (p. 86). Legends or myths convey family identity in a narrative form and include information about the performance of rituals that, nevertheless, can be altered over time. However, there is also a danger that a family myth will become a closed belief system that will prevent the integration of new narrative components. Such a situation is especially likely when the family feels a threat to its survival, as in transitional situations. One example is in late life marital status transitions such as divorce and remarriage, when the spouses' former family myths might threaten their newly created family identity. Often older widows reject the option of remarriage because of such a conflict (Talbott, 1998).

Family identity is acted out through rituals centered in the home, which can be divided into three categories: celebrations, including rites of passage such as weddings and holidays that might be related to ethnicity and subculture; traditions, which are more idiosyncratic to the particular family, such as visits to and from extended family members; and everyday routines, such as dinner time or leisure activities on weekends. All are part of the family life experience and are condensed versions of family life as a whole (Wolin & Bennett, 1984). Rituals usually involve all family members and have a pervasive power to organize the family. Their role is to transmit family culture from one generation to the other. The concept of daily routines encompasses individual, family, and societal time. It serves as the domain for the activities and interactions that accrue to constitute a life. Observing daily life before and after such transitions as retirement or grandparenthood enhances the understanding of individual and family development (Altergott, 1988). It reveals changes in role performance; changes in rituals, such as grandparents spending time with grandchildren on a regular basis whereas while working they could not do it; and changing themes, such as changed interpersonal involvement between spouses or with the rest of the family after retirement.

Family history, which is part of the familial identity, reflects both inter-generational continuity, on the one hand, and the specific historical experiences of different generations that are likely to shape their values, expectations, and outlook (Hagestad, 1981). In coping with conflict and ambivalence, family members sometimes try to steer clear of sensitive topics in the interest of preserving family harmony. Hagestad suggested that family members who occupy both parent and child roles simultaneously in the multigenerational families might bridge intergenerational differences, thus acting as "brokers." The historical dimension of the family life-course perspective provides an appreciation of the multiple contributions of time that impinge on the lives of individuals and their families and on the coalescence of their family identity (Hareven, 1980). If family commitment bridges the individual and familial levels, the perception of the family as central in its members' lives bridges the familial and societal levels.

## Societal Level

The expansion of the welfare state intervention into areas that in the past were managed autonomously by the family has shifted the boundaries between public and private. The distinction between state solidarity and family solidarity has become uncertain, engendering a multiplicity of relationships and circumstances that do not fall completely within either the public sphere, or the private one. Accordingly, the family ethic and family identity have changed as well. Although the family still fulfills a broad series of care tasks, some of the responsibility of caring for the elderly, for example, is now entrusted to the state. This transfer of responsibility applies in particular to the obligations of children toward elder parents, where there is an expectation now that the state should shoulder the burden of care (Sgritta, 1997). Social care of the elderly has come to mean the existence of both formal and informal caregiving networks side be side, providing support for activities of daily living (Cantor, 1989, 1991).

The type of welfare state influences social policy and legislation and reflects the role of the family on the societal level. In Israel, which is considered a family-centered society, social policy reflects high level of familism. Research indicated that policy and legislation that reinforce family support do not erode family identity and the perception of the centrality of the family in care situations (Katan & Lowenstein, 1999). Similarly, a comparative study of services and policies for the elderly in Denmark, Norway, and Sweden showed that family caregiving is substantial, and that collective responsibility through available public services has not discouraged family care. This is so despite a growing preference for formal services relative to family care as a response to changing family norms, and female roles, along with increased availability of services (Daatland, 1990, 1997). By contrast, the shift in emphasis in the United States to market productivity, or "exchange value," rather than "use value" (Hendricks & Leedham, 1991) has resulted in appreciating more autonomy for individual family members. However, accompanying changes to long-term care policies, have resulted in social and nursing care costs having to be paid largely by the family.

Fundamentally, the modern welfare state is the most dominant institutional safety net over the life course, legally regulating the span of careers, funding retirement, and thereby having an important impact on family identity in transitional situations (Kohli & Meyer, 1986). Significantly, the interface of the individual-societal circles demonstrates changing perceptions and timing of life transitions, such as delayed marriage and parenthood, which also impact on grandparenthood. Another example of the interface of the individual-societal circles is the changing nature of women's participation in the labor market, where upon the transition of their husbands into retirement they focused more on housework as part of their family daily routines and their family satisfaction increased (Szinovacz, 2000).

The links between the individual, familial, and societal levels/circles in the model are mostly influenced by culture, which shapes perceptions and creates values and norms, including cultural age deadlines for family and individual transitions (Settersten & Hagestad, 1996). Societal institutions such as work or family thus incorporate meaningful cultural values and norms. Since the life course is a conscious and purposive cultural product of the modern system, and institutional systems are infused with cultural meanings, cultural norms and values inevitably have an impact on individual and familial identity (Meyer, 1988).

## CONCLUSIONS:
## TESTING THE FAMILY-IDENTITY FRAMEWORK

An ideal conceptual and measurement scheme for various types of identities as Burke (1980) proposed, would meet these requirements: 1) It should chart the full spectrum of possible identities and thereby locate individuals based on their self-meanings. Such an approach means that empirical research to test a family-identity framework needs to assess the self-meanings of as many individual family members as possible in relation to their identities within the various levels. 2) Since identities are relational, the importance and desirability of each identity should be assessed by focusing on transitions in later-life families, based on the premise that family identities in later life both reflect the prior organization of the life course and help determine current changes related to specific transitions. Moreover, such late life family identities are affected by changes in other domains, for example, a reflection of retirement, the importance of the work domain. 3) Since identities are also reflexive, and are subject to adjustment relative to expectations embedded in identity, multiple quantitative and qualitative measures over time should be used to assess how identities change, especially during transitional periods.

In light of the frequent shifts today in the timing of transitions, in family structures and types, and in societal norms, family identity may be differentially expressed by different family members. It is therefore important to empirically examine the narratives of many dyads and triads in the family regarding family identity, and to test the proposed model longitudinally within a variety of family formats, during different transitions in the lives of the family members involved, and in a variety of cultural and societal contexts. Modern society both demands an appreciation of the complexity and diversity of family life and family changes, and has an impact on these changes. An important element that serves as a bridge between individual lives and social change is transitions within the family. Former identities are challenged, both for individual family members and for the family as a whole, as rituals defining family boundaries change. It should be the job of formal support services to help during these periods of change.

Developing models such as the family identity model, which consider the interlocking forces of the individual, the familial-generational, and the societal levels and testing the models empirically, will help link theory and research and will enrich the understanding of the complexity of family life in modern society.

Conceivably, obtaining measurements of hierarchical rankings of identities that are consistent across time and place may be difficult, as individuals may provide different rankings depending on the context in which measurements are taken (e.g., home versus work). Thus, identities during different family life-transitions in diverse families, and at different time points should be studied. As Dittmann-Kohli (1990) suggested: "Different socio-cultural and material life conditions, as well as biological age, have an influence on which is represented in the personal meaning system (personal identity) and on the hierarchy of importance and affective or cognitive evaluation of things" (p. 292). Notably, the exploration and testing of the model should be undertaken bearing in mind differences not only between individuals and families in different societies, but also between different ethnic and minority groups. Such studies are needed in light of evidence that lower-level socioeconomic populations and certain racial and ethnic minorities tend to experience life transitions such as retirement and widowhood, at younger ages, on average, than their peers in other groups. In short, the model should be tested for different family structures using both quantitative and qualitative methods in order to examine families in their own contexts as they deal with issues related to later life and later-life family transitions.

To sum up, the proposed framework of family identity attempts to respond to the need for model and theory building, to answer some of the shortcomings inherent in both family development theory and life course theories and to bridge the gaps between the fields of aging and the study of the family in later-life.

## REFERENCES

Altergott, K. (1988). Daily life in late life: Concepts and methods for inquiry. In K. Altergott (Ed.), *Daily life in late life: Comparative perspectives* (pp. 11-22). Newbury Park, CA: Sage.

Aryee, S., & Luk, V. (1996). Balancing two major parts of adult life experience: Work and family identity among dual-earner couples. *Human Relations, 49*(4), 465-487.

Atchley, R.C. (1992). Retirement and marital satisfaction. In M. Szinovacz, D. Ekerdt, & B. H. Vinick (Eds.), *Families and retirement* (pp. 145-158). Newbury Park, CA: Sage.

Becker, H. (1960). Notes on the concept of commitment. *American Journal of Sociology, 66,* 32-40.

Bedford, V. H., & Blieszner, R. (1997). Personal relationships in later-life families. In S. Duck (Ed.), *Handbook of personal relationships* (2nd ed., pp. 523-537). New York: Wiley & Sons.

Bengtson, V. L. (2000). Beyond the nuclear family: The increasing importance of multigenerational bonds. *Journal of Marriage and the Family, 63,* 1-16.

Bengtson, V. L., & Allen, K. R. (1993). The life course perspective applied to families over time. In P. G. Boss, W. J., R. LaRossa, W. R. Schumm, & S. K. Steinmetz (Eds.), *Sourcebook of family theories and methods: A contextual approach* (pp. 469-498). New York: Plenum.

Bengtson, V. L., & Harootyan, R. A. (1994). *Intergenerational linkages.* New York: Springer.

Bengtson, V. L., Rosenthal, C. J., & Burton, L. M. (1995). Paradoxes of families and aging. In R. H. Binstock & L. K. George (Eds.), *Handbook of aging and the social sciences* (4th ed., pp. 253-282). San Diego, CA: Academic Press.

Bennett, L. A., Wolin, S. J., & McAvity, K. J. (1988). Family identity, ritual and myth: A cultural perspective on life cycle transitions. In C. J. Falicov (Ed.), *Family transitions* (pp. 211-234). New York: The Guilford Press.

Berger, P., & Kellner, H. (1974). Marriage and the construction of reality. In R. L. Coser (Ed.), *The family: Its structures and functions.* New York: St. Martin's Press.

Brubaker, T. H. (1990). Families in later life: A burgeoning research area. *Journal of Marriage and the Family, 52,* 959-981.

Burgess, E. W. (1926). The family as a unity of interacting personalities. *The Family, 7,* 3-9.

Burke, P. J. (1980). The self: Measurement requirement from an interactionist perspective. *Social Psychology Quarterly, 43,* 18-29.

Burke, P. J., & Reitzes, D. C. (1981). The link between identity and role performance. *Social Psychology Quarterly, 44,* 83-92.

Byng-Hall, J. J. (1973). Family myths used as defence in conjoint family therapy. *British Journal of Medical Psychology, 46,* 239-250.

Byng-Hall, J. J. (1988). Scripts and legends in families and family therapy. *Family Process, 27,* 167-179.

Cantor M. H. (1989). Social care: Family and community support systems. *Annals of the American Academy of Political and Social Sciences, 503,* 99-112.

Cantor, M. H. (1991). Family and community: Changing roles in an aging society. *The Gerontologist, 31,* 337-346.

Chapman, N. J. (1989). Gender, marital status, and childlessness of older persons and the availability of informal assistance. In M. D. Petersen & D. L. White (Eds.), *Health care for the elderly: An information source book* (pp. 102-120). Newbury Park, CA: Sage.

Connidis, I. A. (2001). *Family ties and aging.* Thousand Oaks, CA: Sage.

Cowan, P. A. (1991). Individual and family life transitions: A proposal for a new definition. In P. A. Cowan & M. Hetherington (Eds.), *Family transitions* (pp. 3-30). Hillsdale, NJ: Lawrence Erlbaum Associates.

Cowan, P. A., & Hetherington, M. (Eds.) (1991). *Family transitions.* Hillsdale, NJ: Lawrence Erlbaum Associates.

Daatland, S. O. (1990). What are families for? On family solidarity and preferences for help. *Ageing and Society, 10,* 1-15.

Daatland, S. O. (1997). Family solidarity, popular opinions and the elderly: Perspective from Norway. *Ageing International, 1,* 51-62

Dittmann-Kohli, F. (1990). The construction of meaning in old age: Possibilities and constraints. *Ageing and Society, 10,* 279-294.

Doherty, W. J., Boss, P. G., LaRossa, R., Schumm, W. R., & Steinmetz, S. K. (1993). Family theories and methods: A contextual approach. In P. G. Boss, W. J. Doherty, R., LaRossa, W. R. Schumm & S. K. Steinmetz (Eds.), *Sourcebook of family theories and methods: A contextual approach* (pp. 3-30). New York: Plenum Press.

Duvall, E. (1971). *Family development* (4th ed.). Philadelphia: J. B. Lippincott.

Duvall, E., & Hill, R. (1948). *Report of the committee on the dynamics of family interaction.* Paper presented at the National Conference on Family Life, Washington, DC.

Ekerdt, D. J., & Vinick, B. H. (1991). Marital complaints in husband-working and husband-retired couples. *Research on Aging, 13*(3), 364-382.

Elder, G. H., Jr. (1978). Family history and the life course. In T. K. Hareven (Ed.), *Transitions: The family and the life course in historical perspective* (pp. 17-64). New York: Academic Press.

Elder, G. H., Jr. (1985). Perspectives on the life course. In G. H. Elder (Ed.), *Life course dynamics: Trajectories and transitions, 1968-1980* (pp. 23-49). Ithaca, NY: Cornell University Press.

Elliott, M. (1996). Impact of work, family and welfare receipt on women's self esteem in young adulthood. *Social Psychology Quarterly, 59,* 80-95.

Ferreira, A. (1966). Family myths. *Psychiatric Research Reports, 20,* 85-90.

Ford, F., & Herrick, J. (1974). Family rules: Family life styles. *American Journal of Orthopsychiatry, 44*(1).

George, L. K. (1993). Sociological perspectives on life transitions. *Annual Review of Sociology, 19,* 353-373.

George, L. K., & Gold D. T. (1991). Life course perspectives on intergenerational and generational connections. *Marriage and Family Review, 16,* 67-88.

Giarrusso, R., Feng, D., Silverstein, M., & Bengtson, V. L. (2001). Self in the context of the family. In K. W. Schaie & J. Hendricks (Eds.), *The aging self and social structure.* New York: Springer.

Goffman, E. (1963). *Stigma: Notes on the management of spoiled identity.* Englewood Cliffs, NJ: Prentice-Hall.

Gwartney-Gibbs, P. A. (1986). The institutionalization of premarital cohabitation: Estimates from marriage license applications, 1970 and 1980. *Journal of Marriage and the Family, 48,* 423-434.

Hagestad, G. O. (1981). Problems and promises in the social psychology of inter-generational relations. In R. Fogel, E. Hatfield, S. Kiesler, & J. March (Eds.), *Aging: Stability and change in the family* (pp. 11-48). New York: Academic Press.

Hagestad, G. O. (1990). Social perspectives on the life course. In R. H. Binstock & L. K. George (Eds.), *Handbook of aging and the social sciences* (3rd ed., pp. 151-168). San Diego: Academic.

Hagestad, G. O., & Neugarten, B. L. (1985). Age and the life course. In R. H. Binstock & E. Shanas (Eds.), *Handbook of aging and the social sciences* (2nd ed., pp. 35-61). New York: Van Nostrand Reinhold.

Handel, G. (1967). *The psychological interior of the family.* Chicago: University of Chicago Press.

Hareven, T. K. (1980). The life course and aging in historical perspective. In K. W. Back (Ed.), *Life course: Integrative theories and exemplary populations* (pp. 9-25). Boulder, CO: Westview Press.

Hareven, T. K. (1995). Historical perspectives on the family and aging. In R. Blieszner & V. H. Bedford (Eds.), *Handbook of aging and the family* (pp. 13-31). Westport, CT: Greenwood Press.

Hendricks, J., & Leedham, C. A. (1991). Dependency or empowerment: Toward a moral and political economy of aging. In M. Minkler & C. L. Estes (Eds.), *Critical perspectives on aging: The political and moral economy of growing old* (pp. 51-64). Amityville, NY: Baywood.

Hess, R., & Handel, G. (1959). *Family worlds: A psychological approach to family life.* Chicago: University of Chicago Press.

Hill, R. (1970). *Family development in three generations.* Cambridge, MA: Schenkman.

Hill, R., & Hansen, D. A. (1960). The identification of conceptual frameworks utilized in family study. *Marriage and Family Living, 22,* 299-311.

Katan, J., & Lowenstein, A. (1999). *A decade of the implementation of the Long-Term Care Insurance Law.* Jerusalem: The Center for Policy Research (Hebrew).

Keilman, N. (1987). Recent trends in family and household composition in Europe. *European Journal of Population, 3,* 297-325.

Klein, D. M., & White, J. M. (1996). *Family theories.* Thousand Oaks, CA: Sage.

Knipscheer, C. P. M. (1988). Temporal embeddedness and aging within the multi-generational family: The case of grandparenting. In J. E. Birren & V. L. Bengston (Eds.), *Emergent theories of aging* (pp. 426-446). New York: Springer.

Kohli, M., & Meyer, J. W. (1986). Social structures and social construction of life stages. *Human Development, 29,* 145-180.

Lowenstein, A. (submitted). Attitudes of young adults towards family identity. *Research on Aging.*

Lowenstein, A., & Ron, P. (1999). Tension and conflict factors in spousal abuse in second marriages of the widowed elderly. *Journal of Elder Abuse and Neglect, 11*(1), 23-45.

Lowenstein, A., & Ron, P. (2000). Adult children of elderly parents who remarry: Aetiology of domestic abuse. *The Journal of Adult Protection, 2*(4), 22-32.

Luescher, K., & Pillemer, K. (1998). Intergenerational ambivalence: A new approach to the study of parent-child relations in later life. *Journal of Marriage and the Family, 60,* 413-425.

Mangen, D. J., & McChesney, K. Y. (1988). Intergenerational chohesion: A comparison of linear and nonlinear analytical approaches. In D. Mangen, V. L. Bengtson, & P. H. Landry, Jr. (Eds.), *Measurement of interngenerational relations.* Beverly Hills, CA: Sage.

Mattessich, P., & Hill, R. (1987). Life cycle and family development. In M. B. Sussman & S. Steinmetz (Eds.), *Handbook of marriage and the family* (pp. 437-469). New York: Plenum.

Martin-Matthews, A. (1994). Widowhood no longer an expectable life event. *Linkage: The Canadian Aging Research Network, 4*(2), 2-5.

McCall, G. J., & Simmons, J. T. (1978). *Identities and interaction.* New York: Free Press.

Meyer, J. W. (1988). The life course as a cultural construction. In M. W. Riley (Ed.), *Social structures and human lives* (pp. 49-62). Newbury Park, CA: Sage.

Parke, R. D. (1988). Families in life-span perspective: A multilevel developmental approach. In E. M. Hetherington, R. M. Lerner, & M. Perlmutter (Eds.), *Child development in lifespan development.* Hillsdale, NJ: Lawrence Erlbaum Associates.

Rapoport, R. (1989). Ideologies about family forms: Towards diversity. In K. Boh, M. Bak, C. Clason, M. Pankratova, J. Qvortrup, G. Sgritta, & K. Waerness (Eds.), *Changing patterns of European family life* (pp. 53-69). New York: Routledge.

Reiss, D. (1971). Perceptual and cognitive resources of family members. *Archives of General Psychiatry, 24,* 121-133.

Reiss, D. (1981). *The family's construction of reality.* Cambridge, MA: Harvard University Press.

Richlin-Klonsky, J., & Bengtson, V. L. (1996). Pulling together, drifting apart: A longitudinal case study of a four-generations family. *Journal of Aging Studies, 10*(4), 255-279.

Riley, M. W., Johnson, M., & Foner, A. (1972). *Aging and society: Volume 3. A sociology of age stratification.* New York: Russell Sage.

Riley, M. W., & Riley, J. W. (1993). Connections: Kin and cohort. In V. L. Bengtson & W. A. Achenbaum (Eds.), *The changing contract across generations* (pp. 90-169). New York: Aldine de Gruyter.

Rodgers, R. H., & White, J. M. (1993). Family development theory. In P. G. Boss, W. J. Doherty, R. LaRossa, W. R. Schumm, & S. K. Steinmetz (Eds.), *Sourcebook of family theories and methods* (pp. 225-254). New York: Plenum Press.

Rossi, A. S. (1980). Life-span theories and women's lives. *Signs, 6,* 4-32.

Salancik, G. (1977). Commitment and the control of organizational behavior and belief. In B. Staw & G. Salancik (Eds.), *New directions in organizational behavior.* Chicago: St. Clair.

Settersten, R. A., & Hagestad, G. O. (1996). What's the latest? Cultural age deadlines for family transitions. *The Gerontologist, 36*(2), 178-188.

Sgritta, G. B. (1997). The generation question: State solidarity versus family solidarity. In J. Commaille & F. de Singly, *The European family* (pp. 151-166). Dordrech, Netherlands: Kluwer.

Smith, D., & Moen, P. (1998). Spousal influence on retirement: His, her, and their perceptions. *Journal of Marriage and the Family, 60,* 734-744.

Stacey, J. (1990). *Brave new families.* New York: Basic Books.

Stryker, S. (1968). Identity salience and role performance: The relevance of symbolic interaction theory for family research. *Journal of Marriage and the Family, 30,* 558-564.

Stryker, S. (1980). *Symbolic interactionism: A social structural version.* Menlo Park: Benjamin/Cummings.

Stryker, S., & Serpe, R. (1982). Commitment, identity salience and role behavior, theory and research examples. In W. Ickles & E. Knowles (Eds.), *Personality, roles and social behavior.* New York: Springer.

Stryker, S., & Serpe, R. T. (1994). Identity salience and psychological centrality: Equivalent, overlapping, or complementary concepts. *Social Psychology Quarterly, 57*(1), 16-35.

Szinovacz, M. E. (2000). Changes in housework after retirement: A panel analysis. *Journal of Marriage and the Family, 62,* 78-92.

Talbott, M. M. (1998). Older widows' attitudes towards men and remarriage. *Journal of Aging Studies, 12*(4), 429-449.

Treas, J. (1995). Older Americans in the 1990s and beyond. *Population Bulletin, 50*(2), 1995.

Troll, L. (1995). Forward. In R. Blieszner & V. H. Bedford (Eds.), *Handbook of aging and the family* (pp. xi-xxi). Westport, CT: Greenwood Press.

Tuma, N. B., & Sandefur, G. D. (1988). Trends in the labor force activity of the elderly in the United States, 1940-1980. In R. Ricardo-Campbell & E. P. Lazar (Eds.), *Issues in contemporary retirement* (pp. 38-75). Stanford, CA: Hoover Inst. Press.

Turner, J. (1988). *The structure of sociological theory* (2nd ed.). Homewood, IL: Dorsey Press.

Van Gennep, A. (1960). *The rites of passage.* London: Routlege and Kegan Paul.

Wamboldt, F. S., & Reiss, D. (1989). Defining a family heritage and a new relationship identity: Two central tasks in the making of a marriage. *Family Process, 28,* 317-335.

Wheaton, B. (1990). Life transitions, role histories, and mental health. *American Sociological Review, 55,* 209-223.

White, J. M. (1991). *Dynamics of family development.* New York: Guilford Press.

Wolin, S. J., & Bennett, L. A. (1984). Family rituals. *Family Process, 23,* 401-420.

# CHAPTER 7

# The Aging Paradox: Toward Personal Meaning in Gerontological Theory

*Gerben J. Westerhof, Freya Dittmann-Kohli, and Christina Bode*

One might expect that the quality of life of older adults is negatively affected by age-related losses of roles and relationships, age-related declines in psychophysical functioning, approaching finitude of life, as well as widespread ageism in our society. Yet, research has found remarkably few age differences in self-esteem, conceived as general evaluations of the own person (Brandstädter & Greve, 1994). Studies on life satisfaction, i.e., cognitive evaluations of one's own life in general, have likewise found that older persons do not see themselves as less well off than younger or middle-aged persons (Diener & Suh, 1998). There appears, then, to be a remarkable stability in the experience of aging, self, and life, in spite of the risks associated with old age. These findings represent the key paradox for contemporary gerontology.

In the recent literature on aging, this "aging paradox" has gained much attention. Psychological lifespan theories have focused on the strategies by which individuals adapt to age-related changes in order to maintain a positive outlook on self and life (Baltes & Baltes, 1990; Brandstädter & Greve, 1994; Filipp, 1996; Staudinger, Marsiske, & Baltes, 1995). Empirical studies have been carried out in order to identify the nature of the adaptation strategies which aging individuals use and to find out which strategies are successful in the aging process. These studies have documented the resilience of aging individuals.

Adaptation processes imply a reorganization of one's interpretations and goals concerning self and life (Dittmann-Kohli, 1995). However, the content of interpretations and goals has not often been studied empirically across age groups.

Such an empirical study is important for at least two reasons. First, the assumptions inherent in the aging paradox can be critically evaluated by comparing them to the perspectives of aging persons themselves. This raises questions, such as whether aging individuals also see aging as a process of loss and decline and whether self-esteem and life satisfaction are the most relevant criteria in judging oneself and one's life. Second, interpretations and goals concerning self and life might be closer related to the life contexts of persons of different ages than judgments about self and life in general. The content of interpretations and goals might therefore reveal the age differences that are lacking in studies on self-esteem and life satisfaction.

## MEANING CONSTRUCTION

Studying these issues suggests the need for a phenomenological turn in aging research. A perspective on the construction of meaning provides a theoretical basis to this turn. Over the last decade, there has been an increasing interest in the study of personal meaning (Bruner, 1990; Dittmann-Kohli, 1990, 1995; Reker & Chamberlain, 2000; Wong & Fry, 1998). This interest is grounded in observations that personal meaning plays an important role in basic psychological processes such as cognitive processing of information, emotional regulation, goal realization, and identity formation.

The study of personal meaning is of particular interest to gerontologists, because it is considered an inherently temporal and dynamic process. Persons do not only attribute meaning to the present situation, but they also reflect about their past and future. In this process they continually reorganize the content of meanings in response to perceived and expected changes in their own person and life world.

In the following sections we discuss empirical findings with regard to the content of the interpretations and goals concerning self and life. We review findings from the German Aging Survey, a representative survey of the German population in midlife and old age (40–85 years; Dittmann-Kohli, Bode, & Westerhof, 2001). To provide a lifespan perspective on the construction of meaning, findings from a study comparing younger apprentices and students (15–34 years) to older adults (60–90 years) will also be discussed (Dittmann-Kohli, 1995; Dittmann-Kohli & Westerhof, 2000). A common aspect in this research is the use of the SELE-instrument, a sentence completion questionnaire which asks individuals to describe what they consider to be true and important about themselves and their life in the past, present, and future (Dittmann-Kohli, 1995; Dittmann-Kohli & Westerhof, 1997). Hierarchical content analysis was carried out in order to classify the meaning content of the sentence completions. Age differences between the resulting categories were statistically analyzed.

The empirical findings provide evidence about the aging paradox from the perspective of aging persons themselves and about age differences in interpretations and goals in life. The first three sections give an overview of the meanings which individuals attribute to aging, self, and life. They critically review the assumptions of the aging paradox and address age differences in the content of interpretations and goals. The fourth section discusses the processes of meaning construction that can be used to interpret the observed findings. The fifth section draws a conclusion about our findings in view of the aging paradox and similarities and differences between age groups. The theoretical, methodological, and practical implications which derive from the study of personal meaning will be discussed in the last section. It is concluded that the empirical findings substantiate the proposition that theories on personal meaning provide an important new perspective in the study of aging.

## MEANINGS OF AGING

The first assumption of the aging paradox is that aging is a process of loss and decline. However, one might ask to what extent aging individuals share this assumption. What are the meanings which aging individuals attribute to their own aging process? Relatively little is known about this question (Montepare & Zebrowitz, 1998). Existing research has focused mainly on subjective age, i.e., on how old a person feels. It has been consistently found that individuals feel younger than they actually are, especially at older ages (Barak & Stern, 1986; Dittmann-Kohli et al., 2001; Montepare & Zebrowitz, 1998). Such a rejection of one's age suggests that individuals see the aging process in negative terms and that they do not want to identify with conceptions of aging as loss and decline.

However, in our studies we found ample evidence that aging persons do realize and accept that they are growing older (Dittmann-Kohli, 1995, 2001; Dittmann-Kohli et al., 2001; Steverink, Westerhof, Bode, & Dittmann-Kohli, 2001; Timmer, Steverink, & Dittmann-Kohli, 2002; Westerhof, 2001b). First, aging adults report negative aspects of their own aging process when they are asked about it. Age-related decline includes changes in one's appearance, one's health and general functioning, as well as in a variety of specific problems in psychophysical functioning. Increasing loneliness and losses in social relations as well as loss of autonomy and respect are also often mentioned. Second, the experience of growing older is reflected in an increasing use of temporal adverbs such as "still," "no more," or "no longer." These temporal adverbs are found in particular in relation to biological decline. For example, persons say "I am proud that . . . I am *still* vital for my age" or "Later, when I am older . . . I will be *no longer* fit." Third, older adults express themselves in terms of a relatively closed time perspective. An open future in which all kinds of goals can be realized is found among the young and in part also among the middle-aged, but it has lost its obvious character among the old.

Yet, aging does not only have a negative face for aging adults. Individuals also mention positive aspects of aging. They identify character growth (e.g., becoming more calm), self-determination as well as wisdom and experience as the most important psychological gains of aging. Aging persons like retirement, tranquility, having more time, and being able to do what they want to. Furthermore, many older adults do expect gains in the near or distant future and they do not anticipate more losses than middle-aged adults.

Sociological theories have often described age-graded transitions, such as retirement or empty nest, in negative terms as role losses. Society has also failed to compensate for these losses and to provide other meaningful opportunities for older persons. This failure is seen as the result of a structural "lag" whereby society takes time to catch up with the graying of its population (Riley, Kahn, & Foner, 1994). Our study shows that role losses and the lack of societal regulations in old age are experienced by many older persons in positive terms. They appreciate freedom from responsibilities in work and family as well as autonomy in deciding what they want to do in the rest of their lives. Hence, transitions that have been described in negative terms in aging theories can even have positive meanings for aging individuals.

To summarize, individuals do realize their own process of growing older and do not simply reject their chronological age. Aging persons are aware of ageism, age-related losses, and declines as well as the diminishing time perspective that is a fundamental part of the aging paradox. However, they also attribute positive meanings to aging, and even to transitions that theories have described in negative terms.

## SELF-ESTEEM AND MEANINGS OF SELF

The aging paradox assumes that self-esteem is the most important criterion in evaluating oneself. But what about other aspects of the self? Traditional psychological theories have conceptualized the self mainly in terms of self-esteem, personality traits, and other aspects of psychological functioning. Such conceptualizations of the self separate mind from body and individuals from social contexts. Since psychological theories often failed to emphasize that human selves are both embodied and social, they have been criticized for reproducing specific Western concepts of the person at the level of scientific theories (Kempen, 1996; Sampson, 1988). Furthermore, by separating the self from the body and the social context a priori, psychologists have had difficulties in bringing them together again.

A theoretical perspective on personal meaning goes beyond the definition of the self in terms of self-esteem and personality and provides a theoretical integration of the embodied and social nature of the self. From this perspective, selves can be recursively directed toward their own psychological functioning, but they can also be directed to aspects of one's life context that are personally important. As James (1890/1983) has already observed, self-concepts do not only refer to the psychological "me" but also to what is considered "mine." In our studies we found that the body and social relations are the most important parts of the self-concept besides the psychological self. In the following we will describe age differences in the meaning of the psychological, physical, and social self.

## Psychological Self

Individuals of all ages evaluate their own psychological functioning (Bode, 2003; Bode, Westerhof, & Dittmann-Kohli, 2001; Dittmann-Kohli, 1995; Dittmann-Kohli et al., 2001). In line with research on self-esteem we found no major age differences in the positive or negative outcomes of this evaluation. However, self-esteem is found to be only one of many aspects of the psychological self. Other meanings refer to character traits, emotions, coping, and personal growth. Whereas self-esteem can be characterized as an evaluation of the self in general, these other meanings refer to specific aspects of psychological functioning. These more specific aspects of the self result more often in negative evaluations than generalized evaluations of oneself. Focusing only on self-esteem might therefore give too rosy a picture of the psychological self at different ages.

Whereas other studies showed that self-esteem is a rather stable characteristic, we found large age differences in other aspects of the psychological self. Psychological aspects of the self are less important in the construction of meaning among older than among younger or middle-aged adults. Qualitative differences in the meaning of the psychological self are found as well. The older adults' psychological self is mainly focused on the question "how do I feel?" They state for example "I often feel . . . good." By contrast, middle-aged and younger adults focus more on their own traits, competencies, and weaknesses in coping with emotions, life problems, and other persons. Middle-aged and younger adults are more like lay psychologists than older adults in that they reflect on how they deal with themselves and their lives in order to find possibilities for psychological growth.

## Physical Self

Although a massive gerontological literature on health and its subjective evaluation exists, relatively little research has focused on the meaning of the physical self. In fact, research on the body was only making its way into gerontology in the last years of the twentieth century (Öberg, 1996).

In our studies we have found clear age differences with regard to the relevance, diversity, and content of meanings of the body (Dittmann-Kohli, 1995; Dittmann-Kohli et al., 2001; Westerhof, Kuin, & Dittmann-Kohli, 1998). The physical self is more important, differentiated and comprehensive in meaning in older than in younger or middle-aged adults. Furthermore, the physical self of the elderly is more focused on health and functioning than that of younger age groups. The elderly do not only regret age-related symptoms more often (e.g., "What's been bothering me recently is . . . my back"; "It is difficult for me . . . to walk"), they also evaluate their health more frequently in a positive way (e.g., "In comparison to others . . . my age, I am rather fit and healthy"). Interestingly, illness is mentioned no more often by older adults than it is by middle-aged adults. Apparently, the physical limitations that are experienced as a consequence of aging are not interpreted as illness by older adults. By contrast, the young are in particular concerned about sports, physical pleasures, as well as their looks. The middle-aged are somewhat in between the old and the young. They refer to age-related changes in appearance as well as the first threats to their physical integrity and they mention physically demanding activities more often than older adults.

## Social Self

Research on social aspects of the self comes from different psychological disciplines: social psychology, cross-cultural psychology, and personality psychology. Each of these disciplines has used somewhat different concepts with different connotations, such as the relational self (Sedikides & Brewer, 2001), the interdependent self (Markus & Kitayama, 1991), and the dialogical self (Hermans, 2001). They have in common that they refer to the process of inclusion of others into one's sense of self. For example, social psychological experiments have shown that threats to important others elicit similar reactions as threats to individuals themselves. Recent studies have found that relatedness is not the opposite of individuality as has often been assumed in earlier research. Human beings give meaning to their lives through individual *and* social aspects of the self (Bode, 2003; Bode et al., 2001; Singelis, 1994; Westerhof, Dittmann-Kohli, & Katzko, 2000). Unfortunately, most of the research on the social self lacks a lifespan or gerontological perspective.

In our studies we found that the social aspects of the self are about equally important to all age groups (Bode, 2003; Bode et al., 2001; Dittmann-Kohli, 1995; Dittmann-Kohli et al., 2001). Nevertheless, the more specific meanings differ between age groups. First, age differences concern the persons who are included as part of the social self. Middle-aged persons include friends and acquaintances as well as family members beyond the nuclear family more often in their social self than older persons. Younger persons are more likely to include only friends and partners into their social selves than other age groups. Second, the age differences concern the way in which the relationships are described. For example, the meaning of autonomy shows interesting age differences. For young adults, autonomy means becoming independent from their parents and finding their own way of life. Among the middle-aged, autonomy is used especially in the sense of assertiveness. For them it is important, for example, to be able to say "no." In old age, autonomy means being able to care for oneself and not be a burden on others. Hence, we find an alliance between the physical and social self only for the older adults.

To summarize, the aging paradox treats self-esteem as the most important criterion in judgments about the self. From the subjective perspective of aging persons themselves, more specific aspects of the psychological, physical, and social self are important with regard to the construction of meaning as well. Self-esteem is only one among many criteria and it is found to be a relatively rosy one at that. Although general self-esteem shows few age differences, other aspects of the psychological, physical, and social self differ strongly between age groups.

## LIFE SATISFACTION AND MEANINGS OF LIFE

Subjective well-being has been defined in many different ways in the social science literature. There is currently widespread agreement that subjective well-being at least contains an emotional component, which relates to one's affective state, as well as a cognitive component, which includes evaluations of one's own life (Diener, Suh, Lucas, & Smith, 1999). In contrast to the emotional component, the content and structure of the cognitive component has received relatively little attention (Westerhof, Dittmann-Kohli, & Thissen, 2001). It is most commonly defined and operationalized as life satisfaction. About two-thirds of the studies on subjective well-being in later life have used life satisfaction as a criterion (Pinquart & Sörensen, 2000). One might ask however whether satisfaction with life is the only criterion that is important to aging individuals when they assess the quality of their lives.

Over the past decade a number of studies on lay conceptions of well-being have addressed this question (Dittmann-Kohli, 1989, 1990, 1995; Ryff, 1989a; Thomas & Chambers, 1989; Van Selm & Dittmann-Kohli, 1998; Westerhof, Dittmann-Kohli, & Thissen, 2001). In the German Aging Survey we found that lay conceptions of well-being include life satisfaction, but this is certainly not the only criterion that is used to assess the quality of life as a whole. Other criteria include retrospections on one's life, achievements in life, adaptation to life, life as hard or filled with problems, enjoyment of life, a calm and peaceful life, and leading a normal life. Even more important is the finding that judgments in terms of life satisfaction are more positive than judgments in terms of other criteria. Whereas people do not readily admit that they are *not* satisfied with their life, it appears to be easier for them to acknowledge that the quality of their life is less than optimal on other dimensions of judgment (e.g., "When I think about myself . . . I would have done things differently in retrospect"). Furthermore, life satisfaction plays a more important role in the meanings of well-being that are used by older, rather than younger and middle-aged adults. Since satisfaction is a positively laden category of meaning it might help older individuals to keep a positive view on their own life, even in spite of unfavorable conditions.

What becomes clear from this research is that the concept of life satisfaction is just one of many lay conceptions of well-being and again one that is positively skewed. It is not so much the level of life satisfaction that differs between age groups, but the ways in which different aspects of well-being are important to them. In the following section we will discuss the process of meaning construction that might account for our findings.

## THE PROCESS OF MEANING CONSTRUCTION

The aging paradox holds that stability in the experience of aging, self, and life exists despite age-related changes in life circumstances. In the German Aging Survey, we found that the apparent stability in self-esteem and life satisfaction goes together with large age differences in other meanings of aging, self, and life. These findings are in line with other research, which found age differences in dimensions of well-being other than self-esteem and life satisfaction (e.g., Kunzmann, Little, & Smith, 2000; Ryff, 1989b). We also found that interpretations and goals in terms of self-esteem and life satisfaction are more positive than other interpretations and goals concerning self and life. This pattern of findings suggests an intricate dynamic in the construction of personal meaning by aging individuals.

On the one hand, individuals try to keep their general meanings, such as self-esteem and life satisfaction, positive (Westerhof, Dittmann-Kohli, & Thissen, 2001). These generalized meanings provide the positive bias that has also been described in psychological theories on positive illusions (Taylor & Brown, 1988), self-affirmation (Steele, 1988), and unrealistic optimism (Klein & Weinstein, 1997). Similarly, lifespan research has documented the resilience of aging individuals when it comes to self-esteem and life satisfaction (Baltes & Baltes, 1990; Brandtstädter & Greve, 1994; Filipp, 1996; Staudinger, Marsiske, & Baltes, 1995). It can be concluded that individuals generally judge themselves and their lives to be better than objective conditions might warrant. More realistic evaluations are even associated with depression and maladaptation (Alloy & Abramson, 1988; Steele, 1988). Hence, positive judgments of oneself and one's life in general might neutralize the impact of specific negative life events and conditions, since they have the power to transcend them.

On the other hand, by focusing on more specific meanings of negative life events and conditions, a person can avoid having to draw negative conclusions about her/himself and life as a whole. Theories on lifelong adaptation assume that individuals can only maintain self-esteem and life satisfaction when adjustments in interpretations and goals concerning self and life are made on a more specific level (Baltes & Baltes, 1990; Brandtstädter & Greve, 1994; Filipp, 1996; Staudinger, Marsiske, & Baltes, 1995). Hence, there is a much more dynamic picture underlying the manifest stability in self-esteem and life satisfaction. The age differences, which we found in the content of meanings of aging, self, and life on a more specific level, correspond to this more dynamic picture.

Although only a longitudinal design could reveal changes in personal meanings, two patterns of findings of the German Aging Survey make it likely that reorganizations have taken place. First, we found that the meanings of aging, self, and life on the more specific level are statistically related to age-graded life contexts. For example, the finding that the physical self is more important for older adults and that its meanings are more directed toward health and functioning is related to the higher prevalence of health impairments among older adults (Westerhof, Kuin, & Dittmann-Kohli, 1998). One might therefore expect that middle-aged persons will also begin to focus more on health and functioning when they experience physical impairments in later life (Dittmann-Kohli & Westerhof, 2000). Second, the particular meaning content that is found among different age groups often suggests that they are sensitive to changing life circumstances (Westerhof & Dittmann-Kohli, 2000). For example, middle-aged persons will only complain about age-related changes in the physical self (e.g., "What I don't like about aging . . . wrinkles") after they experienced such changes.

This is not to say that meanings of aging, self, and life are mere copies of the life circumstances in which aging persons are living. Individuals evaluate their situation as positive or negative and express hopes, plans, wishes, and fears with regard to how things should be or not. Individual differences are found even between individuals who live in similar life circumstances (Westerhof, 2001a). Hence, individuals relate actively to the situation in which they find themselves at a certain age and creatively envision how their further development and life course might look like (Dittmann-Kohli et al., 2001).

The construction of meaning is at the same time an individual and a socio-cultural process. Individual meanings of aging, self, and life are found to be related to existing societal structures and cultural values. First, one's position in societal structures, such as social class, gender, and residence in East or West Germany, is related to the meanings of aging, self, and life (Dittmann-Kohli et al., 2001). Second, cross-cultural studies show that aging individuals make use of cultural values in attributing meaning to life circumstances (Westerhof et al., 2000; Westerhof, Katzko, Dittmann-Kohli, & Hayslip, 2001; Westerhof & Dittmann-Kohli, 1997). For example, health problems in old age raise concerns about becoming a burden to one's children in the United States (a value of autonomy), but they raise concerns about receiving care of one's partner or children in Congo/Zaire (a value of lifelong reciprocal support). Furthermore, cultural values and social regulations, applying to aging and the life course in particular, are integrated in personal meanings of aging, self, and life (Westerhof, 2001a; Westerhof & Dittmann-Kohli, 2000). Last, differences in early socialization might play a role in the construction of meaning at older ages (Bode, 2003). We found, for example, that individuality is more important than relatedness in cohorts which had their formative years in the sixties or later. This was only the case in West Germany and the Netherlands but not in East Germany. This finding was interpreted in terms of the cultural shift to individualization in the sixties that took place in West Germany and the Netherlands but not in the former German Democratic Republic.

To summarize, the individual and sociocultural process of meaning construction results in a positive outlook on self and life in general despite less favorable life conditions. At the same time it results in the reorganization of interpretations and goals concerning self and life on a more specific level in response to age-graded life contexts.

## THE AGING PARADOX RECONSIDERED

Our research provides ample evidence that the aging paradox is less mysterious than is often suggested. On the one hand, whereas the aging paradox often describes aging in negative terms, it also has positive aspects from a subjective point of view of aging persons. Changes, which theories have described as losses such as work and family responsibilities, are even interpreted by some individuals as gains. Aging is therefore not as negative as assumed in the aging paradox. On the other hand, individuals are not as positive as they appear in studies on self-esteem and life satisfaction. Self-esteem and life satisfaction were found to be exactly the two criteria that resulted more often in positive evaluations than other criteria. This finding suggests that it is important for individuals to maintain a positive outlook on a generalized level of meaning. However, individuals also readily admit negative aspects of aging, self, and life, in particular when it comes to more specific problems. Older individuals may therefore not be as well off in their own experience as is found in research on self-esteem and life satisfaction. By contrast to the more resilient generalized meanings, these specific meanings are constantly reorganized in response to changing life circumstances. As a result of individual and sociocultural processes of meaning construction age differences exist in the content of the meanings of aging, self, and life, in spite of the stability in self-esteem and life satisfaction.

The aging paradox showed a remarkable stability in the experience of aging, self, and life. From a perspective of personal meaning, we found many significant age differences in more specific meanings of aging, self, and life. Besides their statistical significance, these differences are also significant in a number of other ways. First, differences in personal meaning exist even though the same individuals did not show large age differences in a traditional measure of life satisfaction (Dittmann-Kohli et al., 2001). Second, when comparing the age differences to differences according to aspects of one's social position in societal structures, such as gender or social class, we found that age differences are larger in most analyses. Even in cross-cultural comparisons we found that age differences are larger than cultural differences. In a comparison between the Netherlands, East and West Germany, we found larger differences with regard to individuality and relatedness according to age than according to country (Bode, 2003). Furthermore, we found that the meaning constellations even differ between young and old in similar ways in the Netherlands and Congo/Zaire. Older persons are more concerned about health, illness, and finitude of life and they express more maintenance goals, whereas the young are more concerned about self and personality, and express more achievement goals (Westerhof & Dittmann-Kohli, 1997).

These findings show that age differences exist in addition to the apparent stability in self-esteem and life satisfaction. The question how aging individuals maintain high levels of self-esteem and life satisfaction can therefore only be understood if complex dynamics of meaning construction are also considered. Personal meanings reveal how individuals of different ages differ in their emotional and motivational involvement in life and in the core features of their personal identity. We therefore conclude that age matters. In the following section we will explore the theoretical, methodological, and practical implications of this conclusion.

## IMPLICATIONS FOR THEORY, METHOD, AND PRACTICE

### Theoretical Implications

Our findings call for a reflection on theories on adult development and successful aging. Psychological theories on adult development have often stated that the later phases of life are characterized by an increasing individuality and a focus on individual aspects of functioning. Ryff's (1989b) thorough review of theories on well-being shows that lifespan psychologists have focused mainly on individual-psychological developmental outcomes such as autonomy, environmental mastery, psychological growth, self-acceptance, purpose in life, and only more marginally on positive relations with others. Similarly, theories on successful aging have focused on individual aspects such as self-esteem, life satisfaction, or control over one's life as the most important outcomes (Baltes & Baltes, 1990; Baltes & Carstensen, 1996; Brandtstädter & Greve, 1994; Heckhausen & Schulz, 1995).

From the phenomenological perspective of aging individuals themselves, these theories may have focused too much on individual-psychological aspects of functioning in old age at the expense of physical and social aspects of the self (Bode et al., 2001). Of course, lifespan theorists have often stressed that the life course should be studied in terms of psychological, social *and* biological changes. Nevertheless, they have studied these mainly from the outside, in terms of objective changes in personality, self-esteem, cognitive functioning, physiological functioning, illness, social roles, social status, etc. Our study shows that it is also important to include the phenomenological perspective of aging individuals themselves.

We suggest using the concepts of individuality, relatedness, and physical integrity to refer to the subjective construction of psychological, social, and biological domains of functioning. These concepts refer to one's sense of being a person, of being related to other persons and of one's body as an integrated whole. Our findings show that throughout the life-course relatedness and physical integrity are pillars of personal meaning that are at least as important as individuality. It is therefore not only important to study how individuals maintain self-esteem and life satisfaction throughout the life course, but also how they maintain a sense of individuality, relatedness, and physical integrity and thereby an overall sense of meaning in life.

Aging individuals admit weaknesses, problems, and fears on specific levels of personal meaning more readily than with regard to generalized judgments of self and life. Consequently, negative interpretations and goals concerning self and life differ in content and structure from positive ones (Ryff & Essex, 1991; Veroff, 1983; Westerhof, Dittmann-Kohli, & Thissen, 2001). This is particularly important because the concepts and measures of self-esteem and life satisfaction only focus on the positive. Studies on subjective evaluations of aspects of life which are related to individuality, relatedness, and physical integrity have also not paid enough attention to the differences in content and structure between positive and negative meanings of self and life. For example, our findings on physical integrity suggest that the many studies on appraisals of one's physical health in old age may be positively biased and should be complemented with questions on negative aspects of one's physical functioning.

We believe that it is important for individuals to know negative aspects of their own psychological, biological, and social functioning in order to adjust to changing life circumstances. It is only through the realization of such negatively valued aspects of aging, self, and life that individuals can formulate new goals, reorganize their behaviors, and maintain an overall sense of meaning in life. Together, our findings show that personal meanings of individuality, relatedness, and physical integrity go beyond simple ratings in terms of good or bad. Different motives have radically different meanings for persons of different ages living in different life contexts (Veroff, 1983; Westerhof et al., 2000).

The causes and consequences of these age differences in meanings of individuality, relatedness, and physical integrity, also deserve further empirical study. Our findings suggest that the social processes of lifespan development should be closely considered in such empirical studies. Meaning construction serves to make one's life intelligible to oneself *and* to other persons (Hermans, 2001). Successful aging is therefore not a purely individual process, but it is achieved in dialogue with others. Studying the social aspects of aging is especially important, because by attributing meaning, aging individuals contribute to maintenance or change in their existing circumstances. Cultural values and age-graded social structures are only reproduced if aging adults appropriate them as being their own (Westerhof & Dittmann-Kohli, 2000; Westerhof, 2001a).

## Methodological Implications

The finding that age matters also has important implications for methods. When trying to diagnose how successfully people age in the present and the future, it is important to find criteria that are meaningful to aging individuals themselves. It should be kept in mind that the personal meaning of a criterion may be different for individuals of different ages. This is also important in the construction of measurement instruments. One should try to keep questionnaire items as close as possible to the meanings which aging individuals attribute to themselves and their own lives. For example, Singelis' (1994) instrument for assessing independent and interdependent selves includes items such as "I would offer my seat in a bus to my professor" that are not relevant to most older persons. More far-reaching, one might even argue that filling out a psychological instrument is always an act of attributing meaning (Westerhof, 1994). Whereas social scientists often take the answers to questionnaires for mere cognitive representations of reality, it should be kept in mind that individuals of different ages might construe the meaning of similar questions in different ways. In general, we can conclude that methodology is an age-sensitive issue.

## Implications for Practice

Taking meaning construction seriously has also implications for practice. Intergenerational communication might suffer from the different ways in which persons of different ages attribute meaning to self and life. Williams and Nussbaum (2001) have described older adults' under-accommodation to younger adults' conversational needs and younger persons' over-accommodation (patronizing) to older persons as major problems in intergenerational conversations. Younger and older persons are found to be more satisfied with intergenerational relations when both are more attentive to issues that are really meaningful to their interlocutors. Better intergenerational dialogue might evolve when individuals get the chance to understand the different meanings that exist at different ages and why they are so important to them.

In this respect, the development of policies for the aged can be seen as a specific form of intergenerational relations. Younger professionals who are responsible for developing aging policies should therefore be aware not to project their own meanings of aging, self, and life on the aging population for whom they are working. This might be the case with the strong emphasis on illness, autonomy and independence in many aging policies. Although we found that these are important concerns of older people, they are certainly not the only ones. Aspects of relatedness might deserve more attention in aging policies.

With regard to psychological practice individuals of different ages might have different ways of expressing problems in life to psychological professionals. Especially noteworthy in this respect is our finding that older adults do not monitor themselves as much as middle-aged or younger persons in terms of psychological functioning. It has been observed that older adults present symptoms of depression more in somatic terms than younger adults who are more used to the specialist terms of the psychologists. This may have consequences for diagnosing patients from different age groups.

Our studies suggest that processes of meaning construction deserve much more attention in further gerontological theory, research, and practice. Personal meaning proved to be a highly age-sensitive matter. Aging individuals have their own views of being a person in the process of growing old. It is important for gerontologists to take these views into account in order to develop ecologically valid theories, methods and interventions.

## NOTE

The German Aging Survey is an interdisciplinary survey on the present and future generations of German elderly. The purpose of the survey is to study the relations between objective life circumstances and subjective conceptions of self and life in aging adults. The German Aging Survey was carried out at the Department of Psychogerontology at the University of Nijmegen, the Netherlands (Director: Prof. Dr. F. Dittmann-Kohli), and the Research Group on Aging and the Life Course at the Free University of Berlin, Germany (Director: Prof. Dr. M. Kohli). It was sponsored by the Federal Ministry of Family Affairs, Senior Citizens, Women, and Youth. Data collection was accomplished by Infas-Sozialforschung, Bonn, Germany.

## REFERENCES

Alloy, L. B., & Abramson, L. Y. (1988). Depressive realism: Four theoretical perspectives. In L. B. Alloy (Ed.), *Cognitive processes in depression* (pp. 223-265). New York: Guilford Press.

Baltes, P. B., & Baltes, M. M. (1990). Psychological perspectives on successful aging: The model of selective optimization with compensation. In P. B. Baltes & M. M. Baltes (Eds.), *Successful aging: Perspectives from the behavioral sciences* (pp. 1-34). New York: Cambridge University Press.

Baltes, M. M., & Carstensen, L. L. (1996). The process of successful aging. *Ageing and Society, 15*, 397-422.

Barak, B., & Stern, B. (1986). Subjective age correlates: A research note. *Gerontologist, 26*, 571-578.

Bode, C. (2003). *Individuality and relatedness in the second half of life: A comparison between the Netherlands, East- and West-Germany.* Doctoral Dissertation, University of Nijmegen.

Bode, C., Westerhof, G. J., & Dittmann-Kohli, F. (2001). Selbstvorstellungen über Individualität und Verbundenheit in der zweiten Lebenshälfte [Self-conceptions: Individuality and communion in the second half of life]. *Zeitschrift für Gerontologie und Geriatrie, 34*, 365-375.

Brandtstädter, J., & Greve, W. (1994). The aging self: Stabilizing and protective processes. *Developmental Review, 14*, 52-80.

Bruner, J. (1990). *Acts of meaning.* Cambridge, MA: Harvard University Press.

Diener, E., & Suh, E. M. (1998). Subjective well-being and age: An international analysis. *Annual Review of Gerontology and Geriatrics, 17*, 304-324.

Diener, E., Suh, E. M., Lucas, R., & Smith, H. L. (1999). Subjective well-being: Three decades of progress. *Psychological Bulletin, 125*, 276-302.

Dittmann-Kohli, F. (1989). Erfolgreiches Altern aus subjektiver Sicht [Successful aging from a subjective point of view]. *Zeitschrift für Gerontopsychologie und -psychiatrie, 2*, 301-307.

Dittmann-Kohli, F. (1990). The construction of meaning in old age. *Ageing and Society, 10*, 270-294.

Dittmann-Kohli, F. (1995). *Das persönliche Sinnsystem: Ein Vergleich zwischen frühem und spätem Erwachsenenalter* [The personal meaning system: A comparison between early and late adulthood]. Göttingen: Hogrefe.

Dittmann-Kohli, F. (2001, September). *Die kognitive Repräsentation von Verfall und Stabilität in spontanen Selbstbeschreibungen: Eine Untersuchung sprachlicher Ausdrücke für lebenszeitliche Entwicklungsverläufe* [The cognitive representation of decline and stability in spontaneous self-descriptions: A comparison of linguistic expression of life course developmental trajectories]. Paper presented at the 15th Tagung Entwicklungspsychologie, Potsdam, Germany.

Dittmann-Kohli, F., Bode, C., & Westerhof, G. J. (Eds.). (2001). *Die zweite Lebenshälfte-Psychologische Perspektiven. Ergebnisse des Alters-Survey* [The second half of life: Psychological perspectives. Findings from the German Aging Survey]. Schriftenreihe des Bundesministeriums für Familie, Senioren, Frauen und Jugend, Band 195. Stuttgart: Kohlhammer.

Dittmann-Kohli, F., & Westerhof, G. J. (1997). The SELE-sentence completion questionnaire: A new instrument for the assessment of personal meaning in research on aging. *Anuario de Psicologia, 73*, 7-18.

Dittmann-Kohli, F., & Westerhof, G. J. (2000). The personal meaning system in a life span perspective. In G. T. Reker & K. Chamberlain (Eds.), *Exploring existential meaning: Optimizing human development across the life span* (pp. 107-123). Thousand Oaks, CA: Sage.

Filipp, S. H. (1996). Motivation and emotion. In J. E. Birren & K. W. Schaie (Eds.), *Handbook of the psychology of aging* (4th ed., pp. 218-235). San Diego: Academic Press.

Heckhausen, J., & Schulz, R. (1995). A life-span theory of control. *Psychological Review, 102*, 284-304.

Hermans, H. J. M. (2001). The dialogical self: Toward a theory of personal and cultural positioning. *Culture and Psychology, 7*, 243-281.

James, W. (1890/1983). *The principles of psychology.* Cambridge: Harvard University Press.

Kempen, H. J. G. (1996). Mind as body moving in space: Bringing the body back into self psychology. *Theory and Psychology, 6*, 717-733.

Klein, W. M, & Weinstein, N. D. (1997). Social comparison and unrealistic optimism about personal risk. In B. P. Buunk & F. X. Gibbons (Eds.), *Health, coping, and well-being: Perspectives from social comparison theory* (pp. 25-63). Mahwah: Erlbaum.

Kunzmann, U., Little, T. D., & Smith, J. (2000). Is age-related stability of subjective well being a paradox? Cross-sectional and longitudinal evidence from the Berlin Aging Study. *Psychology and Aging, 15*, 511-526.

Markus, H. R., & Kitayama, S. (1991). Culture and self: Implications for cognition, emotion, and motivation. *Psychological Review, 98*, 224-253.

Montepare, J. M., & Zebrowitz, L. A. (1998). Person perception comes of age: The salience and significance of age in social judgments. *Advances in Experimental Social Psychology, 30*, 93-161.

Öberg, P. (1996). The absent body: A social gerontological paradox. *Ageing and Society, 16*, 701-719.

Pinquart, M., & Sörensen, S. (2000). Influences of socioeconomic status, social network, and competence on subjective well-being in later life: A meta-analysis. *Psychology and Aging, 15*, 187-224.

Reker, G. T., & Chamberlain, K. (Eds.) (2000). *Exploring existential meaning: Optimizing human development across the life span.* Thousand Oaks, CA: Sage.

Riley, M. W., Kahn, R. L., & Foner, A. (Eds.) (1994). *Age and structural lag: Society's failure to provide meaningful opportunities in work, family, and leisure.* New York: Wiley.

Ryff, C. D. (1989a). In the eye of the beholder: Views of psychological well-being among middle-aged and older adults. *Psychology and Aging, 6*, 286-295.

Ryff, C. D. (1989b). Happiness is everything, or is it? Explorations on the meaning of psychological well-being. *Journal of Personality and Social Psychology, 57*, 1069-1081.

Ryff, C. D., & Essex, M. J. (1991). Psychological well-being in adulthood and old age: Descriptive markers and explanatory processes. *Annual Review of Gerontology and Geriatrics, 10*, 144-171.

Sampson, E. E. (1988). The debate on individualism: Indigenous psychologies of the individual and their role in personal and societal functioning. *American Psychologist, 43*, 15-22.

Sedikides, C., & Brewer, M. B. (Eds.). (2001). *Individual self, relational self, and collective self.* Philadelphia: Psychology Press.

Singelis, T. M. (1994). The measurement of independent and interdependent self-construals. *Personality and Social Psychology Bulletin, 20*, 580-591.

Staudinger, U. M., Marsiske, M., & Baltes, P. B. (1995). Resilience and reserve capacity in later adulthood: Potentials and limits of development across the life span. In D. Cicchetti & D. J. Cohen (Eds.), *Developmental psychopathology* (Vol. 2, pp. 801-847). New York: Wiley.

Steele, C. M. (1988). The psychology of self-affirmation: Sustaining the integrity of the self. *Advances in Experimental Social Psychology, 21*, 261-302.

Steverink, N., Westerhof, G. J., Bode, C., & Dittmann-Kohli, F. (2001). The personal experience of growing old, resources and subjective well-being. *Journals of Gerontology: Psychological Sciences, 56B*, P364-P373.

Taylor, S. E., & Brown, J. D. (1988). Illusion and well-being: A social psychological perspective on mental health. *Psychological Bulletin, 103*, 193-210.

Thomas, L. E., & Chambers, K. O. (1989). Phenomenology of life satisfaction among elderly men: Quantitative and qualitative views, *Psychology and Aging, 4*, 284-289.

Timmer, E., Steverink, N., & Dittmann-Kohli, F. (2002). Cognitive representations of future gains, maintenance, and losses in the second half of life. *International Journal of Aging and Human Development, 55*, 317-335.

Van Selm, M., & Dittmann-Kohli., F. (1998). Meaninglessness in the second half of life: The development of a construct. *International Journal of Aging and Human Development, 47*, 81-104.

Veroff, J. (1983). Contextual determinants of personality. *Personality and Social Psychology Bulletin, 9*, 331-343.

Westerhof, G. J. (1994). *Statements and stories: Towards a new methodology of attitude research.* Amsterdam: Thesis Publishers.

Westerhof, G. J. (2001a). "I'm afraid that I'll loose my job before I retire": Personal narratives about employment and the social structures of the life course. *Hallym International Journal of Aging 3*, 55-79.

Westerhof, G. J. (2001b, September). *Culture, self and the meaning of aging.* Paper presented at the 15th Tagung Entwicklungspsychologie, Potsdam, Germany.

Westerhof, G. J., & Dittmann-Kohli, F. (1997). Zingeving, levensloop en cultuur: Verschillen en overeenkomsten tussen jong en oud in Nederland en Zaïre [Personal meaning, life course and culture: Differences and similarities between young and elderly adults in the Netherlands and Zaire]. *Medische Antropologie, 9*, 115-136.

Westerhof, G. J., & Dittmann-Kohli, F. (2000). Work status and the construction of work-related selves. In K. W. Schaie & J. Hendricks (Eds.), *The evolution of the aging self: The societal impact on the aging process* (pp. 123-157). New York: Springer.

Westerhof, G. J., Dittmann-Kohli, F., & Katzko, M. (2000). Individualism and collectivism in the personal meaning system of elderly adults: USA and Zaire as an Example. *Journal of Cross-Cultural Psychology, 31*, 649-676.

Westerhof, G. J., Dittmann-Kohli, F., & Thissen, T. (2001). Beyond life satisfaction: Qualitative and quantitative approaches to judgments about the quality of life. *Social Indicators Research, 56*, 179-203.

Westerhof, G. J., Katzko, M., Dittmann-Kohli, F., & Hayslip, B. (2001). Life contexts and health-related selves in old age: Perspectives from the United States, India and Zaire. *Journal of Aging Studies, 15*, 105-126.

Westerhof, G. J., Kuin, Y., & Dittmann-Kohli, F. (1998). Gesundheit als Lebensthema [Health as a dominant concern]. *Zeitschrift für Klinische Psychologie, 27*, 136-142.

Williams, A., & Nussbaum, J. F. (2001). *Intergeneration communication across the lifespan.* Mahwah: Erlbaum.

Wong, P. T. P., & Fry, P. S. (Eds.). (1998). *The human quest for meaning.* Mahwah: Erlbaum.

## CHAPTER 8

# Negotiating Aging Identity: Surface, Depth, and Masquerade

## Simon Biggs

### THE CRITICAL STATE OF AGING THEORY

Theories of age and identity are undergoing considerable change. This chapter constitutes an attempt to understand some of these trends and their implications for the study of adult aging. It poses the question of how the often-contradictory influences on an aging identity are themselves "made sense of" both personally and socially. In so doing, it is argued that a combination of factors would need to be taken into account, including social agism, enhanced personal integration and novel forms of uncertainty associated with the creation of identity in later life.

The question of how older adults develop strategies for negotiating an aging identity would have important implications for policy, the practice of helping professionals and the development of appropriate research methodologies.

I start this exploration by drawing attention to two trends that have emerged in social gerontology and appear to be pulling in different directions. Each has important implications for the state of aging identity within a critical perspective. The first includes work that has emphasized negative social effects on adult aging. This trend can be seen within a political economy approach, developed by Estes (1979, 1993, 2001) and Minkler and Estes (1998) in the United States and Townsend (1981), Phillipson (1982, 1998), and Walker (1986, 1996) in the United Kingdom, who have critically addressed the social construction of old age and the institutionalization of disadvantage. Social agism (Butler, 1963; Bytheway, 1995; Moody, 1998), can be seen as the attitudinal correlate of those constructions. This viewpoint has drawn attention to older age as a time of marginalization and resistance to a dominant discourse emphasizing social, physical, and economic decline. The second holds a very different interpretation of aging, drawing on work in the fields of psychotherapy, social psychology, and the humanities, and emphasizes the possibilities for self-development in later life. It can be recognized in the work of Jung (1934/1967), Neugarten (1968), Guttman (1987), in Tornstam's (1996) exploration of gerotranscendence as a form of personal integration, and Gergen and Gergen's (2001) celebration of creativity in later life. Here, aging identity is seen as holding potential for a positive re-appraisal of the self and it is suggested that the ground upon which identity is built differs from that of other parts of the adult life course.

Cole (1992), has observed the tendency for concepts of aging to split into two independent and contradictory patterns, a dualism which separates out positive and negative attributions. And, while both the trends noted above critique negative constructions of aging and encourage positive ones, there has been something of an institutional division within the gerontological academy which has perpetuated an absence of dialogue and integration (Cole, Kastenbaum, & Ray, 2000). If each reflects an aspect of contemporary adult aging, then it seems reasonable to suggest that the experience of later life encompasses both and that a critical gerontology should reflect this.

Theorizing age and identity is, among other things, a meeting point for social and personal construals of the self. It increasingly needs to grapple with the complexities and contradictions that arise from a simultaneous possibility of enhanced personal potential and an environment tacitly or explicitly hostile toward old age. Katz (2000), for example, has critiqued notions of active and positive aging as "busy bodies." He suggests that the discovery of the "gray" consumer has made a straightforward distinction between negative ageism and positive aging less distinct. Biggs (2001) has examined the influence of anti-ageist rhetoric in social policy. This is seen to contain ambiguous moral injunctions, embedded within emerging narratives of aging and the construction of self as a useful citizen. Lebouvie-Vief (2000) indicates that adult aging may provoke emotional adjustment and integration. However, she points out that this does not necessarily correspond to an increase in personal contentedness. What is striking about these analyses is that they suggest a world in which positive exhortations to age well and negative undercurrents co-exist and require further conceptual explanation.

Writers such as Phillipson (1998) and Polikva (2000) have argued that the ground on which age is socially constructed is changing rapidly, and that theories of postmodernity should be taken seriously as a legitimate field for critical enquiry. Just as the development of critical gerontology has been uneven, it is reasonable to assume an unevenness of cultural change, the co-existence of different trends in contemporary aging leading to novel forms of complexity, options, and variability within the experience of aging itself. This variability has been associated with a shift from identities built on production to those built on consumption (Bauman, 1995; Giddens, 1991). It can be argued (Gilleard & Higgs, 2000) that consuming in the "grey market" allows a new freedom for older adults that their occupational or retirement identities did not, and that this is part and parcel of increased flexibility when choosing the sort of identity one wishes to adopt. However, it has also been suggested that aging identity is threatened whether social and personal aspects are defined primarily by "what I do" or by "what I buy into" (Phillipson & Biggs, 1998). On the one hand, protection is required to safeguard the self from relatively fixed social-cultural stereotyping that may deny or restrict possibilities for personal growth and social inclusion, once older people are no longer seen as being productive. This is most often referred to in the discussion of ageism as an absence of a person's use-value in societies based on capitalist production. On the other, the growth of consumption has added a second source of assault. This arises from the fragmentation of reliable ground on which to resist dominant constructions of aging. Building an identity then becomes fraught with uncertainty, as increasingly fluid sources of external support makes personal coherence difficult to maintain. If this argument is accepted, then an aging identity has to protect itself from both an excess of structure and an excess of flux.

This chapter will take as its central concern the growth of a masking motif within theories of aging, ideas which can be traced to a wider debate on the condition of postmodernity, and the view that identity has become disconnected from material reality and is increasingly a matter of surface and performance. They have emerged within gerontology and cast a distinctive light on the question of the relation between positive and negative aspects of aging and identity. Finally, some implications will be drawn for the future of critical gerontological theory and research.

## SOCIAL MASKING AND AGING IDENTITIES

Social masking is common to all people. It may appear at its most extreme in cases where a group or individual becomes socially marginalized from a dominant ideal, one form of which is in relation to age. It has become a popular means of interrogating the multiple options available to contemporary identity and as a way of thinking about identity as a performance. Here I will examine the work of Jean Baudrillard and Judith Butler, both of whom have made influential commentary on the post-modernization of identity, as a way into the uses of masquerade within critical gerontology itself.

### Baudrillard, Social Masking, and Fluid Aging

The work of Jean Baudrillard (1976/1993, 1983/1999) has significantly influenced the climate within which contemporary ideas about identity have been debated. This has inevitably extended to theories of age (Gilleard & Higgs, 2000; Featherstone & Hepworth, 1983; Holstein & Gubrium, 2000), and an interest in consumerism as a lens though which to understand aging (see Kastenbaum, 1993;

Katz, 1999; Sawchuck, 1995). Sandwell (1995) notes that Baudrillard's key contibution to an understanding of contemporary identity is that "signifiers are totally 'emancipated' from the signified and referrential" (p. 126).

In other words, identifying statements, such as "youthful," "old," or "aging," may no longer refer back to particular positions or attributes that can be considered real or authentic, but are swapped around as desire or circumstance dictates.

Admittedly, when applied directly to age, such fluidity of identity appears an unlikely possibility. However, it follows that a variety of identities and personal images can be adopted by social actors, who can then arguably take on any appearance that they wish. According to Baudrillard (1993), this is less an issue of adopting a different role as one moves from situation to situation and more an issue of the changing nature of social images themselves. These have disconnected from their original meanings and effectively become simulations of those originating points of reference. Further, what we usually think to be "real" is often nothing more than a product of an unrecognized simulation.

Baudrillard (1993) outlines a loosely historical progression in which representation has detached itself from a base in material reality. I have added in parenthesis how this might translate as an observation on age.

First, representations are mimetic in so far as they are seen to reflect a pre-existing basic reality (signs of aging are the same as physical aging). Second, representations are masks that disguise or pervert a basic reality (signs of age are disguised by other identities signifing not-age). Next, masking takes place to hide an absence of any core reality (aging, which is itself only an artifice, covers up an absence of meaning); leading to a final "epoch" in which signs cease to bear any relationship to an underlying reality whatsoever (aging is just one of many identities, none of which are any more appropriate than any other). In this context, of arguing that society is moving from representations of actual states of affairs (associated with production) to simulation for its own sake (associated with consumption), Baudrillard briefly touches on the notion of a "third age" in later life. His discussion of adult aging appears to be stuck in a very "modern" version of old age, as a period of non-production: "Old age has merely become a marginal and ultimately asocial slice of life—a ghetto, a reprieve, and the slide into death. Old age is literally being eliminated. In proportion as the living live longer, as they 'win' over death, they cease to be symbolically acknowledged" (1993, p. 163).

The third age, then, becomes empty of meaning and dependent upon representations from other parts of the life course. Insofar as adult aging is considered at all, it would appear to provoke disguise or disguise of a social void. If links can be drawn with contemporary gerontology, they would appear closest where aging is associated with the pursuit of "agelessness" ( Andrews, 1999; Kaufman, 1986). It follows that one can take on any identity except aging because aging itself is construed as an absence. This may be because it is not recognized for purposes of consumption other than as something to be avoided, and has no value as a source of production.

Baudrillard also uses the concept of a mask in *Fatal Strategies* (1999), under a section entitled "the obscene." He argues that it is almost impossible to shed appearances. The face, stripped of its masks, constitutes a type of psychological nudity where there exists an emotionally raw state of looking and being looked at. It is this emotional, and for Baudrillard, sexual transparency which lends the absence of social affectation a sense of revulsion. Beyond emotional vulnerability exists an awareness of personal emptiness because there are, within the Baudrillarian universe, no personal truths, reasons or meanings. It follows that any search for an authentic existence beyond the mask is condemned to "vacuous decipherment." "Only appearances, that is to say, signs that do not let meanings filter through, protect us from this irradiation, this loss of substance in the empty space of truth" (1999, p. 60).

This interpretation of masquerade is difficult to grasp partly because it subsists upon a supposed absence of deeper meaning, even though the very way that Baudrillard poses the question suggests a distinction between depth and surface. The mask simply hides emptiness, which when translated into the language of identity, describes a personal void, reminiscent (although Baudrillard would probably reject this) of existential uncertainty. From an existential point of view, the answer would lie in creating one's own meanings in order to make sense of the emptiness of social convention. From Baudrillard's viewpoint, there is no meaning beyond a particular "appearance" which includes the acceptance that appearances is all that one has to hold on to. Unfortunately little is said here about what is being protected from existing meanings and which substance is in danger of being lost. As such, this perspective draws attention to the surface appearances available to aging identity, hinting at an emptiness that lies beyond. However, it does not address the seemingly intractable physicality of aging. It does not tell us whether we can choose not to age although it hints at such a possibility, and it is this proposal and the contradictions that surround it that has been reflected in contemporary gerontological thinking.

Featherstone and Hepworth have noted that contemporary lifestyles of older people allow: "Individuals who look after their bodies and adopt a positive attitude toward life . . . to avoid the decline and negative effects of the ageing process and thereby prolong their capacity to enjoy the full benefits of consumer culture" (1983, p. 87).

In Featherstone and Hepworth's view, adult aging is no longer a transition from productivity to disengagement. Rather, it has become a life course plateau, allowing continual re-invention from midlife into deep old age. The turn to lifestyle, reinforces the view—most forcefully expressed by Featherstone and Hepworth as a "Blurring of what appeared previously to be relatively clearly marked stages and the experiences and characteristic behaviour which were associated with those stages" (1989, p. 144).

As part of this process, older adulthood is liberated from a forced withdrawl from society. Thus:

> Popular perceptions of ageing have shifted, from the dark days when the "aged poor" sat in motionless rows in the workhouse, to a modernising interwar phase when "the elderly" were expected to don the retirement uniform, to postmodern times when older citizens are encouraged not just to dress "young" and look youthful, but to exercise, have sex, take holidays, socialise in ways indistinguishable from those of their children's generation. There are no rules now, only choices. (Blaikie, 1999, p. 104)

Such observations fit well with McAdams' (1993) view that adults are now required to "story" the life course from their own imaginative resources, or personal myths, as the certainties of stage-appropriate codes of behavior appear to be dissolving. "Defining the self through myth may be seen as an ongoing act of psychological and social responsibility. Because our world can no longer tell us who we are and how we should live, we must figure it out on our own" (McAdams, 1993). The trick of identity management under such conditions is arguably to discover techniques whereby a multiplicity of options for identity can be negotiated in the absence of binding cultural guidelines.

## Butler, Aging Identity, and Performance

A second stream of thought associated with postmodernity has viewed identity as a performance. A common thread with the discussion above exists in an interest in social flux and how to negotiate uncertainty as traditional categories of identity are undercut. This is evident in the work of Judith Butler (1990, 1996). Butler's main interest has been the analysis of gender and sexuality as performances that are culturally enforced. Identities, she argues, acquire stability through matrices of expected behavior that define the space in which they can be enacted. In the case of gender, this matrix has taken the form of a binary distinction between masculine and feminine, to the exclusion of other possibilities. A similar binary distinction could be argued to exist between youth and age, although Butler's interests do not extend this far. In such spaces ones "inner" sense of self is often filled by what it is not, an opposite that is externally defined. Butler follows Lacan's (1994) psychodynamic view here, of women's identity as a "lack" of something that is defined as "other." Viewing identities as perfomative, however, injects elements of creativity and transgressive freedom into that same space. "What I'm trying to do," Butler says, "is think about performativity as that aspect of discourse that has the capacity to produce what it names" (1996, p. 112).

In other words, a performance is a "vehicle" through which personal identity can be established. Identity becomes itself through this of act of performance. In so doing, a mechanism emerges as to how self-invention can take place within an otherwise hostile space, as performance is sufficiently fluid to allow resistance and parody of the stereotyped identity being performed.

Nussbaum (1999) suggests that in this reading of identity, it is not always clear whether we are talking about language or about action. She attempts to clarify the situation by saying: "when we act and speak in a gendered way, we are not simply reporting on something that is already fixed in the world, we are actively constituting it. . . . At the same time, by carrying out these performances in a slightly different manner, a parodic manner, we can perhaps unmake then just a little" (1999, p. 52).

It must be said that Nussbaum is critical of the lack of ambition that such a model holds, particularly in terms of social action. Key to Butler's contribution, however, is an exploration of "how to take an oppositional relation to power, that is admittedly, implicated in the very power one opposes" (Disch, 1999). There is an element of inevitability to this approach that assumes one can never quite shake off the problems that identity poses, nor the social constructions that form the basis of oppressive spaces.

It is relatively easy to see how older identities might be stuck in the contradiction that Butler describes, in the sense that we are the same people who will age or who have been young. We cannot easily escape into a split between self and other to avoid this problem. We are thus identified with and simultaneously resist the aging process, evidenced by the observation that adult aging rarely provokes a rejection of the cult of youth but often colludes with it. Much as Butler suggests with respect to gender, we take an oppositional relation to the power of age as it is socially defined, while being implicated in the definitions of age that we oppose. Performances around age can be interpreted as a strategy for managing the problem of increased personal integration, whilst negotiating a path through socially constructed agism. Butler's model does not, however, explain the particular circumstances that accompany adult aging. Neither does it suggest how the relationship between these opposing issues is resolved through masquerade.

Two facets, hypothesised as key to the management of contemporary identity, arise from the work of Baudrillard and Butler, which may inform debate on adult aging. First, is the perception that identity is becoming increasingly fluid. Many social gerontologists appear to have picked up on the implication that such fluidity increases choice, without addressing the corollary that there is an underlying emptiness to the experience, or even to the existence, of selfhood. Second, aging can be viewed as a performance, in ways similar to gendered identities. However, this analysis has not been fully extended by the authors, to draw out its implications for later life.

## Masquerade and Aging

The core contradiction that any theory of aging has to encounter is that mutability and performance eventually have to accommodate finitude and the restraints imposed by aging itself. Postmodern identity, in other words hits a wall, when adult aging is encountered. It faces limits that challenge a tendency toward narcissistic omnipotence and an intolerance of limitation. There is an element of unbuckability about aging which occurs in a way that is subtly different from other identity markers. However much it may be desired, one cannot choose not to grow old.

The implications of an aging identity become increasingly salient in midlife and extend into old age. Observations have been made by a number of writers concerning the relationship between the hidden and the surface of aging identities that such a realization provokes. Benson's (1997) study of the divergence between media and private perceptions of adult aging, Gullette's (1998) view of midlife as the beginning of "automatic decline and compulsory optimism" and McAdams' (1993) comments on "a curious blend of resurgence and decline," each hint at this layering of the self.

The question of masquerade and hidden identity are increasingly being used, in gerontological literature, to examine the relationship between social and personal potential in later life (Biggs, 1993, 1999; Hepworth, 1991; Woodward, 1991, 1995). While masking has been employed to interpret the management of an aging self in an uncertain and unequal world, the relationship between hidden and surface differs significantly between these authors.

Hepworth (1991) characterizes the distinction between surface and depth in terms of an opposition between age and youth, maintaining that: "At the heart of the difficulty of explaining what its like to be old lies the awareness of an experiential difference between the physical processes of ageing, as reflected in outward appearance and the inner, or subjective sense of a 'real self' which paradoxically remains young" (1991, p. 93).

This "mask of aging" position, at it has become known, holds that the aging body becomes a cage from which a younger self-identity cannot escape (Featherstone & Hepworth, 1989). Here, the mask motif and the problem of aging are couched in terms of a tension between the aging body and a youthful "inner" self. The body, while it is malleable, can still provide access to a variety of consumer identities and thereby engage in the performance of identity. However, as aging gathers pace, it becomes increasingly difficult to "re-cycle" the body through cosmetics, surgery, props, and prostheses thus denying access to that world of choice. An endgame emerges with older people being at war with themselves, an internalized battle between a desire to express oneself and the aging body. Aging, as a mask, thus becomes a nightmare for the consumer dream as aging reverses its libertarian possibilities. The mask emerges as a contradiction between the fixedness of the body and the fluidity of social images.

Both Woodward (1991, 1995) and Biggs (1993, 1999) draw on a psycho-dynamic understanding of the relationship between depth and surface in their use of the masquerade motif. Here, masquerade consists of language games, body language, and forms of personal adornment which contribute to the performance of self. Masquerade is of particular interest because it occurs at the meeting point of both the personal and social worlds and that of surface appearances and an interior sense of identity. It is, in this sense, a bridge between the inner and outer logics of adult aging. Everyone masquerades to some extent, but with increasing age, masking takes on a characteristic nuance.

Within the psychodynamic tradition, Joan Riviere's (1929) paper on "womanliness" has proved a fruitful starting place from which to consider masquerade. Here, femininity is seen as a mask developed by women as a staged performance, which facilitates negotiation of a patriarchal environment. Masquerade becomes a means of participating in a world defined by others, which exacts the cost of denying personal identity in favor of one legitimized by the gaze of those others. "Femininity" is performed as a means of deflecting the possible reprisals that participation might provoke in men and the anxiety that would be felt as a result. This interpretation can translate relatively easily into the language of ageism as it addresses the task of having to become an acceptable aging person through participation in a world defined by values of youth or perpetual midlife. The performance would need to deflect possible reprisals from the not-yet-old that may take the form of envy, disgust, and a reaction against the reminder of personal aging.

Woodward picks up on the notion of masquerade "as a submission to dominant social codes and as a resistance to them," and is particularly interested in youthfulness as a masquerade in old age. As she draws from the story of Aschenbach in Mann's "Death in Venice" as well as other sources, it can be concluded that when it comes to aging, masquerade becomes the preserve of both sexes. Indeed, it is suggested that because each individual ages, the question is not as clearly cut as it is in the case of an impossibly distant "other." For Woodward, aging constitutes a 'masquerade of defiance over the masquerade of pathos' and it appears that, in old age, masking both conceals and reveals the marks of age. A key factor here is a recognition that:

> Masquerade has to do with concealing something and presenting the very conditions of that concealment. A mathematics of difference is posited between the two terms—an inside and an outside, with the outside disguising what is within. . . . As "pretense," masquerade is a form of self-representation. But I also want to call into question the unequivocal notion of the mask as "mere outward show" that hides a "truth." A mask may express rather than hide a truth. The mask itself may be one of multiple truths. (1991, p. 148)

Woodward's description of masking is both subtle and complex. The notion of multiplicity is used to suggest that there is no one mask, but rather that masquerade varies depending upon its audience. Further, the disguise is permeable. It is as much a statement of recognition of aging as a state that something has to be done about, as it is a wish to deny aging as such. She emphasizes the element of play involved in creating a convincing aging identity, while hinting at the possible sanctions that make masquerade necessary.

In my own work (Biggs, 1997, 1999) masquerade preserves the distinction between hidden and surface elements of identity. However, this is not seen as an inevitable part of the aging process, but rather as a tactical manoeuvre to negotiate the contradiction between social ageism and increased personal integration. Indeed under certain conditions the self-integration that comes with maturity should allow a more settled identity to come into play, without the need for masquerade other than as a means of connection to other people. This would be particularly the case in non-threatening, non-ageist environments.

Rather like the persona in Jungian psychology (*Collected Works*, Vol 7, 1967), masking acts as a bridge between inner psychological and external social logic. However, whereas Jungian psychology emphasizes the conventional and ultimately superficial characteristics of masquerade, it is argued that with adult aging, a protective role comes into play. The mask is not so much left behind, as adapted to fit new circumstances. Thus, an element of social protection occurs for parts of the self that cannot be expressed without transgressing contemporary expectations around age. The experience of a long life and the existential questions that aging brings with it are conceived as provoking an expanded and more grounded sense of self. However, because this new and evolving process of the "Mature Imagination" (Biggs, 1999) still exists, within a predominantly ageist society, masquerade is used to cloak socially unacceptable aspects of aging. In such circumstances, the mask is seen as a source of in-authenticity, which nevertheless protects this mature self from external attack, and becomes a somewhat perverse vehicle for self-expression in its own right. Accordingly, relationships underscored by age can provoke a machiavellian use of masking phenomena.

The masquerade also creates a necessary inner space in which to build a stable identity and a stance from which to assess and connect with the social world. In this respect, masquerade can be helpful to social actors because it allows identity to be grounded within that protected inner space. Accordingly, facilitative social environments can now be defined as ones that enhance a sense of harmony between inner and outer worlds, where one can "be oneself" with minimal resort to artifice or masquerade. An ideal situation, in which masquerade is entirely unnecessary probably doesn't exist. Rather, one is dealing in degrees of likelihood that the need for masquerade might be attenuated, from one situation to another.

In both Woodward and Biggs, masquerade becomes part of a coping strategy to maintain identity and a means of keeping one's options open. Rather than being the sum of attributes through which a sense of otherness can be deduced, the mask is simply a device through which an active agent looks out at and negotiates with the world. It leaves the viewer to unravel the fact from the fiction and controls the distance between oneself and other people. Masquerade, then, is largely a result of an irony of later life: that a withdrawal of psychological inhibition and an increase in social restriction are experienced simultaneously by many mature adults.

Thinking in terms of masquerade also has certain advantages for critical gerontologists, in so far as it opens up a critical distance between appearances and underlying experience. It is no longer possible simply to equate structural/functional role performance with the nature of aging—and that's it. The distance identified between internal and external worlds and the relationship between them allows an interrogation of that space, its form, depth, and the power relations that maintain it. It allows room to manoeuvre both for the critical theorist and for resistance and personal expression as aging takes place. Attention is drawn, then, to psychological spaces that possess some degree of freedom from everyday conformity and social control. The possibility of fluidity and choice of identity is "held" by this approach at surface levels of masquerade, while simultaneously opening the opportunity to ask questions about more grounded sources of identity that exist deep within the psyche.

Such an approach to identity mediated by masquerade emphasizes the importance of maintaining a dialogue between the personal and the social. If masquerade can be seen as a strategy used to outwit social ageism, it also contains the danger of becoming inward-looking and thus solipsistic. This may occur if the inner world is perceived to be sufficiently threatened or to contain greater rewards and satisfactions than would result from interaction with the social world. The bridge between the inner and the outer, the psyche and the social, would then become increasingly precarious. One's sense of self would become progressively fixed and self-referential.

An erosion of the mask would leave the psyche vulnerable and without strategies with which to negotiate the world. Masquerade creates a protected inner space within which a sense of core self-identity can emerge. However, in taking this too far, solipsism holds the danger of becoming "out of touch." Both extremes, an eroded mask and an exclusive preoccupation with protected contents, would reduce the possibility of interaction based upon a secure and grounded age-identity.

What holds true for psychic equilibrium in this case also holds true for the development of critical gerontology. Currently, critical gerontology appears to separately recognize the negative social construction of adult aging and the potential for personal growth and potential in old age. Using the metaphor of masquerade provides one way of achieving dialogue between these two observations.

## CONCLUDING COMMENTS

There has been a tendency in gerontological theory to concentrate upon the surface elements of an aging identity, on appearance and the props that can be used to maintain a certain presentation of self to an external audience. This has arguably occurred to the extent that some positions, tacitly or explicitly, are maintained in the belief that the surface appearances are all there is to it. The great seduction of thinking in terms of surfaces is that it allows choice from a multiplicity of identity statements, and at root the promise that the supposedly negative effects of aging can be postponed or ignored. It is also an approach that privileges the interface between external social realities and the self as observed, and as such minimizes the tension between socially structured statements about aging and subjective experience.

Part of the translation of contemporary and specifically post-modern theorizing on identity into the realm of aging studies has been an increasing awareness of the inadequacies of that proposal. Adult aging, at the most visible level of an aging body, creates a tension between surface appearance and elements of the self that are hidden from view. This has raised a number of new directions for a critical gerontology of identity which has re-discovered the distinction between surface and depth and the deployment of masquerade as a means of negotiating the spaces between these two poles of attraction. Whereas attention to appearances emphasizes inter-changeable options for the performance of identity, depth anchors the self in memory, continuity, desire, and enduring motivation. There are few of us, after all, who would like to be thought of as lacking depth. The interchange between these different levels of identity raises a number of interesting questions, including:

• The form that a masquerade might take, given its function as a personally protective maneuver, but also as a bridge that connects to wider social realities.
• The status of an inner logic, existing beneath the surface forms and elisions that masking suggests.
• The circumstances that affect the likelihood that different elements of an aging identity being expressed.

First, masquerade, as an act of performance, may take on different characteristics depending upon the circumstances older adults find themselves in. It may connect with others, while still protecting the self and the degree to which one function is in the ascendant may depend upon whether interaction takes place with a social worker, doctor, loved or disliked family member, friend, or rival. Structural factors arising from class, gender, and cultural inequalities would be expected to mediate the deployment of masquerade—how far one feels safe in being oneself.

Second, the relationship between appearances and deeper elements of identity, raises the question of the nature of the internal world of aging and how it can be accessed by researchers and helping professionals. The question of an inner existence, which may be in some way more core, central of genuine than reactions to particular situations or transient wishes raises the issue of whether it is possible to identify an authentic way of being in later life. Such an undertaking would be fraught with difficulty. A starting point may be to locate adult aging within a life course trajectory, thus provoking existential issues that arise from the point someone has reached. It would need to avoid simply reflecting contemporary norms and scientific fashion while nevertheless retaining some grounding in what is special about late life.

Third, and the degree to which deeper aspects are allowed to surface, may be key to understanding well-being in later life. This may be based on an ability to meaningfully express a sense of personal continuity, memory, belonging, emotional commitment, and experience that might otherwise be suppressed. The degree to which older people feel able to openly experience their own individuation, gero-transcendence, and increased personal integration would provide a conceptually clear, if empirically sophisticated means of judging the value of initiatives both in policy and in professional practice.

This struggle, in effect to find tools that help us critically engage with the issues raised by aging identities, also suggests a number of important themes for contemporary social gerontology as a whole. These themes, I believe, are key to taking forward critical gerontological thinking and would include:

- A consideration of both personal and structural factors in our understanding of aging identity, without reducing one to the other.
- An accommodation of both depth and surface elements within an understanding of aging identity.
- Grounding aging identity, in such a way as to take account of both fluidity and fixity.
- The elaboration of circumstances that enable the expression of a nuanced, yet authentic performance of self.

If the arguments above are accepted, there are key issues raised for research into aging which are not currently emphasised by large scale survey data nor the turn to qualitative narrative approaches. These would include whether it is possible to work out which level of identity research picks up. Certain methods may pick up different layers of identity, depending on generational and other power relations between researcher and respondent. It may be possible to work toward environments that increase the likelihood that deeper, and perhaps less superficial elements of the aging experience are expressed. To begin this task one has to accept that a first response, or a developed and workable narrative may only alert us to the surface performance of identity without addressing more profound existential questions about the late course. This is particularly the case if there is a cultural contradiction between self-integration in old age and social ageism.

Our theorizing and our interpretation of empirical findings must, then, take into account that the performance of an aging identity as inevitably layered. Some older adults may have had the opportunity over a long life to achieve a greater integration and clarity of self-expression. They may require suitably facilitative environments in which to express it. The degree to which researchers, policymakers, and helping professionals can establish a rapport with more authentic expressions of the aging experience, and eventually the achievement of greater well-being within an aging society, will depend on the development of methods of inquiry sensitised to the complexity of this mature imagination.

## REFERENCES

Andrews, M. (1999). The seductiveness of agelessness. *Aging & Society, 19*(3), 301-318.

Baudrillard, J. (1976, trans. 1993). *Symbolic exchange & death.* London: Sage.

Baudrillard, J. (1983, trans. 1999). *Fatal strategies.* London: Pluto.

Bauman, Z. (1995). *Life in fragments.* Oxford: Blackwell.

Blaikie, A. (1999). *Aging & popular culture.* Cambridge: Cambridge University Press.

Benson, J. (1997). *Prime time.* Wolverhampton: Wolverhampton University Press.

Biggs, S. (1993). *Understanding aging.* Bucks: Open University Press.

Biggs, S. (1997). Choosing not to be old? *Aging & Society, 17*(5), 553-553.

Biggs, S. (1999). *The mature imagination.* Bucks: Open University Press.

Biggs, S. (2001). Toward critical narrativity: Stories of aging in contemporoary social policy. *Journal of Aging Studies, 15,* 1-14.

Butler, J. (1990). *Gender trouble.* London: Routledge.

Butler, J. (1996). Gender as performance. In P. Osbourne (Ed.), *A critical sense.* London: Routledge.

Butler, R. (1963). *Why survive? Being old in America.* San Francisco: Harper & Row.

Bytheway, B. (1995). *Ageism.* Bucks: Open University Press.

Cole, T. (1992). *The journey of life.* New York: Springer.

Cole, T., Kastenbaum, R., & Ray, R. (2000). *Handbook of the humanities & aging.* New York: Springer.

Disch, L. (1999). Judith Butler and the politics of the performative. *Political Theory, 27*(4), 545-550.

Estes, C. (1979). *The aging enterprise.* San Francisco: Jossey-Bass.

Estes, C. (1993). The aging enterprise revisited. *The Gerontologist, 33*(3), 292-298.

Estes, C. (2001). *Social policy & aging.* Thousand Oaks: Sage.

Featherstone, M., & Hepworth, M. (1983). The midlifestyles of George and Lynne. *Theory, Culture & Society, 1*(3), 85-92.

Featherstone, M., & Hepworth, M. (1989). Aging and old age; Reflections on the postmodern lifecourse. In B. Bytheway, T. Keil, & P. Allatt (Eds.), *Becoming and being old.* London: Sage.

Gergen, K., & Gergan, M. (2001). Positive aging newsletter. www. healthandage-positive@www.e-newsboomerang.com

Giddens, A. (1991). *Modernity & self-identity.* Oxford: Polity.

Gilleard, C., & Higgs, P. (2000). *Cultures of aging.* London: Prentice-Hall.

Gullette, M. (1998). Midlife discourses in twentieth century United States. In R. Shweder (Ed.), *Welcome to middle age.* Chicago: University of Chicago Press.

Guttman, D. (1987). *Reclaimed powers.* London: Hutchinson.

Hepworth, M. (1991). Positive aging and the mask of age. *Journal of Educational Gerontology, 6*(2), 93-101.

Holstein, J., & Gubrium, J. (2000). *The self we live by: Narrative identity in a postmodern world.* New York: Oxford.

Jung, C. (1932/1967). *Collected works.* Vol. 7. London: Routledge.

Kastenbaum, R. (1993). Encrusted elders. In T. Cole (Ed.), *Voices and visions of aging.* Charlottesville: University Press of Virginia.

Kaufman, S. (1986). *The ageless self.* New York: Meridian.

Katz, S. (1999). Fashioning agehood: Lifestyle imagery and the commercial spirit of seniors culture. In J. Povlsen (Ed.), *Childhood & old age.* Odense: Odense University Press.

Katz, S. (2000). Busy bodies: Activity, aging and the management of everyday life. *Journal of Aging Studies, 14*(2), 135-152.

Labouvie-Vief, G. (2000). Emotions in adulthood. In V. Bengtson & K. Schaie (Eds.), *Handbook of theories of aging.* New York: Springer.

Lacan, J. (1994). *Le seminar. Livre IV La relation d'objet* [Seminar: Book four: The relation to the object]. Paris: Seuil.

McAdams, D. (1993). *The stories we live by.* New York: Morrow.

Minkler, M., & Estes, C. (1998). *Critical gerontology.* New York: Baywood.

Moody, H. (1998). *Aging: Concepts & contoversies.* Thousand Oaks: Pine Forge.

Neugarten, B. (1968). *Middle age & aging.* Chicago: Chicago University Press.

Nussbaum, M. (1999). The professor of parody. *New Republic, 220*(8), 37-46.

Phillipson, C. (1982). *Capitalism & the construction of old age.* London: Macmillan.

Phillipson, C. (1998). *Reconstructiong old age.* London: Sage.

Phillipson, C., & Biggs, S. (1998). Modernity and identity; themes and perspectives in the study of older adults. *Journal of Aging & Identity, 3*(1), 11-23.

Polikva, J. (2000). Postmodern aging and the loss of meaning. *Journal of Aging & Identity, 5*(2), 225-235.

Riviere, J. (1929). Womanliness as masquerade. In V. Burgin (Ed.), *Formations and fantasy.* London: Methuen.

Sandwell, B. (1995). Forget Baudrillard? *Theory, Culture & Society, 12*(1), 125-152.

Sawchuck, K. (1995). From gloom to boom: Age, identity and target marketing. In M. Featherstone & A. Wernick (Eds.), *Images of aging.* London: Routledge.

Tornstam, L. (1996). Gerotranscendence: A theory about maturing into old age. *Journal of Aging & Identity, 1*(1), 37-50.

Townsend, P. (1981). Structured dependency of the elderly. *Aging & Society, 1*(1), 5-28.

Walker, A. (1986). Pensions and the production of policy in old age. In C. Phillipson & A. Walker (Eds.), *Aging & social policy.* Aldershot: Gower.

Walker, A. (1996). *The new generational contract.* London: University College Press.

Woodward, K. (1991). *Aging & its discontents.* Indiana: Indiana University Press.

Woodward, K. (1995). Tribute to the older woman. In M. Featherstone & A. Wernick (Eds.), *Images of aging.* London: Routledge.

# SECTION THREE

# Theorizing Macro Relations

# CHAPTER 9

# Globalization and the Reconstruction of Old Age: New Challenges for Critical Gerontology

## Chris Phillipson

This chapter explores the various challenges for critical gerontology created by the social, economic, and cultural changes linked with the development of globalization. Despite the fact that attention is just recently increasing, globalization has become an influential force in the construction of old age, most notably in the framing of social and economic policies designed to manage and regulate population aging. It is no longer sufficient to confine analyses of aging issues to local, or even national policies. Growing old has been relocated within a transnational context, with international organizations (such as the World Bank and International Monetary Fund) and cross-border migrations, creating new conditions and environments for older people. At the same time, employment opportunities and policies affecting workers and retirees reflect the global context within which labor markets now operate (Held, McGrew, Goldblatt, & Perraton, 1999). These developments have underlined the importance of theorizing about age, notably in respect of the complex interaction between individuals and groups, and changes at the level of nation states and international governmental organizations.

The main argument of this chapter is that the phenomenon of globalization, which seem to produce new risks and dangers to people's lives, raises important new concerns for social gerontology and critical gerontology in particular. In general, the focus on globalization confirms the importance of locating individuals within the orbit of social and economic structures (a central feature of political economy perspectives within gerontology), these increasingly subject to forces lying beyond the boundaries of the nation state. At the same time, globalization has also been linked to the abandonment of those routines and institutions established in what Giddens (1991) and others refer to as "the first phase of modernity." Anthony Giddens (1991) and Ulrich Beck (2000a) argue that we are now living in a "post-traditional society," where in comparison with the past there is greater emphasis on developing new lifestyles and making fresh choices about the conduct of daily life. Taking these various themes, this chapter explores the implications of globalization for theorizing about the nature of growing old in the twenty-first century.

The chapter is divided into three main sections. The first summarizes key phases in the development of old age as it has evolved over the past 50 years. The analysis traces the institutionalization of aging in the period immediately following the ending of the Second World War, and the subsequent de-stabilization of old age with the move from "organized" to "disorganized" capitalism (Lash & Urry, 1987). The second section then examines the rise of globalization and the influence of international governmental organizations (IGOs), this viewed as bringing forth a new phase in the construction of later life. The third section considers the implications of global perspectives for developing theories within social gerontology.

## INSTITUTIONALIZING OLD AGE

The first task is to consider the way which growing old was transformed in the two decades following the ending of the Second World War. In virtually all industrialized societies, with varying degrees of emphasis, responses to aging were formed around the institutions and relationships associated with state supported public welfare, retirement, and the intergenerational contract (Phillipson, 1998). In general terms, this period is associated with the emergence of retirement as a major social institution, with the growth of entitlements to pensions and the gradual acceptance of an extended period of leisure following the ending of full-time work. Retirement, along with the development of social security and pensions, provided the basis for a reconstructed and standardized life course built around what Best (1980) described as the "three boxes" of education, work, and leisure. This arrangement was reinforced by the theme of "intergenerational reciprocity," with older people receiving care and support as part of the "moral economy" underpinning an extended life course (Hendricks & Leedham, 1991). Kohli (1991) summarizes this development as follows:

> It is by the creation of lifetime continuity and reciprocity that the welfare system contributes to the moral economy of the work society. This becomes especially clear when we look at retirement. The emergence of retirement has meant the emergence of old age as a distinct life phase, structurally set apart from active life and with a clear chronological boundary. But the other parts of the welfare system can be viewed in this perspective as well:

as elements in the construction of a stable lifecourse, covering the gaps ("risks") that are left open by the organization of work. (pp. 277-278)

In fact, what Kohli (1991, p. 274) refers to as the "institutionalisation of the life course" lasted a relatively short span of time in historical terms, with the period from 1945 to 1975 defining its outer limits. From the mid-1970s a number of changes can be identified arising from the development of more flexible patterns of work and the emergence of high levels of unemployment. These produced what may be termed the reconstruction of middle and old age, with the identification of a "third age" in between the period of work ("the second age") and that of a period of mental and physical decline ("the fourth age"). A characteristic feature of this new period of life is the ambiguity and flexibility of the boundaries between work at the lower end, and the period of late old age at the upper end of the life course. Both now have complex periods of transition, with the ambiguity associated with the ending of work (Schuller, 1989) in the first period, and the blurring of dependence and independence in the second (Bernard & Meade, 1993). This period is not defined by individual attributes, but by the nature of key forms of engagement with economic and social roles. It is the latter that are most affected by a shift toward globalization (Beck, 2000b).

In the case of the retirement transition, the template of previous generations—long work, short retirement—has undergone substantial alteration (Schuller, 1989). For many (mostly male) workers, the predictability of continuous employment is being replaced by insecurity in middle and late working life—an experience shared with the majority of women workers (Itzin & Phillipson, 1993). The effects of this shift have yet to receive the full attention of researchers concerned with social aging. The retirement transition itself has become elongated and of greater complexity with the emergence of different pathways (e.g., unemployment, long-term sick, redundancy, disability, part-time employment, self-employment) which people follow before they describe themselves or are defined within the social security system as "wholly retired" (Phillipson, 1998). The result has been greater uncertainty in the position of older workers, both in their attitudes toward leaving work and in terms of their status within society.

But these developments can also be viewed as part of a new political economy shaping the lives of present and future generations of older people. The change here has been variously analyzed as a move from "organized" to "disorganized capitalism," to a shift from "simple" to "reflexive modernity," or to the transformation from mass assembly ("fordist") to flexible/service-driven ("post-fordist") economies. Lash and Urry (1987) identify the period from 1970 as marking the "end of organised capitalism," the latter characterized by full employment and expanding welfare states (the core elements underpinning the growth of retirement). With the period of disorganized capitalism comes the weakening of manufacturing industry and the creation of a "mixed economy of welfare" (Johnson, 1987). Industrial de-concentration is accompanied by spatial de-concentration, as people (the middle classes in particular) and their jobs leave the older industrial cities (Byrne, 1999; Wilson, 1997). In fact, large multi-national corporations are able to move capital and labor intensive productive activities around the globe, seeking the most favorable economic conditions (Hutton & Giddens, 2000). These developments reflect a heightened degree of instability running through capitalist social relations:

> The world of "disorganized capitalism" is one in which the "fixed, fast-frozen relations" of organized capitalist relations have been swept away. Societies are being transformed from above, from below, and from within. All that is solid about organized capitalism, class, industry, cities, collectivity, nation state, even the world, melts into air. (Lash & Urry, cited in Kumar, 1995, p. 49)

Living in the period of what has been termed "late modernity" is, then, about experiencing a world where, as noted in the introduction, traditional routines and institutions are abandoned, and national boundaries become less salient. In the face of these global shifts, individuals are faced with distinctive pressures in respect of the management of everyday life (Bauman, 2000; Giddens, 1991). These changes affect all individuals—no one can escape their global reach and consequences. But people clearly differ in respect of how they respond to a world where traditional institutions are pulled apart, and where day-to-day interaction is governed by a greater degree of openness as well as uncertainty. For some older people, the implication of these changes may be highly positive. Featherstone and Hepworth (1989), for example, analyze what they describe as the "modernisation of aging," this involving a distancing from the period of "deep old age." They see this process as involving three important characteristics: first, the development of new, more youthful images of retirement, these providing a challenge to conventional models of aging. Second, what they describe as "the social construction of middle age," this becoming more fluidly defined as "mid-life" or "the middle years." Finally, there is the development of the contemporary period of extended mid-life into a complex of statuses of "being," "development," and personal growth mediated by *transitional* states or crises. Featherstone and Hepworth (1989, p. 154) conclude that: "this elaboration of mid-life increasingly implies a flexible, individualised, biographical approach which takes into account human diversity."

The above changes reflect the importance of what Hendricks and Leedham (1991) refer to as the "self-structure dialectic," and the way in which individuals can shape or change structures as well as be influenced by them. But while some of the benefits of the new social context may be emphasized, the negative features arising from structural change must also be recognized. This, however, requires a renewed focus within social gerontology on macrosociological variables, notably those relating to global economic and technological change (Hagestad &

Dannefer, 2001). It is to this area that we now turn, examining first of all the emergence of a new phase of aging in the context of the spread and intensification of global social relations (Klein, 2000).

## GLOBALIZATION AND AGING SOCIETIES

Seen from the perspective of the last half-century, the analysis thus far suggests two main phases in the development of old age. First, the emergence of mass retirement (from the late 1940s onwards), underpinned by systems (varying in scope from country to country) of public welfare. This was a time when nations of the developed world singled out older people as beneficiaries of support, mindful of the sacrifices associated with the depression of the 1930s and the world war that followed (Macnicol, 1998; Phillipson, 1998). John Myles (1991, p. 304) characterizes this period in terms of the "institutionalisation of the retirement wage," the major achievement of which was, he suggests, to secure the "right [of working people] to cease working before wearing out." The second period, from the early 70s and through the 1990s, was marked by instability in respect of the images and institutions associated with supporting older people. Old age became fractured into different stages and divisions, these reflecting the unravelling of standardized retirement pathways (Kohli & Rein, 1991).

At the beginning of the twenty-first century, however, it is possible to discern a further stage in the evolution of old age, as nation state-based solutions (and anxieties) about aging run alongside those formulated by global actors and institutions (Cutler & Hendricks, 2001). David Held et al. (1999) define globalization in the following terms:

> Today, virtually all nation-states have gradually become enmeshed in and functionally part of a larger pattern of global transformations and global flows. . . . Transnational networks and relations have developed across virtually all areas of human activity. Goods, capital, people, knowledge, communications and weapons, as well as crime, pollutants, fashions and beliefs, rapidly move across territorial boundaries. . . . Far from this being a world of "discrete civilisations" or simply an international order of states, it has become a fundamentally interconnected global order, marked by intense patterns of exchange as well as by clear patterns of power, hierarchy and unevenness. (p. 49)

This transformed political economy is underscored by the emergence of a more aggressive form of capitalism, one contrasted with the more controlled and regulated capitalism of the 1950s and 1960s. Hutton (1999) describes the essential features of this "turbo-capitalism," as follows:

> Its overriding objective is to serve the interests of property owners and shareholders, and it has a firm belief, effectively an ideological one, that all obstacles to do that-regulation, controls, trade unions, taxation, public

ownership, etc- are unjustified and should be removed. Its ideology is that shareholder value must be maximised, that labour markets should be "flexible" and that capital should be free to invest and disinvest in countries at will. . . . It's a very febrile capitalism, but for all that and its short-termism it has been a very effective transmission agent for the new technologies and for creating the new global industries and markets. It's a tool both of job generation and of great inequality. (pp. 9-10)

Yeates (2001) argues that in the area of social policy, globalization has been uneven in its scope, intensity, and impact. She argues that: ". . . the contradictions of globalization points to the complexities of what 'globalization' is and how other states and other interests respond to it and shape it" (p. 168). Yeates suggests that the relationship between social policy and globalization is best conceived as "dialectical" or "reciprocal": ". . . far from states, welfare states and populations passively 'receiving' [and] adapting to globalization . . . they are active participants in its development" (p. 2). At the level of the state, globalization may influence economic and social policy in a variety of ways. Kargalitsky (1999) notes, on the one hand, a weakening role for nation-states within the context of the growing importance of global markets and international governmental organizations (IGOs). Yet on the other hand: ". . . it is equally indisputable that despite this weakening, the state remains a critically important factor of political and economic development. It is no accident that transnational corporations constantly make use of the nation state as an instrument of their policies" (Kargalitsky, 1999, p. 294). And Yeates also makes the point that the growth of global financial capital does not in itself deny states the power to regulate it or any other fraction of capital.

On the other hand, states vary greatly in their ability to control and influence the process of globalization. Moreover, it is undoubtedly the case that global institutions (notably multi-national corporations) have exerted increasing influence in setting agendas around social policy issues (especially when acting in partnership with dominant powers such as the United States). This is especially the case in respect of policies concerning older people, where International Governmental Organizations (IGOs) have started to raise major concerns about the funding of the welfare state. In the developed world, the magnitude and absolute size of expenditures on older people invariably place their programs as one of the first to be targeted with financial cuts—just as they were one of the first beneficiaries of the welfare state (Myles, 1984). In less developed countries, elderly people (women especially) have been among those most affected by the privatization of health care, and the burden of debt repayments to agencies such as the World Bank and the IMF (Help Age International, 2000).

But older people have also been affected by the way in which IGOs have fed into what Carroll Estes and Associates (2001) have identified as the "crisis construction and crisis management" of policies for the elderly. Bob Deacon (2000) argues that globalization generates a discourse within and among global actors on the future of national and supranational policy. He illustrates this theme with the observation that: "The future of social policy at the national and supranational levels is being shaped by a struggle between supranational organisations for the *right to participate* in shaping policy, and within and between supranational organisations for the *content* of social policy" (p. 2). The clearest example here has been in the field of pension policy where Yeates (2001, p. 122) observes that: "Both the World Bank and IMF have been at the forefront of attempts to foster a political climate conducive to the residualization of state welfare and the promotion of private and voluntary initiatives." The report of the World Bank (1994) *Averting the Old Age Crisis* has been influential in promoting the virtues of multi-pillar pension systems, and in particular the case for a second pillar built around private, non-redistributive, defined contribution pension plans. Holtzman (1997), in a paper outlining a World Bank perspective on pension reform, has argued the case for reducing state pay-as-you-go (PAYG) schemes to a minimal role of basic pension provision. This position has influenced both national governments and key transnational players such as the International Labour Organisation (ILO), with the latter now conceding to the World Bank's position with their advocacy of a mean-tested first pension, the promotion of an extended role for individualized and capitalized private pensions, and the call for OECD member countries to raise the age of retirement.

In Deacon's (2000) terms, this debate amounts to a significant global discourse about pension provision and retirement ages, but one which has largely excluded perspectives which might suggest an enlarged role for the state, and those which might question the stability and cost effectiveness of private schemes. The International Labour Organisation (2000) has concluded that: "Investing in financial markets is an uncertain and volatile business: under present pension plans people may save up to 30 per cent more than they need—which would reduce their spending during their working life; or they may save 30 per cent too little—which would severely cut their spending in retirement." Add in as well the crippling administrative charges associated with the running of private schemes, and the advocacy of market-based provision hardly seems as persuasive as most IGOs have been keen to present (Minns, 2001).

While the impact of IGOs on the pensions debate is reasonably well-known, their influence upon questions relating to the delivery of health and social services is much less understood. Increasingly, however, the social infrastructure of welfare states is being targeted as a major area of opportunity for global investors. The World Bank has expressed the belief that the public sector is less efficient in managing new infrastructure activities and that the time has come "for private actors to provide what were once assumed to be public services" (Whitfield, 2001). This view has been endorsed by a variety of multinational companies, for example in their work with the World Trade Organisation (WTO). This is, however, a controversial area given that public sector services have been linked (especially in Europe) with the notion of citizenship and rights to health and social care, as well as minimum levels of social protection. With the exception of the United States, virtually all industrialized countries have established universal systems of health care based upon general taxation or social insurance principles. The public sector also tends to be dominant in the provision of health services, but with some (tightly regulated) for-profit providers (Whitfield, 2001).

Public provision of health and social care has, however, come under intense scrutiny from the WTO (with enthusiastic support from the United States). The WTO enforces more than 20 separate international agreements, using international trade tribunals that adjudicate disputes. Such agreements include the General Agreement on Trade in Services (GATS), the first multilateral legally enforceable agreement covering banking, insurance, financial services, and related areas. Barlow and Clarke (2001, p. 84) note that the current (2001) round of GATS negotiations has put "every single social service on the table and is only the first of many rounds whose ultimate goal is the full commercialization of all services." Indeed, the WTO has itself called upon Member governments to "reconsider the breadth and depth of their commitments on health and social services" (cited in Yeates, 2001, p. 74). According to Pollock and Price (2000):

> The WTO intends a tighter regulatory framework that will make it more difficult for member states to keep rules that protect public services from foreign investors and markets. The ultimate aim is to increase pressure on member states to open their public-sector services to foreign investment and deregulation. (p. 38)

Price, Pollock, and Shaoul (1999) suggest that the WTO have three main objectives: first, to extend coverage of GATS; second, to toughen procedures for dispute settlements so that members can more easily be brought into line; third, to change government procurement rules to create market access. The authors (1999) highlight the call from the U.S.-based Coalition of Service Industries for foreign ownership to be allowed for all health facilities:

> We believe we can make progress [in negotiations on trade] to allow the opportunity for US businesses to expand into foreign health care markets . . . historically health care services in many countries have largely been the responsibility of the private sector. The public ownership of health care has made it difficult for US private-sector health care providers to market in foreign countries. (p. 1990)

Privatization and deregulation will almost certainly be a key area of conflict over the next decade, but with the concerns of older people likely to be somewhat marginal to the debate over shifting responsibilities for the delivery of health and social care (Estes & Associates, 2001).

On a more general note, IGOs have themselves contributed to the theme of "intergenerational conflict," fostered by neo-liberal governments in the 1980s and 1990s (Bengston & Achenbaum, 1993; Walker, 1996). Peter Hicks (1998) (writing as a consultant to the Social Policy Division of the OECD) reviewing the policy challenges of aging populations, invoked the "young versus old" argument when questioning the desirability of spending increasing amounts of money to support people in retirement: ". . . spending money to this end would be at the expense of higher priorities, such as investment to improve the opportunities of poor children or unemployed youth, lifelong learning or better health." His package of reforms included: "reduced growth in government spending on pensions and a slowing or reversal of trends towards longer periods of retirement; more productive investment of private savings for retirement; [removal] of artificial incentives that now favour sudden and earlier retirement." And Nicholas Vanston (1998), Head of the Resource Allocation Division of the OECD Economics Department, concluded his review of the economic impact of aging, with the comment that:

> The demographic bulge of baby boomers, who will start passing into retirement in ten years' time, will put enormous strains on public pensions systems as well as reduce the growth of average living standards. Fortunately, the policy measures that can alleviate the burden—labour-and product-market reforms, fiscal consolidation—are those that governments should favour whether or not there is an ageing problem. (p. 1)

The above discussion confirms that globalization places significant constraints on the actions of governments: creating pressures to expand for-profit providers on the one side; placing restrictions on public welfare on the other side. Financial globalization, while not a direct cause of the erosion of welfare states, nonetheless sets boundaries or restrictions around their development. Moreover, the ideology of globalization supports a more limited view of the state's role in protecting its citizens. Reflecting this, David Held et al. (1999) argue that: ". . . financial globalisation has imposed an external financial discipline on governments that has contributed to both the emergence of a more market-friendly state and a shift in the balance of power between the state and financial markets" (p. 232). But while this has clearly demonstrated major issues for social policy and aging, it also raises important issues for the development of social theory in gerontology. It is this area which we now turn, examining the implications of globalization for theorizing about the nature of old age.

## GLOBALIZATION AND THE NEED
## FOR SOCIAL THEORY

Accepting the social and economic importance of globalization, what implications does this have for theorizing about older people, and for the nature of theory inside social gerontology? In general terms, debates around globalization have focused on issues such as the ecological crisis, the power of multinational corporations, problems of debt repayment, and associated concerns (Klein, 2000). All of these certainly touch the lives of older people (many of whom are involved in campaigns on these themes), yet as a group they have tended to be presented as marginal to the various debates. On the other hand, globalization as a discourse about the nature of economic and social policy, and about the balance between public and private forms of support, is beginning to have a major impact upon the lives of older people (Estes & Phillipson, 2002). Issues relating to pensions and health and social services are a central part of the discussion; equally, however, there are important concerns regarding the development of social theory applied to old age. The argument to be developed here is *that globalization poses a challenge for the construction of theory as much as for social policy.* In relation to critical gerontology, three areas may be of particular importance: first, the need to re-focus theory given trends associated with globalization; second, the implications for theory arising from the emergence of various forms of global governance; third, the changing status of individual actors within the context of a global society. Each of these points will be reviewed before we move to a concluding argument and summary of the chapter.

The impact of globalization may be understood, as has been suggested, at a number of different levels: inter-governmental, state, policy, individual, and theoretical. It is the last of these, however, where we might observe the most radical effects, especially given current trends within gerontology. Hagestad and Dannefer summarize the latter in terms of a trend toward the "microfication" of substantive issues and analytical foci. These researchers suggest that:

> Increasingly, attention has been concentrated on the psychosocial charac-teristics of individuals in microinstitutions, to the neglect of the macrolevel. Apart from population characteristics, macrolevel phenomena of central interest to social scientists, such as social institutions, cohesion and conflict, norms and values, have slipped out of focus or been rendered invisible. (Hagestad & Dannefer, 2001, p. 4)

Yet the paradox, for older people as well as younger generations, is that the macrolevel has become more rather than less important. Indeed, one might argue that while social theory in gerontology has retreated from the analysis of institutions, globalization has moved in to transform the terms of the debate. Even in the case of political economy perspectives, which continue to focus on structural issues (Estes and Associates, 2001), globalization has re-ordered the concepts typically used by researchers. Ideas associated with the state, gender, social class, ethnicity, have retained their importance, but their collective and individual meaning is substantially different in the context of the influence of global actors and institutions.

The first argument, therefore, is that accepting the importance of globaliza-tion also strengthens the case for reinserting macrolevel analysis within geron-tology. Hagestad and Dannefer (2001, p. 15) suggest that the costs of a microlevel focus have been substantial, especially in respect of hampering our "ability to address the aging society in the context of global economic and technological change." Given the explanatory role of theory, globalization is setting major new challenges in terms of the interaction between individuals, communities, and nation-states, and the global architecture within which these are nested. Aging may now be more appropriately analyzed in the context of the networks and flows characteristic of global society, these producing a loosening in those attachments which have traditionally anchored people to specific class, nation-state, and kinship settings (Castells, 1996; Urry, 2000).

Building on this last point, it is possible to outline three distinct phases in the post-war experience of growing old. In the first phase of aging, the nation state introduced new institutions to manage the growth of an aging population. The second phase began their fragmentation, with increasing variation in individual and societal responses to growing old. With the third phase of global aging, these variations are maintained (and indeed enhanced in many respects) but with the influence of transnational communities, corporations, and IGOs producing new agendas as well as new cultures associated with growing old. What influence might this have on theoretical models used in social gerontology, for example social construction perspectives such as political economy? Estes, Linkins, and Binney (1996) suggest that: "A cornerstone of the political economy of public policy and ageing . . . is the social construction of problems and the remedies to deal with them" (p. 349). In her initial formulation of this approach, Estes (1979) presented the argument as follows:

> The major problems faced by the elderly in the United States are, in large measure, ones that are socially constructed as a result of our conceptions of ageing and the aged. What is done for and about the elderly, as well as what we know about them, including knowledge gained from research, are products of our conception of ageing. In an important sense, then, the major problems faced by the elderly are the ones we create for them. (p. 1)

Globalization brings forth a new set of actors and institutions influencing the social construction of public policy for old age. To take one example, the increasing power of global finance and private transnational bodies raises significant issues about the nature of citizenship, and associated rights to health and social care, in old age. In the period of welfare state reconstruction, rights were defined and negotiated through various manifestations of nation state-based social policy (although it is important to emphasize the dominance of the United States via the Bretton Woods system). Globalization, however, transfers citizenship issues to a transnational stage, this driven by a combination of the power of inter-governmental structures, the influence of multinational corporations, and the pressures of population movement and migration. Alongside globalization come provocative questions about the nature of citizen-rights, and the determinants of "life chances" available to members of the global society, including older people. Under the pressures of global capitalism and finance, citizen rights have become a highly contested arena rife with power struggles on multiple levels.

Drawing on the work of Bauman (2000) and Beck (2000a, c), it might also be argued that rights, in the period of late modernity, have become more fragmented as well as individualized. Certainly, the risks associated with aging are relatively unchanged—the threat of poverty, the need for long-term care, the likelihood of serious illness. What has changed, as Bauman (2000) argues in a more general context, is that the duty and the necessity to cope with these has been transferred to individual families (women carers in particular) and individual older people (notably in respect of financing for old age). The new social construction (and contradiction) of aging is, on the one hand, the focus upon growing old as a global problem and issue; on the other hand, the individualization of the various risks attached to the life course. This development suggests an important role for theory in bringing together macro- and microsocial perspectives (Clarke & Marshall, 2001), with new approaches required to understanding how global processes may reshape the institutions and experiences with which aging is associated.

The second major issue to be addressed concerns that of global governance and its impact on aging. This development introduces us to the undoubted complexities of globalization and its impact on daily life. One the one side, the negative effects are well-known: corporations that appear to trample over the rights and needs of individuals and communities; IGOs that put debt repayment before maintaining or improving schemes of social protection; and forms of crisis construction that emphasize the costs associated with aging populations. Ramesh Mishra (1999) summarizes these trends as follows:

> The main problem [appears to be] that those conditions and social forces which made *national* welfare states possible, e.g., the existence of a state with legitimate authority for rule-making and rule-enforcement, electoral competition and representative government, strong industrial action and protest movements threatening the economic and social stability of nations, nationalism and nation-building imperatives, are unavailable at the international-level. Moreover, globalisation is disempowering citizens within the nation-state as far as social rights are concerned without providing them with any leverage globally. At the same time transnational corporations and the global marketplace have been empowered hugely through financial deregulation and capital mobility. (p. 130)

Yet the contrary trends are also important and require analysis and discussion in the framing and development of social theory. Deacon (2000), for example, notes what appears to be the emergence of a "new politics of global social responsibility." He writes:

> Orthodox economic liberalism and inhumane structural adjustment appear to be giving way to a concern on the part of the [World Bank] and the IMF with the social consequences of globalization. International development assistance is concerned to focus on social development. United Nations agencies are increasingly troubled by the negative social consequences of

globalization . . . [there is a shift] away from a politics of liberalism to a global politics of social concern. (p. 13)

In a similar vein, Mishra (1999, p. 130) observes the increasing momentum behind the move toward global governance and reform of existing IGOs, with increasing pressure to make bodies such as the World Bank and IMF more democratic and accountable for their actions.

At the same time, the ability of corporations or other organizations to evade their responsibilities may be constrained by different forms of transnational governance. For example, taking the European context, avoidance by successive U.K. governments of age discrimination legislation has finally been challenged by a European Union directive outlawing discrimination in the workplace on grounds of age, race, disability, or sexual orientation. Similarly, national legislation following the European Convention on Human Rights, also has the potential to be used to challenge age discrimination in areas such as service provision and employment, as well as fundamental issues relating to the right to life, the right not to be subject to inhumane treatment, and the right to a fair hearing. Both examples illustrate the way in which international law may be used to challenge discrimination against older people. They further illustrate the need for new approaches to theorizing about age that can integrate the continuing power and influence of the nation-state, with the countervailing powers of global institutions. As has been suggested at different points in this chapter, aging must be viewed as a global phenomena, one transforming developing as much as developed countries. But we need to be clearer about the way in which global institutions and global governance might be used to promote the needs and rights of older citizens. The task here must be to construct new theories about the nature of citizenship in the light of the more fluid borders surrounding nation-states. The extent to which these developments lead to the emergence of a "global community" and "global citizenship," such as that outlined by John Urry (2000), is unclear. The important question, however, is whether older people are advantaged or disadvantaged by the spread of mobile communities along with more varied forms of citizenship, an issues which can only be settled by the application and development of social theory.

Finally, accepting the influence of globalization suggests new perspectives for understanding the pressures upon aging as a "lived experience." Increasingly, older people (in common with other age groups) experience the world as though they were riding (as Giddens, 1991, expresses it in his description of high modernity) a "juggernaut": "It is not just that more or less continuous and profound processes of change occur; rather, change does not consistently conform either to human expectation, or to human control" (p. 28). But what has to be theorized is how older people (in ways that might be different from other age groups) maintain a sense of security and identity in what Beck refers to as a "runaway world." He describes its main features as follows:

> We live in an age in which the social order of the nation state, class, ethnicity and the traditional family is in decline. The ethic of individual self-fulfilment and achievement is the most powerful current in modern society. The choosing, deciding, shaping human being who aspires to be the author of his or own life, the creator of an individual identity, is the central character of our time. It is the fundamental cause behind changes in the family and the global gender revolution in relation to work and politics. Any attempt to create a new sense has to start from the recognition that individualism, diversity and scepticism are written into Western culture. (Beck, 2000c, p. 165)

The unravelling of traditional institutions has exposed once again the cultural uncertainties that surround old age. Society is beset, as it was in the 1930s and 1940s, with anxieties about the most appropriate way to respond to an aging population (Phillipson, 1998). But these uncertainties are given a particular emphasis by the pressures and insecurities associated with a late modern age. Arguably, older people have had most to lose from the break-up of the relationships associated with "organized capitalism." For elderly people, the extension of individualization in the period of "disorganized capitalism," poses a significant threat to identity itself. As Biggs (1993) notes, modern life raises at least two possibilities: the promise of a multiplicity of identities on the one side, the danger of psychological disintegration on the other. Biggs suggests that in response to these circumstances, individual actors will attempt to find socially constructed spaces that lend some form of predictability to everyday relationships. Yet in a postmodern world such spaces may be increasingly difficult to locate. This point has been powerfully made by Zygmunt Bauman (1996) in his book *Postmodernity and its Discontents*. He argues here:

> In our postmodern times . . . the boundaries which tend to be simultaneously most strongly desired and most acutely missed are those of a rightful and secure place in society, of a space unquestionably one's own, where one can plan one's life with the minimum of interference, play one's role in a game in which the rules do not change overnight and without notice, and reasonably hope for the better. . . . It is the widespread characteristic of men and women in our type of society that they live perpetually with the "identity problem" unresolved. They suffer, one might say, from a chronic absence of resources with which they could build a truly solid and lasting identity, anchor it and stop it from drifting. (p. 26)

The type of argument advanced by Bauman points to some of the major issues that social theory applied to aging will need to tackle: where do older people stand in a society in which priorities and values are constantly open to revision and change? What is the moral and existential space to which they are entitled, in a world where social integration is achieved through the marketplace? What are the costs and benefits of what Beck (2000c, p. 165) refers to as the "compulsion to lead your own life." How does this "compulsion" play in a world where illness and loss of key relationships threaten? These are practical but also intensely theoretical questions for which gerontology, and critical gerontology in particular, must urgently seek answers.

## CONCLUSION

The aim of this chapter has been to review the implications for older people of the social and economic changes associated with globalization. In addition to its direct economic and social policy implications, globalization is seen to have major consequences for the application of social theory to aging. First, globalization re-emphasizes the importance of a macro-level focus within the field of aging. Dominant global institutions—the World Bank, the World Trade Organisation, the International Monetary Fund—have established distinctive views and policies about the causes, characteristics, and consequences of population aging. The approach taken by these organizations raises significant issues for theories concerning public policy in old age, and in particular attempts to understand the interaction between local, nation state, and global organizations, and their relative influence on the social construction of aging. Second, social theory also needs to acknowledge the activities of supranational bodies in debates on the nature of citizenship. Traditionally, aging has been theorized within the context of the borders of nation states. In the twenty-first century, however, there will be greater fluidity and mobility within and across societies, illustrated by the rise of different kinds of transnational communities. Theorizing about what it means to grow old within this social context is certainly a major priority for understanding new social relations and social patterns of aging. Finally, older people will be faced with the challenge of securing identity within the context of the uncertainty and risks characteristic of late modernity. Globalization undoubtedly adds a further dimension to the nature of such risks and the different way in which they are expressed throughout the life course. Exploring the lives of older people as active participants in this new global environment will be a major challenge for social gerontology in the twenty-first century.

## REFERENCES

Barlow, M., & Clarke, T. (2001). *Global showdown*. Ontario: Stoddart.

Bauman, Z. (1996). *Postmodernity and its discontents*. Oxford: Blackwell.

Bauman, Z. (2000). *Liquid modernity*. Cambridge: Polity Press.

Beck, U. (2000a). *What is globalisation?* Cambridge: Polity Press.

Beck, U. (2000b). *The brave new world of work*. Cambridge: Polity Press.

Beck, U. (2000c). Living your own life in a runaway world: Individualisation, global-isation and politics. In W. Hutton & A. Giddens (Eds.), *On the edge: Living with global capitalism* (pp. 164-174). London: Jonathon Cape.

Bengston, V., & Achenbaum, W. A. (Eds.). (1983). *The changing contract across generations*. New York: Aldine de Gruyter.

Bernard, M., & Meade, K. (Eds.). (1993). *Women come of age*. London: Edward Arnold.

Best, F. (1980). *Flexible life scheduling*. New York: Praeger.

Biggs, S. (1993). *Understanding ageing*. Buckingham: Open University Press.

Byrne, D. (1999). *Social exclusion*. Milton Keynes: Open University Press.

Castells, M. (1996). *The rise of the network society*. Oxford: Blackwell.

Clarke, P., & Marshall, V. (2001). *Social theory and the meaning of illness in later life*. Paper presented at the 17th World Congress of the International Association of Gerontology, Vancouver.

Cutler, S. J., & Hendricks, J. (2001). Emerging social trends. In R. H. Binstock & L. K. George (Eds.), *Handbook of aging and the social sciences* (pp. 462-480). San Diego, CA: Academic Press.

Deacon, B. (2000). *Globalisation and social policy: The threat to equitable welfare*. Occasional Paper no. 5., Globalisation and Social Policy Programme (GASPP), United Nations Research Institute for Social Development. Geneva: UNRISD.

Estes, C. (1979). *The aging enterprise*. San Francisco: Jossey-Bass.

Estes, C. (2002). *Social policy and aging*. Thousand Oaks: Sage.

Estes, C. L., Linkins, K. W., & Binney, E. A. (1996). The political economy of aging. In R. H. Binstock & L. K. George (Eds.), *Handbook of aging and the social sciences* (pp. 346-361). San Diego, CA: Academic Press.

Estes, C. L., & Phillipson, C. (2002). The globalisation of capital, the welfare state and old age policy. *International Journal of Health Services, 32*(2), 279-297.

Featherstone, M., & Hepworth, M. (1990). Ageing and old age: Reflections on the postmodern life course. In B. Bytheway, T. Keil, & P. Allatt (Eds.), *Becoming and being old: Sociological approaches to later life* (pp. 143-158). London: Sage.

Featherstone, M., & Wernick, A. (1995). *Images of aging*. London: Routledge.

Giddens, A. (1991). *Modernity and self-identity*. Cambridge: Polity Press.

Giddens, A., & Hutton, W. (Eds.) (2000). *On the edge: Living with global capitalism* (pp. 1-52). London: Jonathan Cape.

Habermas, J. (1976). *Legitimation crisis*. London: Heinemann.

Hagestad, G., & Dannefed, D. (2001). Concepts and theories of aging: Beyond microfication in social science approaches. In R. Binstock & L. George (Eds.), *Handbook of aging and the social sciences* (5th ed., pp. 3-21). San Diego: Academic Press.

Held, D., McGrew, A., Goldblatt, D., & Perraton, J. (1999). *Global transformations*. Cambridge: Polity Press.

Help Age International (2000). *The mark of a noble society: Human rights and older people*. A briefing paper. London: Help Age International.

Hendricks, J., & Leedham, C.A. (1991). Dependency or empowerment? Toward a moral and political economy. In M. Minker & C. and Estes (Eds.), *Critical perspectives on aging: The perspectives on aging: The political and moral economy of growing old* (pp. 51-64). Amityville, NY: Baywood.

Hicks, P. (1998). The Policy Challenge of aging Populations. *The OECD Observer*, no. 212.

Holtzman, R. A. (1997). *A world bank perspective on pension reform*. Paper prepared for the joint ILO-OECD Workshop on the Development and Reform of Pension Schemes, Paris, December.

International Labour Organisation (2000). Press release, April 28. Geneva: ILO.

Itzin, C., & Phillipson, C. (1993). *Age barriers at work*. Solihull: METRA.

Johnson, N. (1987). *The welfare state in transition: The theory and practice of welfare pluralism.* Sussex: Wheatsheaf Books.

Kargalitsky, B. (1999). The Challenge for the Left: Reclaiming the State. In L. Panitch & C. Leys (Eds.), *Socialist register 1999: Global capitalism versus democracy* (pp. 294-313). New York: Monthly Review Press.

Klein, N. (2000). *No logo: Taking aim at the brand bullies.* London: Flamingo.

Kohli, M. (1991). Retirement and the moral economy: An historical interpretation of the German case. In M. Minkler & C. Estes (Eds.), *Critical perspectives on aging: The political and moral economy of growing old* (pp. 273-292). Amityville, NY: Baywood.

Kohli, M., & Rein, M. (1991). The changing balance of work and retirement. In M. Kohli, M. Rein, A. M. Guillemard, & H. van Gunsteren (Eds.), *Time for retirement: Comparative studies of early exit from the labor force* (pp. 1-35). Cambridge: Cambridge University Press.

Kumar, K. (1995). *From post-industrial to post-modern society.* Oxford: Basil Blackwell.

Lash, S., & Urry, J. (1987). *The end of organized capitalism.* Cambridge: Polity Press.

Macnicol, J. (1998). *The politics of retirement in Britain 1878-1948.* Cambridge: Cambridge University Press.

Minkler, M., & Estes, C. (Eds.). (1991). *Critical perspectives on aging: The political and moral economy of growing old.* Amityville, NY: Baywood.

Minns, R. (2001). *The cold war in welfare: Stock markets versus pensions.* London: Verso.

Mishra, R. (1999). *Globalisation and the welfare state.* Cheltenham: Edward Elgar.

Myles, J. (1984). *Old age in the welfare state: The political economy of public pensions.* Lawrence, KS: University Press of Kansas.

Myles, J. (1991). Postwar capitalism and the extension of social security into a retirement wage. In M. Minkler & C. and Estes (Eds.), *Critical perspectives on aging: The political and moral economy of growing old* (pp. 293-311). Amityville, NY: Baywood.

Phillipson, C. (1998). *Reconstructing old age.* London: Sage.

Price, D., Pollock, A. M., & Shaoul, J. (1999). How the World Trade Organisation is shaping domestic policy. *The Lancet, 354,* 1899-1892.

Pollock, A. M., & Price, D. (2000). Rewriting the regulations: How the World Trade Organisation could accelerate privatisation in health-care systems. *Lancet, 356,* 1995-2000.

Schuller, T. (1989). *Work-ending: Employment and ambiguity in later life.* In B. Bytheway, T. Keil, & P. Allatt (Eds.), *Becoming and being old: Sociological approaches to later life.* London: Sage.

Urry, J. (2000). *Sociology beyond societies.* London: Routledge.

Vanston, N. (1998). The economic impacts of aging. *The OECD Observer,* no. 212.

Walker, A. (Ed.) (1996). *The new generational contract.* London: UCL Press.

Whitfield, D. (2001). www.centre.public.org.uk/briefings/pfi p. 33.

Wilson, W. J. (1997). *When work disappears: The world of the new urban poor.* Chicago: University of Chicago Press.

World Bank (1994). *Averting the old age crisis.* Oxford: Oxford University Press.

Yeates, N. (2001). *Globalisation and social policy.* London: Sage.

# CHAPTER 10

# Theoretical Approaches to Problems of Families, Aging, and Social Support in the Context of Modernization

*Merril Silverstein, Vern L. Bengtson,*
*and Eugene Litwak*

In most nations of the world the process of demographic change is causing a rapid increase in the number of elderly members of society (Kinsella & Velkoff, 2001). At the same time, family structures and functions are changing as a consequence of reduced fertility rates, transnational and internal migration, divorce and step-parenting, and weakening norms of filial piety. When put together, these trends have caused some to question whether "new" family forms are sufficiently equipped to provide care and support to the swelling number of elders who are also living longer lives. This concern is especially acute in many developing nations where systems of formal care and support remain restricted and limited in their availability, and where kin remain the dominant source of care. In more developed nations, the prospect of a large cohort of aging baby-boomers, as well as the imperatives of a global economy that compel governments to retrench their commitments to older citizens has instigated a crisis of confidence, or at least an element of uncertainty, in the ability of state systems to carry the burden of old age support and the ability of families to fill the gap (Phillipson, 1998). While this crisis may have forced the transfer of some support functions of the state back to informal groups—such as the family—one thing is clear: individuals increasingly need to rely on their personal resources to meet their needs for old age support and security.

How are we to understand the shifting balance between informal family groups and formal government systems given recent social change, the emergence of new family forms, and the changing role of the state in the context of a new economic order? Do venerable theories in social gerontology have sufficient explanatory power to incorporate such modern contingencies? Do these theories need to be retooled for current social realities, or are altogether new theories necessary? In this chapter we review several theoretical models concerning families, intergenerational mechanisms, and support to older generations in the context of societal modernization and postmodern conceptualizations of the family. We focus on several explanatory models—intergenerational solidarity and task-specific theory—that have promise for explanation in light of emerging historical contingencies and contemporary social change in state and family systems that support the elderly.

## MODERNIZATION AND AGING FAMILIES

Modernization theory emerged out of social gerontology in the 1970s as a way to understand how societal development served to lower the social status, resources, and privileges of the elderly (Cowgill, 1986). This theory rests on the proposition that industrialization, urbanization, and the growth in technology resulted in a status inversion that disadvantaged the aged relative to the youth of society. While ambitious in scope, the theory lost its luster as an explanatory framework for the simple reason that the empirical facts appear to contradict the basic predictions made by the theory. For instance, it is irrefutable that the health and wealth of the elderly in developed societies have never been better, standing in stark contrast to the status of the elderly in less developed nations. This is keenly seen in the more generous pension coverage of older populations in developed nations of the world (World Bank, 2001). Formal systems of care in the modern welfare state have done much to minimize old age poverty (Walker, 1993) and make health care an entitlement of old age (Donelan et al., 2000). Further, empirical data showing the continued importance of kin as emotional supports to the elderly in developed nations belies the prediction that older adults lose status within the family of modernized countries (Bengtson, Giarusso, Silverstein, & Wang, 2000). Any weakening in filial obligation toward the elderly of developing nations may be off-set by some of the benefits that economic growth brings in terms of enhancing the ability of those nations to institute or expand formal mechanisms of care for the older population.

Instead of focusing on the status of the elderly as the outcome of modernization, we suggest that it is more fruitful to focus on qualitative differences across nations in the mechanisms by which the elderly are supported—particularly differences in family structure (and by extension kinship support) and in the use of redistributive public policies that pool the risk for old age support across tax payers in the population. We suggest that *task-specific theory* and the *intergenerational solidarity paradigm* hold useful theoretical principles to guide our understanding of how macro-societal change has altered the implicit contract between families and the state in supporting and benefitting older citizens.

Modernizing economies are generally characterized by rapid increases in the importance of technical knowledge and specialization of the workforce. Such changes often require adult children to move away from their families of orientation in order to maximize their educational and occupational attainment. This mobility has resulted in greater geographic separation between the generations and a decline in the amount of contact between older parents and their adult children (Crimmins & Ingegneri, 1990; Stearns, 1989). Indeed, adult children in more developed nations tend not to coreside with their parents, and often live far from them. The rise in prominence of the nuclear over the extended family household coincides with economic growth, and the transition from an agricultural to an industrial, and then to a post-industrial, information based economy (Goode, 1963).

Families are also guided by cultural beliefs or ideologies that guide which family forms are preferred and which are considered inappropriate. Variation in these beliefs is typically found between more highly and less highly developed societies. The strong obligation toward elders in more rural nations is thought to derive from the power that land ownership and control confers on the elderly (Nason, 1981; Nydegger, 1983; Salamon & Lockhart, 1980; Tsuya & Martin, 1992).

Although filial piety—unquestioned respect, responsibility, and sacrifice for family elders—is considered by some to be eroding as a central norm governing intergenerational relations in developing nations (Caffrey, 1992; Cheung, Lee, & Chan, 1994; Foner, 1993), it is often characterized as having been completely lost in modern Western nations. Yet studies have consistently identified adult children as key sources of interaction and support for older parents in the most highly modernized societies (Duffy, 1984; Hashimoto, 1993; Johnson, 1995). Although older parents in developed countries have less contact and are less likely to live with their children when compared with their counterparts in less developed and developing countries, neither do they appear to have been abandoned by their offspring (D'Costa, 1985; Shanas, 1973). In Western industrialized countries intergenerational solidarity—including intimacy, contact, the exchange of some instrumental services—is maintained in spite of geographic separation (Litwak & Kulis, 1987; Silverstein & Litwak, 1993; Warnes, 1994). This type of family that is cohesive over large geographic distances has been heralded as an ideal intergenerational structure insofar as it meets the needs of dependent family members while serving the demands of a modern economy for a mobile labor force (Litwak, 1985).

We turn to a discussion of two sociological theories that have informed many empirical analyses of kinship structures of the elderly: task specific theory and the intergenerational solidarity paradigm. We review the basis of each theory, discuss how each approaches the issue of social support with regard to the elderly in modern society, and discuss overlapping and unique elements in their explanatory coverage.

## TASK-SPECIFIC THEORY

Task-specific theory provides a systematic approach to the study of social support to the elderly by focusing on the complementary roles played by families and by formal systems of care. This approach rests on the proposition that families and formal organizations seek unique but complementary goals (Litwak et al., 1989; Messeri, Silverstein, & Litwak, 1993). The task specific theory starts with an analysis of Weber's rationale for the effectiveness of the monocratic bureaucracy, namely that it concentrates technical knowledge and resources far better than the family (Litwak, 1985; Litwak & Szelenyi, 1969). The theory rejects the assumption that formal organizations and kinship groups are in complete conflict in a zero-sum game, and instead suggests that, while their *structures* are in conflict, they are mutually dependent on each other for achieving common goals (Litwak, 1978, 1985; Litwak & Meyer, 1966; Litwak, Meyer, & Hollister, 1977).

On what basis are functions divided between families and organizations? To answer this question it is necessary to examine the structures of each of these groups and then match these structures to the tasks each can best perform.

### Technical Abilities vs. Everyday Knowledge

The monocratic bureaucracy limits its requirements to its members' technical abilities, that is, workers must maintain the technological standards set for the job. By contrast, members of the nuclear family have virtually unlimited lifelong commitments to the relationship as an end in itself. Prototypical of such lifelong commitments are those between parents and child, which are heavily based on biological and legal definitions, that have little if anything to do with technical criteria. When the nuclear family does expel someone, e.g., divorce, estrangement, it does not typically use the degree of technical knowledge as the basis for expulsion.

### Size and Division of Labor

Bureaucratic organizations tend to have large size, and a detailed division of labor. A detailed division of labor permits specialization, which allows staff limit the number of fields they must cover. This enables specialists to increase their technical knowledge in one field. For instance, in a nursing home geriatric aides, nurses, and physicians possess specialized technical knowledge about the health needs of older people that make them especially useful for managing the chronic diseases found in the long-term care population.

In addition, a detailed division of labor permits the breaking down of complex behavior into their simpler components, giving staff advantages in speed, accuracy, and efficiency. In human services the detailed division of labor is accomplished by the standardization of idiosyncratic behavior so that one specialist can handle a larger volume of services. This is illustrated in the nursing home where a small staff can cook for 100 patients as long as they can standardized the menu, the eating time, and the eating place. By contrast, the nuclear family is very small with only two adults and many different activities. It has what Cooley (1955) referred to as diffused relations and what network analysis called multiplex relations (Hall & Wellman, 1985). Family members may substitute for each other fairly freely, as their goals and abilities often overlap and do not require technical knowledge. Because families are small and able to solve problems with an immediacy only possible with few hierarchical distinctions, family members can generally react more quickly than formal organizations, as well as coordinate efforts more easily.

## Coordination of Labor

Because of their large size, formal organizations make use of written rules or hierarchical authority to coordinate activities among bureaucratic units and personnel. Families, by contrast, rely on the flexibility inherent in their small size, diffuse relationships, and (sometimes) frequent contact to coordinate based on intimate knowledge of each other. A formal organization that relies exclusively on face-to-face contact and intimate knowledge to manage its personnel would be lose efficiency because an inordinate amount of resources would have to be diverted to coordination.

## Motivation

Yet another dimension of group structure is the way they motivate their members. The monocratic bureaucracy motivates its members in a way to insure the competence of its labor force. Typically, formal organizations emphasize civil but impersonal relationships because intense relations of love or hate will distort objective judgments based on merit. Within that context, the main incentive used by the formal organization is economic—an expedient exchange between hours of work and financial rewards. By contrast, the nuclear family motivates its members by internalized commitments of duty and/or affection to the relationship, and not by monetary gain.

The formal organization recruits people on the basis of merit, and then motivates and coordinates them in ways that avoid nepotism of favoritism. This is evidenced in the strategy used by organizations to recruit members on the basis of skill or credentials. By contrast, the family recruits members through birth or courtship, both of which are heavily based on non-technical considerations. The family is far more effective in managing non-technical tasks because it motivates its members more quickly and at lower cost than formal organizations in this area.

Why are families better for managing non-technical tasks? A brief illustration can make the point. If an elderly Alzheimer patient falls asleep in bed with a lighted cigarette, all that is needed to save him is for someone to remove the cigarette from his hand. This is an non-technical task. If society required that only a person with a firefighter's technical training and skill could perform this task, the efficiency of the activity would not be enhanced and the cost would increase substantially. Furthermore, having a family member who has an internalized commitment to the older person is more likely to guarantee that they will be diligent in monitoring their elderly relative, as contrasted with a home care worker who is motivated by economic incentives. The virtue of an internalized motivation is that it needs little supervision to be done well. Finally, because the family member has intimate knowledge of the older person, they are more likely than a paid home care worker to know if and how the older relative is likely to obtain matches and cigarettes. In short, the very attributes of internalized commitment and intimacy that would be a handicap in a formal organization, turn out to be most effective for managing non-technical tasks in the family. This principle has far reaching consequences in terms of the division labor between bureaucratic organizations and families in society—the two basic structures from which the vast majority of support and care is received by the elderly.

## Task-Specific and the Modern Family

How does task-specific theory address the problem of modernization and family change? We start with traditional concerns about modernization that occupied the efforts of family sociologists in the first half of the twentieth century. Much of this traditional analysis of the family's roles implicitly relied on theories of organizational effectiveness by citing how families abdicated many essential tasks, such as education and work, to formal organizations. Scholars of the time such as Ogburn (1932) and Burgess (1916) wrote about formal organizations taking over *all* functions of the family but two: early socialization of the child and adult companionship. Implicit in their analysis was the assumption that formal organizations were more effective then primary groups in managing most tasks and accomplishing most goals. But they never explained *why* large-scale organizations were more effective nor did they empirically document that families no longer played substantial roles.

Parsons (1944) explicitly introduced group effectiveness as a major causal factor in his analysis of the emergence of the isolated nuclear family and the decline of the extended family. Parsons' justification for the survival of the nuclear primary household is very explicit in its focus on group effectiveness. In his formulation, developed economic organizations required a geographically mobile labor force that favored small families with only one breadwinner (Parsons & Bales, 1955). This family model precluded multi-generational households (as well as dual-earner households) and required that the nuclear family essentially "abandon" its members in older generations. This implicit organizational effectiveness analysis was an eloquent theoretical justification for the traditional view that nuclear families would emerge as the dominant family form in modern industrial society.

However, much empirical evidence has contradicted this model of family life in developed societies. Contemporary studies expand on earlier work in gerontology, which showed that in the vast number of cases older people were helped by kin in most developed nations, including the United States (Cantor, 1980; Litwak, 1985; Shanas, 1979), France (Attias-Donfut & Arber, 2000), and Germany (Kohli, Kunemund, Motel, & Szydlik, 2000). When support was economic in nature, or was instrumental and chronic, family members often partnered with formal organizations. Formal organizations shored up the ability of families to accomplish their goals of meeting the needs of their older members, but families typically provided the bulk of the care.

While the extended family also plays a major role in providing economic transfers to the elderly (Spilerman, 2000), welfare states have become distributors of wealth through state pension programs. As Anderson's (1977) historical analysis of pensions in England reveals, the emergence of large formal organizations to support the elderly strengthened kinship ties by removing the obligation of financial support from filial relationships. The important distinction is that families and the state both transfer economic resources, but operate under completely different principles. Social Security payments are, at least partially, redistributive in nature and reflect a standardized formula that is routinized by computer-fed algorithms, and administered by a large bureaucracy. By contrast, families provide money transfers idiosyncratically based on need, ability, and preference. Similarly, formal long term care relieved many families from the time, physical, emotional, and financial burdens of care for older relatives. Chronic care tasks could be accomplished efficiently by professional staff operating within the context of organizational rules, principles of merit, and with an economy of scale, but were onerous and burdensome when delivered by adult children or other relatives. Families would then left to perform tasks that required affection and long-term internalized commitment to the relationship, such as buying gifts, making social visits, and monitoring the quality of the formal care received by impaired older persons.

The task-specific framework raises the question of how kinship and formal organizational structures can coordinate their activities when their basic operating principles are in conflict. One answer is that the family has adapted its functions to be congruent with the functions of formal organizations. The *modified-extended family* is a particularly modern type of kinship structure characterized by moderate to infrequent face-to-face contact, relatively large distances between family members, but also high rates of communication, and strong norms of filial obligation. This family type is well suited to be in partnership with bureaucracies that are equipped to deliver services requiring specialized knowledge and/or that can be standardized. In order for family members to maintain their ability to be flexible and fluid in a modern economy, these partnerships are crucial for optimizing the achievement of family goals while maintaining family resources. For instance, older adults who receive home care services are less likely to make demands on their adult children for instrumental support; however adult children will likely arrange and supervise such care, as well as provide emotional support and intermittent "personal" assistance that can only come from idiosyncratic knowledge of the parent and a long standing reciprocal relationship.

In summary, task specific approach focuses on the different, but complementary group structures of families and organizations that allow each to uniquely accomplish tasks that are necessary for solving most human problems. With regard to support and care of the aged, this scheme provides a powerful elaboration of how to effectively establish partnerships between families and organizations. In this framework, modernization does not herald the demise of the family, but signals a redistribution of efforts between families and organizations. While formal organizations are best equipped to can deal with complex tasks that can be broken down, routinized, or that require technical knowledge, families can manage idiosyncratic tasks that require only everyday knowledge, that are diffuse in nature, and that are motivated by affection and long-term commitment.

## INTERGENERATIONAL SOLIDARITY
## AND CONFLICT

Intergenerational solidarity is a framework to characterize the behavioral and emotional dimensions of interaction, cohesion, sentiment, and support between intergenerational relationships over the course of the adult life-span. This includes parent-child relations, as well relationships between non-adjacent generations. The framework consists of six conceptual dimensions of intergenerational solidarity (Bengtson & Mangen, 1988; Bengtson & Schrader, 1982; Roberts, Richards, & Bengston, 1991): (a) *Affectual solidarity:* The sentiments and evaluations family members express about their relationship with other members: (b) *Associational solidarity:* The type and frequency of contact between intergenerational family members. (c) *Consensual solidarity:* Agreement in opinions, values, and orientations between generations. (d) *Functional Solidarity (Assistance):* The giving and receiving of support across generations, including exchange of both instrumental assets and services as well as emotional support. (e) *Normative solidarity:* Expectations regarding filial obligations and parental obligations, as well as norms about the importance of familistic values. (f) *Structural solidarity:* The "opportunity structure" for cross-generational interaction reflecting geographic proximity between family members. The theoretical rationale for these six dimensions and the adequacy (or limitations) of their measurement in survey research have been described at length in a volume by Mangen, Bengtson, and Landry (1988) and in subsequent articles (Roberts & Bengtson, 1990; Roberts et al., 1991; Silverstein, Parrott, & Bengtson, 1995).

The solidarity model has informed the scholarly debate concerning the "decline of the family" in American society (Bengtson et al., 2000). David Popenoe (1993), the most articulate proponent of the "decline" position, has argued that there has been a striking weakening in the family's structure and functions in American society, particularly since 1960. Moreover, his hypothesis is that recent family decline is "more serious" than any decline in the past, because ". . . what is breaking up is the nuclear family, the fundamental unit stripped of relations and left with two essential functions that cannot be performed better elsewhere: Child-rearing and the provision to its members of affection and companionship" (Popenoe, 1993, p. 527). This comment might seem familiar as it almost perfectly echoes those made by Burgess (1926), Ogburn (1932), Davis (1941), and Parsons (1944) several generation earlier. Supporters of the family decline hypothesis have focused on the negative consequences of changing family structure—resulting from divorce and single-parenting—for the psychological, social, and economic well-being of children. Further, they suggest that social norms legitimating the pursuit of individual over collective goals, and the availability of alternate social groups for the satisfaction of basic human needs, have substantially weakened the social institution of the family as an agent of socialization and as a source of emotional succor for family members (Lasch, 1979; Popenoe, 1993).

Proponents of the solidarity model—by focusing attention on the systematic study of the ties that bind the generations—posit that adult intergenerational relations tend to be less subject to the types of social change that the "decline" theorists claim have weakened the fabric of family life. Research shows strong connections between elderly family members and their children on all dimensions of solidarity (Bengtson & Roberts, 1991) and further, these connections have remained strong over the last 30 years (Bengtson, Biblarz, & Roberts, 2001). Ignored by the "decline-of-family" proponents is the longevity revolution that has created longer years of shared lives between generations, and the consequences of co-survival for the well-being of family members across several generations (Bengtson & Silverstein, 1993; Uhlenberg, 1996). Based on this demographic principle, Bengtson (Bengtson et al., 2000) proposes an alternative hypothesis: that relations across two or more adult generations are becoming increasingly important to individuals and families in American society. Indeed, opportunities for cross-generational exchanges have never been greater. These long-lived relations are generally characterized by strong cohesion (high effectual solidarity and normative solidarity) over the entire life-span. However, in some instances they are characterized by ambivalence, strains, and even conflict. In the next section, we will discuss an alternative specification of the solidarity model that allows for incongruent patterns of intergenerational engagement that may better characterize the structure of the post-modern family.

## Solidarity and Conflict in the Modern Family

In developing the solidarity model over the last decade it has become clear that solidarity is less a single unifying construct that can be additively measured on a single scale, and more a puzzle of interlocking pieces, the exact configuration of which varies across families. By considering the dimensions of solidarity as intersecting components of a *typology* of family structure, it then becomes possible to distinguish those dimensions that have withered from those that have remained stable or strengthened over historical time (Bengtson & Silverstein, 1993).

Considering solidarity more as a heuristic than a strict measurement model has opened the door to understanding the paradoxical, contradictory, and discrepant aspects of intergenerational relationships. Consistent response patterns across dimensions of solidarity—perhaps more typical of families pre-modern societies—has given way to more loosely connected dimensions within families today. For instance, proximity and affection have to a large degree become uncoupled in modern families due to geographic mobility that has scattered family members across wide distances. Similarly, the functional dimension of intergenerational solidarity may have shifted to formal organizations in some families, with no corresponding loss in the affective component of these relationships. In the United States, as in almost all developed nations, state pension programs, and to a more limited extent social services, have freed the elderly from dependence on family members for their economic well-being. Thus, the absence of functional support does not necessarily imply the lack of affection in family relationships.

Recent advances in the solidarity model have focused on developing a multi-dimensional typology of intergenerational family ties. Previous work using national data has demonstrated that three meta-dimensions characterize intergenerational family relations: 1) *affinity* (emotional closeness and perceived agreement between generations); 2) *opportunity structure* (frequency of contact and residential propinquity between generations); and 3) *functional exchange* (flows of instrumental assistance between generations) (Silverstein & Bengtson, 1997). From these three meta-dimensions, intergenerational relations can be categorized into five underlying types: tight-knit, sociable, intimate-but-distant, obligatory, detached. The latent categories are described as follows with their representation in the population shown for relations of adult children with mothers followed by relations with fathers: 1) *Tight-knit:* connected on all five dimensions of intergenerational solidarity (32 percent, 22 percent); 2) *Sociable:* connected only on associational, structural, effectual, and consensual dimensions of solidarity (27 percent, 24 percent); 3) *Intimate-but-distant:* connected only on effectual and consensual dimensions of solidarity (20 percent, 14 percent); 4) *Obligatory:* connected on associational, structural, and functional solidarity (15 percent, 16 percent); 5) *Detached:* connected on none of the five dimensions of intergenerational solidarity (7 percent, 25 percent).

This paradigm has be condensed into an even simpler two-dimensional paradigm reflecting the construct of *latent support* (the latent reserve or capacity to provide support) and *enacted support* (functional exchanges between generations). Latent support *enables* functional exchange (through good-will, normative obligation, or an appropriate opportunity structure), but does not neces-sarily imply that relations are functional (see Berkman, Oxman, & Seeman, 1991). Using this simpler scheme to interpret the typology, we can see that 40–50 percent of relationships can be characterized as intimate-but-distant or sociable—two types that have latent reserve of support, but little enacted support. These two types share the underlying structure of the modified-extended family that task-specific theory hypothesizes to be the best "fit" to a developed society.

An important elaboration of the solidarity typology is that family structures are dynamic, such that relationships characterized by latent support have the potential, under certain conditions, to become enacted over time. This dynamic aspect of family life is captured in a similar way by the latent-kin matrix (Riley & Riley, 1993), a family network that remains dormant, or in reserve, until a need arises to activate its support potential. What remains to be investigated is how, when, and under what conditions these latent family intergenerational networks become activated, how one charts the complex ebb and flow of inter-generational support over time in families, and how the macro-social, cultural, political, and economic environment conditions the sensitivity with which latent support is triggered into enacted support. The decoupling of these dimensions by itself represents the particularly modern notion that the family is a complex and evolving social institution whose members continually negotiate with each other to achieve both enduring and ephemeral intergenerational arrangements.

## THEORETICAL INTEGRATION

Task specific theory is essentially an effectiveness theory that predicts which social organization or primary group is most effective for which task. It predicts for all families which types of tasks can be managed by which types of kinship system and formal organizations. The theory also recognizes the role of tech-nological change in its formulation. For instance, rapid transportation (e.g., inexpensive air travel) and communication (e.g., Internet) technologies have allowed families a greater latitude to fulfill functions that formerly required continuous proximity (Litwak & Kulis, 1987). This idea resonates with the solidarity model with its emphasis on the mechanisms by which latent support gets triggered into enacted support. Both theories are informative as to adjustments required of families to cope with the contradictions and cross-pressures inherent in modern family forms.

The solidarity theory consists of a series of dimensions along which kinship is measured. As such it does not make predictions about optimal kinship systems, but lays out a method for distinguishing family types or structures. For instance, the "intimate-but-distant" type is one that is characteristic of societies with geo-graphic mobility but strong family cohesion. Both task-specific and solidarity theories delineate this type as one that has distinct properties, and that is func-tional under particular conditions. Tasks that require continuous proximity, such as caregiving, are typically delivered during or following a crisis in the family that requires a dramatic adjustment (such as moving to be closer to the care recipient). Task specific theory, because it incorporates a wider array of group structures than solidarity theory, makes the additional stipulation that formal services may be brought to bear in order to dovetail with what families are best able to provide. A closer inspection reveals that dimensions of solidarity resemble several of the dimensions used to characterize group structure in task specific theory, such as internalized and long-term commitment (norms), love (affection), proximity (structure), face-to-face contact (association), common life style (consensus). In addition, solidarity includes a dimension (function) that is typically used as a dependent variable in the task specific model, that is, what is exchanged and the amount exchanged.

Task specific theory and the solidarity paradigm provide congruent and overlapping conceptualizations of the family in the context of modernization and social change. Where the former focuses more on group structures of various types (kinship, friendship, marital, formal), the latter concentrates on family processes. Messeri, Silverstein, and Litwak (1993) performed a meta-analysis finding that structural difference between kin, marital unit, neighbors, friends, and formal organization dictated the tasks they were best able to perform. Solidarity theory state is that there are different kinds of kinship systems as well, and that they differ between families and vary in the same families over time. Thus, one way to view the theoretical coverage of each theory is to consider task-specific a theory about diversity in the structure of social groups, and solidarity a theory about diversity in the structure of one particular social group, the family. Taken together, these frameworks can explicate the ways that the family is shaped by, as well as shapes, social and economic development. Scholars using each theory have developed conceptual models of the "post-modern" family that look identical and similarly suited to the contingencies of a modern economy, often in conjunction with a strong welfare state: modified-extended (task-specific) and intimate-but-distant (solidarity). However, there is still theoretical work to be done. Task-specific theory, by focusing on ideal types of social organization and in predicting the most efficient allocation of tasks between these two structures, tends to minimize the influence of culture and demography in its evaluation of outcomes. Less than efficient balances between family and state structures may be the result of: 1) economic deprivation that prevents the development of formal services (e.g., African nations); 2) cultural values that put primacy on family care (e.g., Asian nations); 3) conservative state governments that curtail social spending (including globalization that has caused retrenchment in many national commitments to elder care and elder benefits; and 4) demographic change, such as low fertility that increases the dependency ration, putting a burden on the working age population. These features are assumed to be constant in the task-specific model. What are the demographic, economic, and cultural forces that determine the actual balance or mix between state and family support of the elderly in a given nation? What are the "costs" to society of "inefficiency" when social factors cause the actual mix and the ideal mix to be discrepant? For its part, the solidarity model has typically focused on the micro-social world of the family. Only recently have attempts been made to bridge the micro-macro divide by adding contextual or ecological factors to its theoretical coverage. Extending the concept of solidarity to incorporate ambivalence and discrepant family forms provides a promising avenue for understanding the dynamic and negotiated nature of families within a larger social context. For example, by including state and formal organizations in its formulation, solidarity (and conflict) between generations in the family can be extended to solidarity (and conflict) between age-groups or birth cohorts, producing configurations of solidarity/conflict with the aged that may or may not correspond between micro-family and macro-cohort levels.

Demographic forces are also important in this regard. Reduced fertility and increases in the dependency ratio of developing nations may create tension in the private/public trade-off for elder care at several levels. That is, adult children in smaller families face greater challenges in providing care for older parents; at the same time smaller cohorts of working age adults may face greater pressure for supporting older cohorts through their tax contributions to emerging state pension systems. How this dilemma is ultimately resolved will depend on many variables, including the economic resources of a nation, cultural norms for family care, tolerance of taxes, immigration patterns, and healthy life-expectancy of the older population.

Social values of a society also play a role in how support of society's dependent members is organized. The political climate in United States reveals a great reluctance to intervene in the private nature of family life, including care for aged individuals and their families (Page & Shapiro, 1992). Indeed, most policies in the United States designed to serve the elderly presume there is a family member available to assist in the older person's care, and that benefit coverage should begin only at the point at which family and individual responsibility have been exhausted. In contrast, a welfare state with a highly developed social insurance program such as Sweden designs its public policies with specific family goals in mind. For instance, the liberal elder care policies are at least partially designed to free women from the responsibility of care and allow them to remain in the labor force (Szebehely, 2000).

In the face of rapid economic modernization and population aging, we are seeing changes in the meaning and expression of "filial piety" in traditional Asian societies. In Korea, China, and Japan, for example, multigenerational household sharing is becoming less prevalent (Bengtson, Biblarz, & Roberts, 2001). What does this imply in terms of Confucian norms about caring for one's parents? Social policies are slowly emerging in response to the growing needs of the elderly in these rapidly changing nations. Paradoxically, it appears that Asian societies are becoming more dependent on state provisions for the elderly, while Western societies are facing declining governmental resources and placing more responsibilities on families (Bengtson et al., 2000). This would imply a convergence in kinship structures between developed and developing nations, and between nations with stronger and weaker familistic orientations. Task-specific theory addresses the state/family division of labor as a matter of maximizing efficiency when each social institution provides services that are suited to its structure. Solidarity theory would address the same public-private partnership in terms of the hidden or latent potential of families as a form of social capital for the elderly, as well as strains that may arise when preferences are at odds with structural constraints on the ability of the family to deliver services. Both theories stress the importance of families as contingent resources for the aged and treat this family form as a particularly modern manifestation.

In summary, we suggest task specific and solidarity theories are viable frameworks for understanding the consequences of modernization and social change for intergenerational relationships of the aged. Task-specific theory provides a framework for understanding the role of group structure in organizing informal and formal care for the elderly, while the solidarity model provides a scheme for understanding the complex of sentiments and behaviors that comprise intergenerational cohesion. The challenge facing contemporary scholars is finding a theoretical linkage between macro-social change and micro-family trends that permits a rendering of the process that is *interactively* dynamic between levels of analysis. The near future will be especially telling. Will economic globalization presage a domination of a "Western" paradigm in terms of elder care and support? Will we see a decline in filial piety in East Asian countries or will cultural traditions persist? What forms will state interventions take when they are instituted in more traditional societies? Will families take on greater responsibilities in the West as government mechanisms become more parsimonious in their allocations to their older populations? Are there aspects to old age support that traditional and modern nations can learn from each other? These questions will likely occupy family sociologists for some time as they continue to grapple with the micro-macro conundrum, as well as the dialectic between agency and structure, using frameworks and concepts in social gerontology that have wide theoretical coverage and strong empirical validation.

## REFERENCES

Anderson, M. (1977). The impact on the family relationships of the elderly of changes since Victorian times in government income-maintenance provisions. In E. Shanas & M. B. Sussman (Eds.), *Family, bureaucracy, and the elderly* (pp. 36-59). Durham, NC: Duke University Press.

Attias-Donfut, C., & Arber, S. (2000). Equity and solidarity across the generations. In S. Arber & C. Attias-Donfut (Eds.), *The myth of generational conflict* (pp. 1-21). New York: Routledge.

Bengtson, V. L., Biblarz, T., & Roberts, R. E. L. (2001). *Generation X and their elders: Family transmission and social change.* Cambridge, MA: Cambridge University Press.

Bengtson, V. L., Giarusso, R., Silverstein, M., & Wang, Q. (2000). Families and intergenerational relationships in aging societies. *Hallym International Journal of Aging, 2*(1), 3-10.

Bengtson, V., & Mangen, D. J. (1988). Family intergenerational solidarity revisited: Suggestions for future management. In D. J. Mangen, V. L. Bengtson, & P. H. Landry (Eds.), *Measurement of intergenerational relations.* Newbury Park, CA: Sage.

Bengtson, V. I., & Roberts, R. E. L. (1991). Intergenerational solidarity in aging families: An example of formal theory construction. *Journal of Mariage and the Family, 53,* 856-870.

Bengtson, V. L., & Schrader, S. S. (1982). Parent-child relations. In D. Mangen & W. Peterson (Eds.), *Handbook of research instruments in social gerontology.* Minneapolis, MN: University of Minnesota Press.

Bengtson, V. L., & Silverstein, M. (1993). Families, aging, and social change: Seven agendas for 21st century researchers. In G. Maddox & M. P. Lawton (Eds.), *Kinship, aging, and social change, Vol. 13, Annual review of gerontology and geriatrics* (Vol. 13, pp. 15-38). New York: Springer.

Berkman, L. F., Oxman, T. E., & Seeman, T. E. (1991). Social networks and social support among the elderly: Assessment issues. In R. B. Wallace & R. F. Woolson (Eds.), *The epidemiologic study of the elderly* (pp. 196-211). New York: Oxford University Press.

Burgess, E. W. (1916). *The function of socialization in social evolution.* Chicago: University of Chicago.

Burgess, E. W. (1926). The family as a unity of interacting personalities. *The Family, 7,* 3-9.

Caffrey, R. A. (1992). Family care of the elderly in Northeast Thailand: Changing patterns. *Journal of Cross Cultural Gerontology, 7,* 105-116.

Cantor, M. H. (1980). The informal support system of New York's inner city elderly: Is ethnicity a factor? In D. Gelfand & A. Kutzik (Eds.), *Theory, research and policy* (pp. 153-174). New York: Springer.

Cheung, C. K., Lee, J. J., & Chan, C. M. (1994). Explicating filial piety in relation to family cohesion. *Journal of Social Behavior and Personality, 9,* 565-580.

Cooley, C. H. (1955). Primary groups. In P. Hare, E. F. Borgatta, & R. F. Bales (Eds.), *Small groups.* New York: Alfred A. Knopf.

Cowgill, D. (1986). *Aging around the world.* Belmont, CA: Wadsworth.

Crimmins, E., & Ingegneri, D. (1990). Interaction and living arrangements of older parents and their children. *Research on Aging, 12*(1), 3.

Davis, K. (1941). Family structure and functions. *American Sociological Review, 8,* 311-320.

D'Costa, R. (1985). Family and generations in sociology: A review of recent research in France. *Journal of Comparative Family Studies, 16,* 319-327.

Donelan, K., Blendon, R. J., Schoen, C., Binns, K., Osborn R., & Davis, K. (2000). Elderly in five nations: The importance of universal coverage. *Health Affairs, 19,* 226-235.

Duffy, M. (1984). Aging and the family: Intergenerational psychodynamics. *Psychotherapy, 21,* 342-346.

Foner, N. (1993). When the contract fails: Care for the elderly in nonindustrial cultures. In V. L. Bengtson & W. A. Achenbaum (Eds.), *The changing contract across generations* (pp. 101-117). Hawthorne, NY: Aldine de Gruyter.

Goode, W. (1963). *World revolution and family patterns.* New York: New York Free Press.

Hall, A., & Wellman, B. (1985). Social networks and social support. In S. Cohen & S. L. Syme (Eds.), *Social support and health* (pp. 23-41). New York: Academic Press.

Hashimoto, A. (1993). Family relations in later life: A cross-cultural perspective. *Generations, 17,* 24-26.

Johnson, C. L. (1995). *The parent-child relationship in late life.* Paper presented at the Annual Conference of the American Gerontological Association, Los Angeles, California.

Kinsella, K., & Velkoff, V. A. (2001). *An aging world: 2001.* Washington, DC: U.S. Government Printing Office.

Kohli, M., Kunemund, H., Motel, A., & Szydlik, M. A. (2000). Families apart? Intergenerational transfers in East and West Germany. In S. Arber & C. Attias-Donfut (Eds.), *The myth of generational conflict* (pp. 88-99). New York: Routledge.

Lasch, C. (1979). *The culture of narcissism: American life in an age of diminshing expectations.* Norton, NY: W. W. Norton & Company.

Lee, G. R., Netzer, J. K., & Coward, R. T. (1994). Filial responsibiltiy expectations and patterns of intergenerational assistance. *Journal of Marriage and the Family, 56,* 559-565.

Litwak, E. (1978). Organizational constructs and mega bureaucracy. In R. C. Sarri & Y. H. Hasenfeld (Eds.), *The management of human services.* New York: Columbia University Press.

Litwak, E. (1985). *Helping the elderly: The complementary roles of informal networks and formal systems.* New York: Guilford Press.

Litwak, E., & Kulis, S. (1987). Technology, proximity, and measures of kin support. *Journal of Marriage and the Family, 49*(3), 649.

Litwak, E., Messeri, P., Wolfe, S., Gorman, S., Silverstein, M., & Guilarte, M. (1989). Organizational theory, social supports, and mortality rates: A theoretical convergence. *American Sociological Review, 54,* 49-66.

Litwak, E., & Meyer, H. (1966). Balance theory of coordination between bureaucratic organizations and community primary groups. *Administrative Science Quarterly.*

Litwak, E., Meyer, H. J., & Hollister, C. D. (1977). The role of linkage mechanisms between bureaucracies and families: Education and health as empirical cases in point. In R. J. Lievert & A. W. Immershein (Eds.), *Power, paradigms, and community research* (pp. 121-152). Beverly Hills, CA: Sage.

Litwak, E., & Szelenyi, I. (1969). Different primary group structures and their functions: Kin, neighbors, and friends. *American Sociological Review.*

Mangen, D. J., Bengtson, V. L., & Landry, P. H., Jr. (1988). *The measurement of intergenerational relations.* Beverly Hills, CA: Sage.

Marshall, V., Cook, F., & Marshall, J. (1993). Conflict over intergenerational equity: Rhetoric and reality in a comparative context. In V. L. Bengtson & W. A. Achenbaum (Eds.), *The changing contract across generations* (pp. 119-140). New York: Aldine de Gruyter.

Messeri, P., Silverstein, M., & Litwak, E. A. (1993). Choosing optimal support groups: A review and reformulation. *Journal of Health and Social Behavior, 34*(2), 122-137.

Nason, J. (1981). Respected elder or old person: Aging in a Micronesian community. In P. Amoss & S. Harrell (Eds.), *Other ways of growing old.* Standford, CA: Stanford University Press.

Nydegger, C. N. (1983). Family ties of the aged in cross-cultural perspective. *The Gerontologist, 23*, 26-32.

Ogburn, W. F. (1932). The family and its functions. In W. F. Ogburn (Ed.), *Recent social trends*. New York: McGraw-Hill.

Page, B. I., & Shapiro, R. Y. (1992). *The rational public: Fifty years of trends in american policy preferences*. Chicago, IL: University of Chicago Press.

Parsons, T. (1944). The social structure of the family. In R. N. Anshen (Ed.), *The family: Is function and destiny* (pp. 173-201). New York: Harper.

Parsons, T., & Bales, R. F. (1955). *Family, socialization and interaction process*. Glencoe, IL: Free Press.

Phillipson, C. (1998). Social construction of retirement: Perspectives from critical theory and political economy. In C. L. Estes & M. Minkler (Eds.), *Critical gerontology: Perspectives from political and moral economy* (pp. 315-327). Amityville, NY: Baywood.

Popenoe, D. (1993). American family decline, 1960-1990: A review and appraisal. *Journal of Marriage and the Family, 55*, 527-541.

Riley, M. W., & Riley, J. W. (1993). Connections: Kin and cohort. In V. L. Bengtson & W. A. Achenbaum (Eds.), *The changing contract across generations*. New York: Aldine de Gruyter.

Roberts, R. E. L., & Bengtson, V. L. (1990). Is intergenerational solidarity a unidimensional construct? A second test of a formal model. *Journal of Gerontology: Social Sciences, 45*, S12-S20.

Roberts, R. E. L., Richards, L. N., & Bengtson, V. L. (1991). Intergenerational solidarity in families: Untangling the ties that bind. *Marriage and Family Review, 16*(1/2), 11-46.

Salamon, S., & Lockhart, V. (1980). Land ownership and the position of elderly in farm families. *Human Organization, 39*, 324-331.

Shanas, E. (1973). Family-kin networks and aging in cross-cultural perspective. *Journal of Marriage and the Family, 35*, 505-511.

Shanas, E. (1979). The family as a social support system in old age. *The Gerontologist, 19*, 169-174.

Silverstein, M., & Bengtson, V. L. (1997). Intergenerational solidarity and the structure of adult child-parent relationships in American families. *American Journal of Sociology, 103*, 429-460.

Silverstein, M., & Litwak, E. (1993). A task specific typology of intergenerational family structure in later life. *The Gerontologist, 33*, 258-264.

Silverstein, M., Parrott, T. M., & Bengtson, V. L. (1995). Factors that predispose middle-aged sons and daughters to provide social support to older parents. *Journal of Marriage and the Family, 57*, 465-475.

Spilerman, S. (2000). Wealth and stratification process. *Annual Reviews of Sociology, 26*, 497-524.

Stearns, P. N. (1989). Historical trends in intergenerational contacts. *Journal of Children in Contemporary Society, 20*, 21-32.

Szebehely, M. (2000). Äldreomsorg i förändring—Knappare resurser och nya organisationsformer [Old-age care in transition: Scarcer resources and new organizational forms]. In M. Szebehely (Ed.), *Välfärd, vrd och omsorg. SOU 2000* [Welfare and care. (SOU) 2000:38]. Stockholm: Fritzes.

Tsuya, N. O., & Martin, L. G. (1992). Living arrangements of elderly Japanese and attitudes toward inheritance. *Journal of Gerontology, 47*(2), 45-55.

Uhlenberg, P. (1996). Mortality decline in the twentieth century and supply of kin over the life course. *The Gerontologist, 36*, 681-685.

Walker, A. (1993) Pensions and living standards in the European community. *Ageing International, 20,* 7-14.

Warnes, A. (1994). Cities and elderly people: Recent population and distributional trends. *Urban Studies, 31*(4-5), 799.

World Bank (2001). *Data and maps: Country data.* World Bank. Available: http://www.worldbank.org/data/countrydata/countrydata.html [2002, January 23].

# CHAPTER 11

# Theorizing Age Relations

## *Toni Calasanti*

Despite their increased sensitivity to diversity, few social gerontologists conduct research on or theorize power relations based on *age,* particularly as these might intersect with other inequalities (McMullin, 2000). Instead, they treat age-based oppression as a given, sometimes added to a list of inequalities, and assume a shared understanding that "we all know what that is." But in fact, we do not really understand age relations. Perhaps because social gerontologists have sought to ameliorate or contradict the vision of old age decline, we do not theorize old age as a political location—on its own, much less as one that intersects with other forms of social inequalities.

By not theorizing age relations, social gerontologists embrace theoretical perspectives based upon midlife experiences that may not adapt well to studying old age. Just as feminists demonstrated that "adding women in" to models based upon men's experiences ultimately depicted women as "other," so too "adding the old in" to theories developed on the basis of younger groups' experiences renders the old as deviant. Because paid labor and "productive activities" serve as a basis of much social valuation and social science research, the middle-aged (who, if White, middle-class men are at the peak of their workplace power) are the implicit comparison group against whom the old are weighed. Using such approaches tell us the extent to which the old conform to middle-aged norms but tell us far less about their lives. It also means they are generally categorized as "unproductive" without thoughtful consideration of alternative forms of productivity. We may know that they are "different" but remain ignorant of the details of their lives. Even though social gerontologists study old age, they can inadvertently exclude aspects of the lives of the old from analysis by not beginning with their experiences and using these to broaden traditional concepts, such as work and retirement. For instance, theories based on middle-aged experiences provide no sense of how the daily lives of older persons are shaped by broader social currents as well as their own actions. Ultimately, social gerontologists implicitly treat old bodies as deviant rather than as products of age relations and so reinforce ageism rather than contribute to more useful pictures of the lives of the old.

In this chapter I will offer one example of this ageism within gerontology that results from ignoring age relations—the issue of successful aging. Then, I will focus on theorizing age relations themselves, outlining what this means and some of the issues we must address. Finally, I give some brief examples of the intersections of age relations with other power relations. Obviously, discussions of power relations, including age, must take into account the unique histories and cultures that shape systems of privilege and oppression; however to keep my task manageable, my primary focus is the United States.

## SUCCESSFUL AGING

I have argued elsewhere (Calasanti & Slevin, 2001) that the quest to "age successfully" (Rowe & Kahn, 1998) has taken center stage in much gerontological theory, research, and practice. Proponents suggest staying *active* as a key to successful aging (Andrews, 1999). Seen "as an antidote to pessimistic stereotypes of decline and dependency," activity has taken on the aura of a moral imperative (Katz, 2000, pp. 135, 137-138). Though advocates encourage many forms of activity, they see economically productive activity as an especially valuable avenue for denying dependence; "productive aging" has therefore received particular attention. At the same time, important but often hidden age-based power relations underlie notions of successful and productive aging.

Rowe and Kahn (1998, pp. 38-39) define successful aging as "avoidance of disease and disability, maintenance of cognitive and physical function, and sustained engagement with life" and maintain that it "can be attained through individual choice and effort." They argue that individuals must go beyond their potential for activity to "behavior that is productive" (p. 40). Their formula implicitly devalues the old in relation to the middle aged as it takes midlife capabilities as the "gold standard" against which older persons are measured. Bodies do change, and physical decline is inevitable, even if individual rates of change vary. Rather than accepting this reality as natural, the emphasis on activity encourages us to define an old person "by what she or he is no longer: a mature productive adult . . ." (McHugh, 2000, p. 104), that is, someone of middle age. This standard is implicit in assertions concerning the *maintenance* of activities; for instance, the old are told to stay busy and "remain both physically and socially active" (McHugh, 2000, p. 112) or as Rowe & Kahn (1998, p. 40) put it, "Just keep on going." To the extent that middle age serves as our implicit yardstick, success-ful aging means *not* aging, not being *old:* "The unspecified but clearly preferred method of successful ageing is, by most accounts, not to age at all, or at least to minimize the extent to which it is apparent that one is ageing, both internally and externally" (Andrews, 1999, p. 305). The implications are that physical changes that accompany the passage of time should therefore be fought, and the old should develop strategies to appear "youthful." The quest for "eternal youth" in order to develop a new image of old age may appear positive (Gergen & Gergen, 2000). However, such a renegotiation of old age remains ageist as it in no way challenges the negative views of old age itself. Instead, it simply asserts that if aging individuals are "not old" that these pejorative labels do not apply without acknowledging that exemptions or exceptions are not normative and not even to be expected.

Indeed, the language we use to talk about successful aging emphasizes the control individuals are implicitly seen to be able to exert in relation to their aging, the attendant mandate to exercise such manipulation, and the "blame" that should accrue if they do in fact become "old." Not only Rowe and Kahn (1998) but also many others stipulate that the ability to age successfully is a result of individual effort and within an individual's purview. We are urged to "fight," "defy," and "deny" aging—exhortations that both convey the need to actively "take charge" and the disdain for those who fail. The assumption is that if one does everything correctly, one will "somehow never age" (Holstein, 2000, p. 331). Thus, we are warned, "don't let this [old age] happen to you." This moralizing discourse ignores structural impediments, including the lack of financial where-withal (Krause, 2000), and individual genetics, just as it excludes passivity and even acceptance.

To a great degree, then, the old are urged to discipline their bodies *to* activity (Katz, 2000); they must seize opportunities and walk briskly the paths to health, happiness, and "success." Research among well-to-do, White old people finds such values embedded in their retirement community: "Productive activity is the route to happiness and longevity; to live otherwise is tantamount to a death wish. Retirement communities, then, provide the ultimate script of successful aging, as seniors rush about as if their very lives depended upon it" (McHugh, 2000, p. 112). The moral emphasis on activity renders those unable or unwilling to engage in it as "problems" to be solved or ameliorated. Rather than coun-tering ageism, then, the stress on activity as an antidote or protection against being labeled "old" simply pushes that negative appellation onto those who are chronically impaired, or who prefer to be contemplative (Holstein, 1999; Katz, 2000). The negativity of "old" itself remains unchallenged.

This successful aging literature ignores the intersection of age relations with other inequalities though these interconnections influence definitions of what successful aging is—what it should look like and the ability to remain active in these ways. That is, the middle-aged standard is drawn from middle-class, White, and male experiences, and the desire and ability to meet this norm is based on far more than individual choice. It is as though in the rush to counter the negativity, an idealized old person has been created and whose resemblance to the range of persons labeled old is purely coincidental, at best.

Beginning with how we define productive activity, we see that, partly as a result of feminist theory and research, conceptions of productivity have expanded in recent decades. Unpaid work, such as volunteerism and domestic labor, *has* increasingly been recognized as economic activity. Despite these broader notions, however, paid labor—the domain and primary experience of White, middle-class men—continues to be most valued and certainly used as the standard against which all other activity is evaluated (Gergen & Gergen, 2000; Holstein, 2000). Hence, the dominant view of productive aging still equates it with paid work.

As a result, members of many groups are hampered in their ability to defy aging through productive activity. If we adopt the value placed on paid activities, we see that women, people of color, and members of the working class carry their disadvantages in the realm of paid work with them into old age. The intermittent paid work history typical of some group members renders it unlikely they would secure any labor in their older years other than low-paid work. In addition, the poorer health of many disadvantaged groups, such as Black men, makes continued labor force participation in old age improbable (Bound, Schoenbaum, & Waidman, 1996). Finally, the diverse unpaid economic contributions of women and people of color tend to be ignored or devalued. That is, even when unpaid activities are acknowledged, they are evaluated like paid labor, with men's occupations having higher status. In the realm of both paid and unpaid work, then, disadvantages over the life course and in old age will make it impossible for some old people to engage in valued forms of productive activity.

In recent decades, we have added ideals of consumerism to notions of productivity as central to White, middle-class men's identity. This shift is quite apparent in marketing toward the old (Minkler, 1989), and they have responded. Indeed, recent U.S. data indicate that those aged 65–74 spent more on consumer items than those aged 25–34; further, the amount spent on entertainment among those aged 55–64 was second only to those aged 45–54 (Cutler & Hendricks, 2001). Recognizing the lucrative prospects in targeting a select group of the old, advertisers promote images of old people pursuing leisure activities (Gergen & Gergen, 2000). The images of the "active elder" promoted in marketing and advertising are themselves bound by gender, race, class, and sexuality. Perhaps this is most obvious in one of the most commercialized images, the marketing of retirement communities geared toward "middle-class whites with sizable pensions and large automobiles." The active lifestyles implicated in this depiction of "'imagineered' landscapes of consumptions marked by 'compulsively tidy lawns' and populated by 'tanned golfers'" (McHugh, 2000, p. 110) can be attained only by men whose race and class make them most likely to be able to afford it, and their spouses. Similarly, various means of disciplining bodies to fight aging require consumption, often at high rates. In this instance, both the mandate to do so and having the necessary economic resources depends on the intersection of social locations. For example, wrinkles will cause women to look "old" sooner than men; research suggests that such markers of age are far more critical to White middle-class women than, say, to Black middle-class women (Slevin & Wingrove, 1998). Ridding the body of such signs of aging require spending large sums on cosmetic surgery, an option more likely available to White, middle-class women. A similar case might be made for exercise that involves joining a gym: the necessity to do so, and the time and money involved will be far more likely to be within the purview of some groups than for others. Race, class, and gender, then, bind both the need and the ability to consume in particular ways. Indeed it is likely that the moral imperative to fight aging itself varies by social location.

How then do we acknowledge the reality of old age, including bodily change, without being ageist and advocating "successful aging"? How do we keep from ending up with constructions of old age that deny this reality, or simply render constructions of decline and dependence? One avenue, and the focus of this chapter, is to theorize age relations themselves, and how these interact with other power relation to shape diverse old ages. Exploring age relations is a first and mandatory step in uncovering our own ageism and eliminating it from our work.

## THEORIZING AGE RELATIONS

Theorizing age relations requires that we address a number of issues, only some of which I will detail here. First, what do I mean by age relations? Second, do age relations structure inequality and in similar ways to other power relations? Third, how should we begin to study age relations? Finally, what groups are involved? Addressing these questions should be a priority for gerontological researchers in all countries, not merely in the United States. All too frequently, these important meta-level issues are sidestepped, to the extent they are addressed at all.

Similar to gender relations, my notion of *age relations* contains three components. First, age serves a social *organizing principle*; second, different age groups gain *identities and power* in relation to one another; and third, age relations *intersect with other power relations*. In addition, just as an examination of gender relations helps us understand not only women but men as well, so too does a focus on age relations enable us to learn more about how all of our positions and experiences rest upon power relations based on age. An examination of these issues will help researchers worldwide realize that age does not merely happen, but is created by societal-level decisions.

The first dimension, which asserts that societies are organized on the basis of age, is widely accepted. Age is, in effect, a master status characteristic that defines individuals as well as groups (Hendricks, this volume). The second and third aspects require greater explanation as each speaks to issues of power: how and why does age-based organization matter for life chances? At the heart of these assertions is the notion that age relations do, in fact, constitute a relation of privilege—unearned advantage—and oppression. Analytically, this means that we would not view old age as simply representing an exacerbation of existing inequalities, but instead it would be seen as a power relation in its own right, conferring a loss of power for all those designated as "old" regardless of their possible advantages on other social hierarchies.

## AGE RELATIONS:
## A RELATION OF PRIVILEGE AND OPPRESSION?

Do age relations constitute a *unique* system of oppression? Sara Irwin (1999) has argued recently that they do not. While old age has an influence, she argues, what matters are life-course *processes* and not life-course *divisions* (into different age strata that she refers to as youth, independent adults, and old). Focusing primarily on conflict over resources between classes (and to a lesser extent, gender), Irwin (1999) argues that age differs from other oppressive relations in two critical ways. First, because we all become old and can compete (on the basis of intersecting power relations) over the course of our lives for resources that will shape our old age, age relations differ from other kinds of power relations. Second, and as a result, the old are extremely diverse, so that it does not make sense to talk about "the old" as a unified group. Irwin maintains that rather than focus on life divisions, we should focus on life-course processes—the conflicts that occur as groups fight to maintain their standards of living. For example, she notes that women are subject to claims made on them throughout their lives by husbands, children, and families and are thus left with poorer pensions. As a result, the inequalities of earlier life are reproduced in old age. She concludes, then, that old people and their treatment are, in a sense, extensions of their entire lives rather than results of a transition from independent adulthood to old age. Focusing on age divisions in examining inequality is therefore inappropriate; instead we ought to focus on the life-course processes that shape old age. She concludes that "the life course can best be seen not as an independent dimension of inequality, cross-cutting other (gender, class, ethnic) divides, but as an integral component of processes which shape general social inequalities" (Irwin, 1999, pp. 692-693).

Irwin's provocative analysis raises important points. However, as insightful as her discussion is, her distinctions between age relations and other power relations, and between life-course processes and life-course divisions, ultimately do not hold. In elaborating these differences, she notes that life-course processes are "integral component[s] of other, gender-and class-related inequalities . . ." (Irwin, 1999, p. 710)—a reasonable claim. Certainly, there are more to power relations than age distinctions; and, further, one does *not* arrive at old age devoid of race, ethnicity class, and gender. To that extent, the parameters of one's old age are shaped by particular social locations. Her implicit challenge of the ways in which life-course divisions are made without reference to gender and the like is also well-taken. However, while the old are certainly diverse, so too are groups divided by the other inequalities (gender and class) that she examines. Working-class women differ from middle-class women in important ways, for instance. Powerful arguments for recognizing the diversity among all these groups that result from their intersections have been made already (e.g., Acker, 1999; Collins, 1990; Glenn, 1999). In this sense, recognizing that age also intersects with other power relations makes age relations similar to, rather than different from, other power relations.

In addition, pointing to the importance of life course and aging processes does not mean that age relations do not exist, nor are they equivalent to the social location of old age. Left out of Irwin's discussion is the reality that all inequalities are also processes: gendering, racing, and so on are enacted in everyday interaction. Further, gendering is not the same as the social location of, say, being a woman. Old age does in fact confer a loss of power, even for those who are advantaged—and thus able to make different "claims" in later life to power and resources—by gender and class. Discrimination and exclusion based on age—across lines of race, class, or gender—does exist. The point at which one becomes "old" varies with these other social inequalities, but once reached brings with it a loss of authority and status. Old age is a unique time of life and cannot be reduced to a result of events occurring in middle age or over the life course.

Finally, Irwin's argument that age relations do not produce analytically distinct inequality ignores several realities. First, bodies grow old inevitably. Second, the old confront unique forms of exclusion, such as laws or formal rules governing paid work that deny privileges solely on the basis of age. Third, the old find themselves in unique circumstances; for instance, the experience of widowhood differs when it occurs early on versus later in life (McMullin, 1995). Ultimately, we can take her insights without having to conclude that age divisions do not matter. In fact, I would strongly concur with her concern that we be attuned to processes and structures. They *are* age relations.

## ARE AGE RELATIONS THE SAME AS OTHER POWER RELATIONS?

Differences between women and men are systematic, as are those between racial groups. Thus, we theorize age and race relations. In thinking about theorizing age relations, then, we are asking, are there important and systematic differences between being an *old* woman and a *young* woman?

We might address this first issue by examining what constitutes a relation of privilege and oppression. Criteria for such a relation might include inequalities in distributions of authority, status, and money, such that oppressors: feel entitled to manage the money that might otherwise go to the oppressed group; stigmatize the oppressed group as dirty and sick; and finally regard these inequalities as determined by a natural order and thus beyond dispute. Do the old experience these inequalities?

Even a cursory analysis demonstrates that age relations are indeed oppressive, as the old do suffer from such inequalities, at least in the Western world. The fact that old people may be in positions of political power can make it appear as if age relations do not influence authority. However, in such instances, the point at which someone should step down or no longer hold political office becomes an issue. Such intangibles as trust and competence are considered, and here we begin to see age relations at work. While such qualities are often hard to define, ageism can be and is in fact used to make such judgments; "ageism . . . undermines even the most powerful, respected, or beloved of politicians" (Bytheway, 1995, p. 45) because of the equation of mental and physical incapacity with old age (Wilson, 2000). For instance, Ronald Reagan's presidency—his ability to govern and perform his duties—was often questioned merely by reference to his age. Other positions of authority can also be denied on the basis of age, such as the ability to be appointed as magistrate or on a jury (Bytheway, 1995, p. 49). Given that wisdom and experience are not necessarily valued in an increasingly globalized world, these attributes of old age "may be seen as signs of obsolescence and so disqualify rather than qualify them to lead" (Wilson, 2000, p. 46). This logic often operates in the workplace as well, where older workers in positions of authority are expected to step aside once they enter their sixth decade.

The old also lose authority and autonomy in terms of their ability to be heard and exert control over personal decisions. This is often seen in relation to their bodies. For instance, doctors consistently treat old patients differently than younger clients. A relative dearth of knowledge about old age among doctors has been documented in many countries and speaks to ageism and a general disregard for this population (Wilson, 2000). As a result, doctors take the complaints of the old less seriously than those of younger people, and undertake therapeutic or medical interventions less quickly and rigorously. Indeed, many doctors will simply ascribe whatever symptoms are reported to "old age" and ignore them (Quadagno, 1999). Conversely, the old may lose their ability to make decisions about medical care and their bodies by doctors who seek to control them through drug use. For example, psychologists tend to treat depression in the old with drugs alone while treating the same symptoms among younger clientele with therapeutic measures (Ray, McKinney, & Ford, 1987). In addition, the medical model is itself disempowering; and the increased biomedicalization of aging in the Western world—wherein situations best understood as a result of social issues are instead seen as medical or personal problems to be addressed by medical intervention—only hastens this loss of power (Estes & Binney, 1991; Wilson, 2000). Finally, a variety of health care policies make de facto rationing of health care for the old commonplace (Wilson, 2000).

Inequalities of status and money are maintained in the paid labor market (Bytheway, 1995). Ageist attitudes and beliefs of employers are certainly implicated in the discrimination faced by older workers (e.g., Encel, 1999), but often ageism is more subtly incorporated into staffing and recruitment policies, career structures, and retirement policies (Bytheway, 1995). As aspects of lives become increasingly influenced by the expansion of market forces, the old will be negatively influenced, given their lack of market power (Wilson, 2000). The inability of many to earn money in old age leads to a reliance on others—family or the state. We can see the oppressive nature of age relations when we briefly consider social policies related to the economic dependence and security of the old. The fiscal policies and welfare retrenchment in many Western countries give us one lens on the discrimination faced by the old as they increasingly face cutbacks. As Wilson (2000, p. 9) notes, "Economic policies are often presented as rational and inevitable but, given the power structure of society, these so-called inevitable choices usually end up protecting younger age groups and resulting in unpleasant outcomes for those in later life (cuts in pensions or charges for health care)." Demographic projections about aging populations are often used to justify such changes, even though evidence upholding dire predictions "is either nonexistent or inconclusive" and neither the public nor decision makers seem willing to consider the counter-evidence. Such counter-evidence includes the fact that, cross-cultural comparisons reveal "very little relation between the increase in the population of pension age and the share of national income devoted to state pensions . . ." (Wilson, 2000, p. 9).

Being old, in and of itself, is a position of low status, and the stigma attached to being old is apparent in the number of people trying to avoid the physical markers of aging through such mechanisms as hours spent at gyms, face lifts, and other forms of cosmetic surgery, and use of special lotions, creams, and hair dyes. Visible signs of aging are taken to indicate that the old are in the throes of physical and mental decline (Gergen & Gergen, 2000). Such is the equation of old age with disease and incapacity that it serves to justify the limited rights and authority of the old. It is, in essence, a "natural" part of life that people age and, as they do so, they "naturally" suffer decrements—an equation apparent in the medical doctors' treatment of symptoms as "just old age." Even the most benevolent form of ageism sees it as a duty to care for those who are infirm because of their age. In the long run, ageism encourages young people to see the old as "other" and not fully deserving of citizenship rights (Wilson, 2000, p. 161). Importantly, to the extent that the old internalize such cultural notions of old age, they too incorporate ageism, thereby making it less likely that they would band together politically to promote age-based power and rights.

Still, age relations differ from other power relations in a critical way. Age is *fluid* and group membership shifts over time. As a result, one can experience both aspects of age relations—advantage and disadvantage—over the course of a lifetime. To be sure, other social locations can be malleable. Individuals might experience class mobility, or "pass" as members of different racial groups or genders, for example. But such changes remain uncommon. By contrast, we all grow old or die first. Although when this (becoming old) occurs varies by the intersection of other social locations, where individuals stand in relation to old age *must* change (Calasanti & Slevin, 2001).

## IDENTIFYING AGE GROUPS

Age categories are dynamic and contested, a situation exacerbated by the fluidity of age. Both personal and collective notions of age change over the course of one's lifetime, and by historical and cultural contexts. As a result, identifying age groups and pinpointing which ones are privileged or disadvantaged remains difficult and ephemeral. For instance, Irwin (1999) wrote of only three age groups (youth, independent adults, and the old); others speak of the middle-aged as well, identifying them as powerful social groups within our society (e.g., Gibson, 1996). Such categories as middle age or "mid-life" are also imprecise and vague with less there than might originally meet the eye or than as used for purposes of contrast (Hendricks, 2002), perhaps as much as "old age."

A similar situation obtains with power relations based on race and ethnicity. That is, from one standpoint we speak of the dominance of Whites, who have power in relation to those who are designated "non-White." At the same time, we recognize that "non-Whites" includes multiple groups, each with different relationships and histories in relation to the dominant group as well as with one another. Further, the designation of groups and members as "non-White" is the result of social constructions and interactions (Glenn, 1999). In like manner, when we look at age relations we see that, at a basic level, the relational groups are the "old" and the "not old." The "not old" is comprised of various age groups, each with different relations to one another and to the old. Groups benefit differently in varying contexts and the same age intervals do not adhere across diverse contextual situations. But frequently, all those who are "not old," including those who are very young, benefit at the expense of the old.

The different position of the very young leads me to not categorize them with the old when discussing ageism, despite the prevalence of theorists who do so. Though exclusion from a wide range of citizenship and other rights obtains, the same sorts of meanings do not accrue to youth. People regard youth as a temporary status—a transition period and a training ground on the way to the authority of adulthood. We accord esteem to youthfulness as our "hope" or "future." By contrast, nothing ultimately halts or tempers the exclusion of the old, who never transcend that status and remain marginalized as "forever other" (Calasanti & Slevin, 2001). Certainly, cosmetic surgery or maintenance of middle-aged activity levels may allow one to be "not old" for a time. Even then, the exemption is usually noted in one way or another. But once so categorized, we do not pass out of this status until death; exclusion based on old age is permanent.

These considerations, then, lead directly to the next issue: how do we study and theorize age relations? I address this question in two ways. First, I discuss the necessity of beginning with the experiences of the old themselves. Then, I outline a general conceptual framework, borrowing in part from scholars who theorize gender and race. Along these lines, some examples of the interaction of age relations with other social inequalities are given.

## EXPLORING AGE RELATIONS: CENTERING ON THE OLD

Because privilege is often invisible, those who are marginalized by power relations are often the best source of information concerning such relations (Collins, 1990). As with other systems of oppression, then, we tend to not see the importance or contours of age relations when we are privileged by being "not old"—even if we are disadvantaged in other ways. Thus, an exploration of age relations must begin by listening to those who are old, as well as those approaching old age. To be sure, those who research age groups such as middle aged or old may define these categories differently than those who live them (Hendricks, 2002). Still, the former must be based in the experiences of the latter.

We can begin to examine age relations by exploring ways the old experience or avoid ageism, including processes of defining age boundaries. For instance, Minichiello, Browne, and Kendig's (2000) investigation of how the old experience ageism—including their denial of it—reveals how they construct the meaning of "old" and where they stand in relation to this construction. Given that we learn ageism while young, and we do not suddenly change our attitudes when we become old, the old are in unique positions as cultural agents who have internalized the beliefs of an ageist society while simultaneously living advanced age. To assess whether or not they have been excluded on the basis of old age requires them deciding the extent to which they "fit" the popular but negative portrayal of "old."

For instance, the expanding definition of middle age (Holstein, 2000) stems from the attempt to deny the reality and stigma of old age. As aging persons work to maintain youthfulness, they may lay claim to being middle aged as a way of contrasting themselves with the pejorative images that attach to being "old." Even those over age 65 may not identify themselves as old (though others around them might); and while reaching age 80 leads some to "admit" to being "old," others will maintain still they do not feel old and "don't want to mix with old people" (Wilson, 2000, p. 11). In theorizing age relations, then, we worry less about affixing the chronological age at which middle age or old age "occur" than about the tensions surrounding the designation of age categories, particularly old age; the contexts in which this occurs; and the results of such labeling. For instance, if an employer or co-workers see a worker as "old," what is the consequence of this designation for the individual? How does it influence outcomes of interest? Further, how does this vary by gender, race, and the like? Are women in the workplace viewed as "old" in the same way as men—at the same point in time, with the same consequences, and so on?

## OLD AGE AS A SOCIAL LOCATION

"I know I look older, but I don't feel old. I haven't arrived at the feeling of feeling old" (Minichiello et al., 2000, p. 260). Recognizing the context of such remarks takes us beyond the apparent "agelessness" expressed in the quotation to a focus on the social location of old age. If, among chronologically old respondents, "Being old . . . is about loneliness, loss of things that were meaningful, being unimportant and irrelevant, or having no role" (Minichiello et al., 2000, p. 260), we would certainly expect that the vast majority would not want to associate themselves with the reality of this devalued and undesirable social location and would seek to distance themselves from it. Similarly, if we focus on the experiences of the old with medical interventions, we can see that although some are meant to improve health and quality of life, many others are undertaken primarily to allow the old to hide aging in an attempt to deflect scorn. Focusing on old age as a social location, then, and drawing from recent work on inequality we might ask, how does the process of defining a visible, identifiable group as somehow inferior to the dominant group occur? We might ask: who is privileged by such ageism, and how? What psychic or material advantages do some people receive from ageism and from ex parte power differentials in general (Schwalbe, 2001)?

Glenn's (1999) recent work on race and gender provides one promising avenue for theorizing age relations based on a critical analysis of the experiences of the old. Recognizing the dynamic and constructed nature of these power relations, she advocates a focus on "*processes* through which racialization and engendering take place, rather than on the elucidation of characteristics of fixed race-gender categories." Noting that racializing and engendering processes occur at the meso, micro, and macro levels, she further elucidates areas for exploration: "*representation,* or the deployment of symbols, language and images to express and convey race/gender meanings; *micro-interaction* or the application of race/gender norms, etiquette, and spatial rules to orchestrate interaction within and across race/gender boundaries; and *social structure,* or the allocation of power and material resources along race/gender lines" (Glenn, 1999, p. 9, italics in original).

Applying Glenn's (1999, p. 5) reasoning, to understand age relations we need to consider simultaneously both age-based meanings—"rhetoric, symbols, and images"—and structure—the distribution of power and resources at all three levels. Thus an examination of "dependence" in old age would involve analyses of such programs as Social Security, other age-based entitlements such as Medicare, public policies that influence both paid labor and care work over the life course, the construction and public presentation of dependency ratios and health care debates, and such cultural images as that of grandparenting as "not work," and of wrinkled bodies as sick or asexual.

An examination of age-based meanings makes it all the more apparent that, despite some similarities, the young and old do not share oppressive experiences. If we look at the relevant rhetoric, images, and symbols attached to the young and old, the distinctions become apparent. How do people respond to the care required of the young versus the frail old? How does the care provider view the work; how do others around (typically) her see them? These different meanings are also embedded in social institutions, apparent in such things as social policies that provide care for the young (through schools) without issue, but not the old. The public debate over "dependence" itself reveals the divergent meanings attached to the old and the young. Even though the 1960s presented a higher dependency ratio than projections for 2050 predict, public outcry over such a "burden" has only sounded in relation to these future numbers (Calasanti & Bonanno, 1986). Yet we know that it is far more likely that a child under age 5 will be "dependent" than a person aged 65–70.

## INTERSECTING POWER RELATIONS

Considering the intersections of power relations have led scholars of gender, among others, to recognize multiple forms of masculinities and femininities, and explore how and why some become dominant ideals (Connell, 1995). In like manner, the intersection of age relations with other social locations leads to multiple "old ages"—discourses and practices that vary by gender, race, ethnicity, class, and sexual preference. One issue of interest is identifying age-appropriate ideals—the age-based standards by which people manage their behavior, whether they live up to them or not. We could then assess the extent to which new constructions of aging along the lines of eternal youth, new forms of control over their lives, and sybaritic pleasures have in fact become ascendant discourses (Gergen & Gergen, 2000). At the same time, these forms of "new aging" are based on at least middle class, male and White advantages in such areas as income, education, and health status; thus, they exclude other forms of old age enacted by those who either are unable or disinterested in these lifestyles (Holstein, 2000; Krause, 2000).

Examining intersecting power relations asks us to consider not only how social hierarchies intertwine with age, but also how age relations themselves alter existing power relations. Although the latter is rarely considered, McMullin (1995) provided an excellent beginning for our reconceptualization of class to include the intersection of age relations with other inequalities. She drew from Acker's (1988) assertion that once we take gender relations into account, we need to expand the notion of class to include relations of both production and distribution. Acker singled out wages, as this is the central means by which distribution occurs in a capitalist society, and showed how wages are gendered: in the workplace, through occupational segregation and wage inequities; at home, through the dependence of unwaged wives on their husbands (their primary connection to production). Gendering also occurs at the level of the State, through welfare programs, such as unemployment, that are tapped when market wages are lacking. In each arena, women and men have differential relations to wages. However, each of these gendered wage arenas are also influenced by age relations (McMullin, 1995). For instance, research suggests that age and gender influence workplace hierarchies, based on the perceived importance of work to identity.

Middle-aged and older men are placed at the top as they are believed to have the highest levels of work commitment, while older women and younger—often low-waged—workers are placed at the bottom, perceived to have less commitment (Skucha & Bernard, 2000). Similarly, McMullin (1995) suggested that teenagers are paid less than adults whose wages are, generally, also influenced by their age; but these age-based relationships are also based on gender. For instance, the wage increases over time for women will be far less, on average, than those for men. When we look at the distribution of deferred wages—in the form of private and public pensions, whose acquisition is also structured by age—we also see a gendered distribution. And because of the ways in which marital relations of distribution are structured into state and private pensions programs, for example, loss of spouse in old age has a different distributional meaning and impact for women than for men (McMullin, 1995).

To this evocative analysis we might add the influences of race relations on wage distribution in capitalist society, again noting the ways in which gender and age intersect in the social relations of distribution through such programs as Social Security. Similarly, distribution based on marriage excludes same-sex couples altogether such that loss of spouse in old age, or pensions policies have far different consequences for heterosexual than for homosexual couples.

In the next section, I provide a few additional examples of how consideration of age relations might influence gerontological concepts and theories as well as the ways in which we view other social inequalities. Because feminist perspectives inform my own work within aging, my examples tend to focus on the experiences of old women or on the ways in which gender intersects with age relations. Thus, I will touch upon the intersections of ageism and sexism, sexuality, issues of gender identity in old age, and care work.

## GENDER, AGE, AND SEXUALITY

Both feminists and gerontologists have noted the gendered double standard that requires women to remain youthful longer than men. Still unchallenged, however, is the fact that the mandate to "remain young" is itself ageist. Why is "old" viewed negatively, and why is this negative evaluation affixed to women at younger ages than to men? It is more than the loss of the "male gaze" and reproductive ability; were old age not so negatively defined then its impact would not be as significant. From this vantage, we see that not only women's beauty and attractiveness but also aging *itself* is male-defined. To be sure, women may purchase cosmetic surgery to maintain their desirability to men; but they are also trying to avoid designation of old; "looking good" has an important age component to it.

The topic of old women's attractiveness and sexual desirability brings up the larger issue of sexuality. Typically, feminists have been concerned with the sexual exploitation of women. However, old women become invisible with age in many respects, to both men and women. In terms of sexuality, their relative powerless and depiction as sexually undesirable has meant not exploitation but instead being cast aside as sexual beings just as many women of color are rejected by White men (Hurtado, 1989). Importantly, younger women benefit from the portrayal of old women as sexual cast-offs. To the extent that women's social value is even partly contingent upon their ability to align themselves with powerful men, the negative sexual imagery of old women enhances younger women's opportunities with privileged men. In addition, although some gerontologists note the growing invisibility of aging women as sexual beings, we have not placed old women's sexuality at the center of our work (Calasanti & Slevin, 2001). We have little knowledge about old women's sexual interests or what sexuality means to them. We also lack knowledge of how these might vary by race, ethnicity, class, and sexual preference such that, for example, many Black retired professional women appear to have a much greater appreciation for themselves as sexual beings than do similar White women (Slevin & Wingrove, 1998; Wingrove & Slevin, 1991).

## AGE AND GENDER IDENTITY

Sexuality is closely tied to gender identity, and gerontologists have tended to discuss gender and gender identity based on notions of androgyny, femininity, and masculinity that were developed in relation to younger (often college-aged) populations. How might taking age relations and old age into account redefine these notions, especially in relation to bodies? What happens when natural, age-related changes in bodies not only affect appearance, but also strength, mobility, and general functional ability? How do individuals negotiate their gendered senses of self in these contexts? Addressing such questions would further broaden notions of gender identity. For example, in old age femininity and masculinity might encompass different forms of expression beyond typical ideas about appearance for women, or performance for men. Indeed, for some old women, femininity may be more about "doing"—for example, performing feminine tasks, such as housework—than appearance (Calasanti & Slevin, 2001). This might help explain why women who suffer from osteoporosis appear to have more difficulty coping with changes in their ability to fulfill family (e.g., mother, housekeeper) roles than with their altered appearance (Roberto & Reynolds, 2001).

Turning the lens the other way, how might a consideration of multiple and competing gender identities that interact with age relations influence the ways we see masculine and feminine identities in later life? In examining organizations, Collinson and Hearn (1994) have described how managerial styles exclude women as well as some groups of men based on race, ethnicity, sexual preference, and class. Age also plays an implicit role. Authoritarian managerial styles, which are based upon seniority, or paternalism, rest upon a "familial metaphor of the 'rule of the father' who is authoritative, benevolent, self-disciplined and wise" (Collinson & Hearn, 1994, p. 13) and favor older men. By contrast, entrepreneurialism favors younger men. A highly competitive and predatory approach that emphasizes "being man enough" to "do whatever it takes" (including working long hours, meeting tight deadlines, and being geographically mobile) to compete, it rests upon a discourse that separates private and public spheres, thereby excluding women as well. Similarly, informalism draws on workplace bonds based on shared masculine values and interests: humor, sports, cars, and sex with women (Collinson & Hearn, 1994, pp. 13-14). Thus age relations are critical in two ways. First, they are embedded in each style of masculinity such that men can be included or excluded based on their age-based abilities to engage in appropriate talk and actions. Second, age relations are implicated in the struggle to posit one managerial style as dominant over the others.

The masculine discourses and practices that underlie managerial styles may also influence old age. For instance, to the extent that some men's masculinity relies upon discourses of sports and sexual objectification of women, how do they negotiate this masculinity in old age? Or if their identity is bound up in competing and winning? Do these hegemonic masculine styles in fact rest upon ageism— the denial of old age? That is, to the extent that White, middle-class, and hetero-sexual middle age is inscribed into proscriptions for successful aging, many old men will be devalued.

## GENDER, AGE, AND DEPENDENCE

In the realm of economic dependence we can see more interactions of age and gender relations in terms of power and identities. Those who are economically active—whether family members or the state—hold power over those who are not, and the latter are thus dependent upon them (Bytheway, 1995). Women are largely dependent upon men or the state (Gibson, 1998), but in old age, men also become dependents of the state, relying upon the redistribution of economic resources through such policies as public pensions. Though many men are cushioned in their fall into dependence by their multiple privileges, old men still end up in a position generally regarded as feminine (Calasanti & Slevin, 2001).

Indeed, the debate concerning the productivity versus dependence of the old begs to be challenged from the standpoint of age relations. Earlier, I noted that ageism affects the meaning of "dependence" such that we see the old but not the young as "burdens." I also discussed the ways in which notions of productivity exclude the economic activities of the old. Feminists have demonstrated women's productivity, and gerontologists have followed suit in relation to the old; but an unchallenged middle-aged bias guides much of this work such that arguments still tend to assume that productive is better than "unproductive." As a result, the old are faced with the requirement that they stay active in order to be valuable. Making age-blind arguments to demonstrate that the old are also productive and hence valuable can result in a sort of tyranny to prove one's productive value, one that is also shaped by gender relations.

For example, we can think about the ways in which the gendered nature of care work in old age intersects with age relations, limiting the freedom old women might otherwise enjoy. Grandmothers may be pressed into service caring for grandchildren so that their mothers may pursue paid labor or other activities that carry greater status. Indeed, the "superwoman" may often depend upon the unpaid labor of mothers/mother-in-law. In this way, younger women exploit their elders, whether they intend to or not. To be sure, grandmothers may enjoy caring for grandchildren; nonetheless, the role confines them as well (Browne, 1998; Facio, 1996). It reinforces women's status as domestic laborers and servers of others; and it exploits women based on their age in that their unpaid labor benefits other family members (Laws, 1995, p. 116). Certainly, some old women may resist too much grandmothering. But the need to demonstrate one's "value" and the emphasis on the importance of reproductive labor makes it all the more difficult for old women to refuse to serve as a source of cheap or unpaid labor.

## CONCLUSION

That age categories are subjective and constructed does not make them and their consequences less real. Exclusion and loss of status accompany the designation of old age in many Western countries. Bodies still matter, for we cannot "construct away" many of the physical changes that old age brings. To this extent, the old are not just like the middle aged, only older. They are different. They are more than their bodies, to be sure; but this physical dimension is part of old age.

Still, examining age relations and its intersections with other inequalities will allow us to explicate the structures that deny power to so many of the old for reasons having less to do with the aging of bodies and more to do with our construction of old age as sickness, dependence, lack of productivity, unattractiveness, and decline. To theorize age relations involves breaking the ethical hold that "activity" and "productive aging" have on our views of aging. Just as feminists have argued for women's emancipation and freedom—for their right to choose on a variety of levels—so too must the old be free to choose lifestyles and ways of being old that suit them, including inactivity as well as activity, contemplation as well as exertion, and acceptance that the old can be vibrant sexual beings. Old people will achieve equality with the middle-aged when "old" carries positive content rather than stigma as disease, mortality, or the absence of value. Only then will old people no longer need to be "exceptional" or spend their time "staying young" to be acceptable; only then will they be free to be frail, or flabby, or have wrinkles—to be old, in all its diversity.

All who do not die young will experience these oppressive age relations. In this sense, these relations carry an emancipatory potential not inherent in other power relations. For instance, those who have been disadvantaged in their earlier lives and have long faced relative powerlessness may actually deal with some aspects of growing old more easily as a result (Slevin & Wingrove, 1998). By contrast, those whose advantages blinds them to their privileges may be most surprised by an age-based loss in power, even if economic resources soften the blow. They may come to see how precarious a privileged position can be, and for the first time see how power relations operate. This heightened awareness may extend beyond the realm of age relations to a realization of privileges accruing to other social locations, and stimulate social change. An understanding of ageism, if coupled with an exploration of the underlying age relations, can help us understand other social inequalities.

Exploring age relations will require that we ask how people variously "do age" and particularly, old age. How are people accountable for doing gender and age at the same time? How does age shape gender identity and actions? How do such identities and activities change over time? How do the old enact/embody masculinity and femininity in old age? These questions are inextricably linked to more macro-level concerns, such as power relations expressed, for example, in family norms and social policies. Thus, the fear expressed by many old people concerning their being a "burden" to their families (Minichiello et al., 2000) is embedded both in family processes and social policies that do not provide public sources of care.

Because concerns about and experiences with ageism often center on bodies—the outward sign of aging—a fruitful approach would be to focus on a wide range of bodily changes occurring from middle age onward, a time when individuals begin dealing with issues of bodily changes that mark them as "getting old." Body images and concerns vary by social location, as do available resources for tending to these; thus, we would seek to answer these questions with as diverse a lens as possible, by race, ethnicity, gender, class, and sexual preference.

This is just the beginning of a potentially long list of topics that we need to explore. Regardless of the area under consideration, hope of serving the old and not just saddling them with new disciplines rests with clear-sighted theories of age relations, built upon the experiences and perceptions of the old, attuned to intersections with many relations of inequality.

## REFERENCES

Acker, J. (1988). Class, gender, and the relations of distribution. *Signs, 13*, 473-497.

Acker, J. (1999). Rewriting class, race, and gender. In M. M. Ferree, J. Lorber, & B. B. Hess (Eds.), *Revisioning gender* (pp. 44-69). Thousand Oaks, CA: Sage.

Andrews, M. (1999). The seductiveness of agelessness. *Ageing and Society, 19*, 301-318.

Bound, J., Schoenbaum, M., & Waidmann, T. (1996). Race differences in labor force attachment and disability status. *The Gerontologist, 36*, 311-321.

Browne, C. V. (1998). *Women, feminism, and aging.* New York: Springer.

Bytheway, B. (1995). *Ageism.* Buckingham, United Kingdom: Open University Press.

Calasanti, T. M., & Bonanno, A. (1986). The social creation of dependence, dependency ratios, and the elderly in the United States: A critical analysis. *Social Science and Medicine, 23*, 1229-1236.

Calasanti, T. M., & Slevin, K. F. (2001). *Gender, social inequalities, and aging.* California: Alta Mira Press.

Collins, P. H. (1990). *Black feminist thought: Knowledge, consciousness, and the politics of empowerment.* Boston: Unwin Hyman.

Collinson, D., & Hearn, J. (1994). Naming men as men: Implications for work, organization and management. *Gender, Work, and Organizations, 1*, 2-22.

Connell, R. W. (1995). *Masculinities.* Berkeley: University of California Press.

Cutler, S. J., & Hendricks, J. (2001). Emerging social trends. In R. H. Binstock & L. K. George (Eds.), *Handbook of aging and the social sciences* (5th ed., pp. 462-480). New York: Academic Press.

Encel, S. (1999). Age discrimination in employment in Australia. *Ageing International, 25*, 69-84.

Estes, C. L., & Binney, E. A. (1991). The biomedicalization of aging: Dangers and dilemmas. In M. Minkler & C. L. Estes (Eds.), *Critical perspectives on aging: The political and moral economy of growing old* (pp. 117-134). New York: Baywood.

Facio, E. (1996). *Understanding older Chicanas: Sociological and policy perspectives.* Thousand Oaks, CA: Sage.

Gergen, K. J., & Gergen, M. M. (2000). The new aging: Self-construction and social values. In K. W. Schaie & J. Hendricks (Eds.), *The evolution of the aging self* (pp. 281-306). New York: Springer.

Gibson, D. (1996). Broken down by age and gender: "The problem of old women" redefined. *Gender & Society, 10*, 433-448.

Gibson, D. (1998). *Aged care: Old policies, new problems.* New York: Cambridge University Press.

Glenn, E. N. (1999). The social construction and institutionalization of gender and race: An integrative framework. In M. M. Ferree, J. Lorber, & B. B. Hess (Eds.), *Revisioning gender* (pp. 3-43). Thousand Oaks, CA: Sage.

Hendricks, J. (2002). The drive to midlife: Are we there yet? *The Gerontologist, 42*, 278-281.

Holstein, M. B. (1999). Women and productive aging: Troubling implications. In M. Minkler & C. L. Estes (Eds.), *Critical gerontology: Perspectives from political and moral economy* (pp. 359-373). Amityville, NY: Baywood.

Holstein, M. B. (2000). The "new aging": Imagining alternative futures. In K. W. Schaie & J. Hendricks (Eds.), *The evolution of the aging self* (pp. 319-332). New York: Springer.

Hurtado, A. (1989). Relating to privilege: Seduction and rejection in the subordination of white women and women of color. *Signs, 14*, 833-855.

Irwin, S. (1999). Later life, inequality, and sociological theory. *Ageing and Society 19*, 691-715.

Katz, S. (2000). Busy bodies: Activity, aging, and the management of everyday life. *Journal of Aging Studies, 14*, 135-152.

Krause, N. (2000). Are we really entering a new era of aging? In K. W. Schaie & J. Hendricks (Eds.), *The evolution of the aging self* (pp. 307-318). New York: Springer.

Laws, G. (1995). Understanding ageism: Lessons from feminism and postmodernism. *The Gerontologist, 35*, 112-118.

McHugh, K. (2000). The "ageless self"? Emplacement of identities in sun belt retirement communities. *Journal of Aging Studies, 14*, 103-115.

McMullin, J. A. (1995). Theorising age and gender relations. In S. Arber & J. Ginn (Eds.), *Connecting gender & ageing: A sociological approach* (pp. 30-41). Buckingham, UK: Open University Press.

McMullin, J. A. (2000). Diversity and the state of sociological aging theory. *The Gerontologist, 40*, 517-530.

Minichiello, V., Browne, J., & Kendig, H. (2000). Perceptions and consequences of ageism: Views of older people. *Ageing and Society, 20*, 253-278.

Minkler, M. (1989). Gold in gray: Reflections on business' discovery of the elderly market. *The Gerontologist, 29*, 17-23.

Quadagno, J. (1999). *Aging and the life course.* Boston: McGraw-Hill.

Ray, D. C., McKinney, K. A., & Ford, C. V. (1987). Differences in psychologists' ratings of older and younger clients. *The Gerontologist, 27*, 82-86.

Roberto, K., & Reynolds, S. (2001). The meaning of osteoporosis in the lives of rural older women. *Journal of Health Care for Women International, 22*, 599-611.

Rowe, J. W., & Kahn, R. L. (1998). *Successful aging.* New York: Pantheon Books.

Schwalbe, M. (2001). The elements of inequality. *Contemporary Sociology, 29*, 775-781.

Skucha, J., & Bernard, M. (2000). "Women's work" and the transition to retirement. In M. Bernard, J. Phillips, L. Machin, & V. H. Davies (Eds.), *Women ageing: Changing identities, challenging myths* (pp. 23-39). London: Routledge.

Slevin, K. F., & Wingrove, C. R. (1998). *From stumbling blocks to stepping stones: The life experiences of fifty professional African American women.* New York: New York University Press.

Wilson, G. (2000). *Understanding old age: Critical and global perspectives.* London: Sage.

Wingrove, C. R., & Slevin, K. F. (1991). A sample of professional and managerial women's success in work and retirement. *Journal of Women & Aging, 3*, 95-117.

## CHAPTER 12

# Theoretical Perspectives on Old Age Policy: A Critique and A Proposal*

## *Carroll L. Estes*

A critical perspective on social policy and aging interrogates the broad socio-cultural, economic and political factors, and structural arrangements that are integral to the understanding and production of old age and aging in contemporary society. It provides an alternative to mainstream approaches in the field that focus on aging at the individual and social level and that do not examine the aging process and its social construction as a problematic of larger social forces of class, status, and power. The limitations of prevailing gerontological theories are briefly described and an alternative critical approach is suggested, which builds upon the theoretical roots of: 1) conflict theory; 2) critical theory; 3) feminist theories; and 4) cultural studies, including social constructionist theory. Finally, the critical theoretical approach is applied to gerontology under the topics of the political economy of aging, feminist theories of the state and aging, and cultural studies in aging such as moral economy and humanistic gerontology.

As interest in social policy and the aging of the population has intensified in Europe and the United States, old age and aging have been constructed and regarded as a problem of the welfare state. With globalization and the increasing strength of world capitalism, the policy focus of developed and developing nations

*Portions of this Chapter are drawn and adapted from Chapters 1, 2, 3, and the Conclusions of Carroll L. Estes & Associates, *Social Policy & Aging: A Critical Perspective*. Thousand Oaks CA: Sage, 2001. The author acknowledges the contributions of three colleagues and co-authors: Karen W. Linkins, Steven P. Wallace, and Elizabeth A. Binney for those parts of Chapters 2 and 3 that are utilized from Estes & Associates, 2001.

is increasingly centered on conflicts over the role of the welfare state in the financing of care and support for the elderly (Kohli, 1988). A critical perspective takes as central the structural arrangements of race, ethnicity, class, and gender that are integral to, and in many ways actually produce, old age and aging as we know it. A central concern is how the institutions of the family, the market, and the state are organized and function in producing social policy and their related individual and aggregate outcomes. Ideology is seen as pivotal role in understanding the debate and direction of social policy and the treatment of the aging and aged around the globe.

## PREVAILING GERONTOLOGICAL THEORIES AND THEIR LIMITATIONS

Since its inception in 1945, the field of gerontology has evolved into a formal interdisciplinary science involving biology, clinical medicine, and the behavioral and social sciences. While researchers, practitioners, policy makers, and the general public agree that aging is a part of the life course, there has been substantial disagreement among and within these groups regarding the definition of old age, the perception of what constitutes normal aging, and the extent and scope of public/private responsibility for optimal, successful, or productive aging. This disparity in perspectives is reflected in the broad and fragmented body of theory that constitutes the field of gerontology where ". . . there is no common thread or tie to a common core of disciplinary knowledge to unify the field" (Estes, Binney, & Culbertson, 1992, p. 50).

One dimension of this fragmented body of work on aging stems from the larger social science debate between "micro" versus "macro," perspectives in which the leading theories of aging emphasize either the individual actor or the structure of society as the primary object of study. A small number of theoretical strands attempt to link both micro and macro perspectives (Bengtson, Burgess, & Parrott, 1997; Marshall, 1996). Newer efforts have attempted also to integrate the meso perspective (Estes, 1998). Another classification dimension of different gerontological theories (also consistent with the larger disciplinary social sciences) is the "normative" versus the "interpretive" perspective (Hendricks, 1992; Marshall, 1996). A third classification dimension that may be contrasted with the previous two is the "critical" or "radical" perspective.

Many of the leading theories of aging, especially those that approach the study of aging from the perspectives of biology and social psychology, focus on the *individual as the primary unit of analysis*. In the early work (1945 to the 1980s), the aging process was most often viewed and assessed in terms of the biological breakdown of the individual, or in terms of the individual personality and process, and the presumed concomitant dependency, loss, and the presumed requisite (normatively determined) adjustment to these states of being.

The "first generation" of gerontological theories (Bengtson et al., 1997; Hendricks, 1992) developed by social psychologists focused on the individual, culminating in disengagement theory and activity theory. Under *disengagement theory*, disengagement is treated as a natural, universal, biologically based and normal part of the life course. Within the dominant functionalist paradigm of the time (late 1950s through 1960s), disengagement was assumed to be positive and "functional" for both the individual and society. Although disengagement theory is no longer the dominant theory of aging, its influence remains in public policy. Social Security, Medicare, and private sector retirement policies are all based on the tacit acceptance of disengagement theory. An alternative, *activity theory* assumes that the more active people are, the more likely they are to be satisfied with their lives. Activity theory stimulated other social psychological theories of aging including continuity theory (Costa & McCrae, 1980) and successful aging (Abeles, Gift, & Ory, 1994; Baltes & Baltes, 1990; Rowe & Kahn, 1987). Drawn from developmental or life cycle theory (Lowenthal, 1975; Neugarten, 1964), continuity theory asserts that aging persons have the need and the tendency to maintain the same personalities, habits, and perspectives developed over the life course. The successfully aging individual maintains a mature integrated personality, which also is the basis of life satisfaction (Neugarten, Havighurst, & Tobin, 1968). More recent theories of successful aging and subsequent theories of productive aging expand the basic framework of activity and continuity theory, incorporating three new positive criteria: the low probability of disease and disease-related disability, high cognitive and physical functional capacity, and active engagement with life (Rowe & Kahn, 1997). These theories seek a positive image of aging through the re-definition of and continuing "productivity" of older individuals. Critics (Estes & Associates, 2001; Holstein, 1992) contend that: 1) the productive aging framework places responsibility on the individual (and individual health behaviors) and may also create expectations for "work" (especially for women), without pay and for many years extended through the end of life; and 2) the framework largely ignores key health and economic liabilities associated with race, class, and gender that would justify policies and programs to compensate for these inequalities, and the physical and mental stresses associated with them.

There is hope for a new line of scholarship concerning individual aging—but not yet charted, much less advanced as necessary—from a more institutional and critical perspective, as gerontologists acknowledge the malleability and reversibility of various biological and behavioral phenomena previously thought to be inevitable with age (Rowe & Kahn, 1987, 1998). There is growing recognition of the influence of social, behavioral, and environmental factors in explaining the processes of aging and health in old age (House, Kessler, & Herzog, 1990). The formidable social and environmental barriers to health and healthy behaviors and lifestyles (e.g., safety and economic security) and institutional racism (e.g., racial segregation in poor urban neighborhoods) have been demonstrated to produce independent negative health outcomes (Collins & Williams, 1999; Robert, 1999). A potentially important, and largely unexamined approach for testing in research on aging and health, comes from epidemiologist John Cassell and his colleagues (Geiger, 1981). They identify three principles governing the relationships between *changes* in the social, biological, and physical environments and the likelihood of increased incidence of disease such as strokes, hypertension, TB, and coronary heart disease: 1) domination and subordination (with the more dominant showing the least deleterious health effects and those who are subordinate having the most extreme responses); 2) social and family disorganization (with those with more of it having more negative health outcomes); and 3) the presence and effectiveness of buffers or protective factors such as group or social supports (with those who are more supported being more protected). To date, only the third, research on buffers and social support, has gerontological attention.

## Theories of the Life Course

While the early social and behavioral work focused on individual aging and the factors in successful aging, life-satisfaction, adaptation, disengagement, and adjustment with advancing years, more recent studies focus on understanding the process of aging from the perspective of the life course, and the relation of coping, social support, personal control, self-efficacy, and focus on the behavioral dimensions of aging. Here aging individuals and cohorts are examined as one phase of the entire lifetime and seen as shaped by historical, social, economic, and environmental factors that occur at earlier ages (Bengtson & Allen, 1993; George, 1993). In the work of George (1990) and others, life-course theory bridges macro-micro levels of analysis by considering the relationships among social structure, social processes, and social psychological states. Nevertheless, the primary focus is intentionally focused on the micro, with an emphasis on how macro level phenomena influence *individuals*. Dannefer and Uhlenberg (1999) point to "three significant intellectual problems in theorizing about the life course: (a) a tendency to equate the significance of social forces with social change; (b) a neglect of intra-cohort variability; and (c) an unwarranted affirmation of choice as an unproblematized determinant of the life course" (p. 309). Insofar as theories of personality and the aging process seek explanations at the individual level, these theories are of limited utility in explaining how old age and aging are shaped by public policies that are a product of the state, the economic system, the sex/gender system, and other social institutions such as racism, or the medical industrial complex influence health and aging in society (Estes, Gerard, Zones, & Swan, 1984).

## Age Stratification and the Aging and Society Paradigm

Two macro-level gerontological theories are age stratification (Riley, Johnson, & Foner, 1972) and its successor the aging and society paradigm (Riley, Foner, & Riley, 1999). *Age Stratification* attends to the role and influence of social structures on the process of individual aging and the stratification of age in society (Riley, 1998; Riley & Riley, 1994a, b). This perspective looks at the differential experiences of age cohorts across time, as well as what Riley and Riley (Riley & Riley, 1994a, b) call the interdependence of changes in lives and changes in social structures.

This theory introduces the concept of structural lag to describe social structures (e.g., policies of retirement at age 65) that do not keep pace with changes in population dynamic and individual lives (such as increasing life expectancy). The age-stratification paradigm is relatively inattentive to institutional racism, sexism, and social class relationships insofar as these both influence and reproduce the social structure—and the policies constituted by it—and ultimately the individual experience of aging (Estes et al., 1984). Quadagno and Reid note the criticism that the theory:

> ... relied on an inherently static concept of social structure, that it neglected political processes inherent in the creation of inequality, and that it ignored institutionalized patterns of inequality. (Quadagno & Reid, 1999, p. 347)

In developing the *Aging and Society Paradigm*, Matilda Riley and her colleagues (1999) address the "unintentionally static overtones of age stratification" by introducing "two dynamisms—changing lives and changing structures— as interdependent but distinct sets of processes" (Riley et al., 1999, p. 333), in which there is an interplay between them. In the tradition of functionalist theorizing, the emphasis is on social homeostasis (and imbalances), age integration, and the formation of norms. Although devoted to "describing and understanding age, as age affects individuals and also is embedded in and influences social structures" (Riley et al., 1999, p. 341), it flows out of the *consensus* rather than the *conflict* approach. In direct contrast, a critical perspective is located within the conflict approach.

## Critical Perspectives on Aging and Health

Critical perspectives emerged in response to the limitations of traditional social gerontological theories of aging that take as given (rather than examining as problematic) many of the characteristics, social problems, and conditions facing the elderly (Estes, 1979). In a sense these theories contribute to the reproduction (rather than alteration of) the conditions of the elderly. At a basic level, disengagement and activity theory may be seen as reinforcing ageist attitudes about the elderly and legitimating policies that reinforce dependency at the expense of empowerment. In addition, the association of age with disease and inevitable decline is better re-framed so that aging is seen as a *social rather than biological process*. Such a view of aging is central to the critical perspective since even the experiences related to distinctly biological phenomenon (e.g., Alzheimer's disease) are being shown to be influenced by socioeconomic conditions and inequalities that are experienced, such as education and mental involvement (and compounded), over the life course.

In attempting to bridge some of the issues of theoretical fragmentation and the macro-micro problem—the critical approach considers the multi-level relationships within and among social structure, social processes, and the population (Bengtson & Schaie, 1999; Estes, Linkins, & Binney, 1996). As applied within the political economy framework, the recursive relationship among levels of analysis are emphasized (Giddens, 1984), providing an avenue for extending and further synthesizing this micro-macro linkage. As such, issues of aging are not perceived as beginning with the individual, the generation, institutions or organizations, or society. Rather, all levels are viewed in terms of mutual dependency, rather than opposition.

Although the field of critical approaches to social policy and aging has grown over the past decade, the promise of the field—namely its incorporation of a variety of disciplinary perspectives—also contributes to the difficulty that the field faces in realizing its potential. As both Baars (1991) and Phillipson (1998) note, critical health and aging is a very broad field concerned primarily with many questions that have fallen outside the mainstream of gerontology and other social science disciplines. These range from examining the role of the state and capital in managing the aging process (e.g., Estes, 1991; Walker, 1999) to questions regarding the meaning and purpose of aging in the context of postmodern societies (Cole, 1992; Gubrium & Holstein, 1999), and identity in globalized society (Phillipson, 1999).

## THEORETICAL PERSPECTIVES IN THE CRITICAL APPROACH

Critical approaches to social policy and aging build upon an array of intellectual traditions, including the works of Karl Marx, Max Weber, Antonio Gramsci, the Frankfurt School, and more recently Jurgen Habermas, state theorists such as Claus Offe and James O'Connor, psychoanalytic perspectives (Biggs, 1997), the contemporary work of Anthony Giddens, and theorists of globalization (Urry, Castells, Appadurai, Piven, and Cloward, among others). Utilizing this theoretical seedbed, a field of critical gerontology has emerged and coalesced over the past decade with work in the United States and Europe. According to the theoretical framework I have proposed (Estes, 2001), four broad theoretical areas constitute and inform the field of political economy: 1) conflict; 2) critical;

3) feminist; and 4) cultural. Scholars writing from any one of these theoretical domains may draw upon the others in pursuing their work.

## Conflict Theories

Those working from a *conflict theoretical approach* contend that society and its social order are held together by the dominance of certain groups and structural interests over others. The outcomes of conflict and power struggles are posited as explanations for how society is organized and functions, while society is seen as held together by constraint, rather than consensus (Collins, 1988). It is argued that societal institutions such as work organizations and medicine are organized and operate the ways they do because some manage to successfully impose their ideas, material interests, and actions on others. Conflict theory is not only about social change; it

> concerns explaining social stability as a general theory of society. But it differs from Functionalist theory in seeing social order as the product of contending interests and the resources groups have for dominating one another and negotiating alliances and coalitions. Its basic focus . . . [is] (in Dahrendorf's terms) latent conflict; it deals with social order as domination and negotiation. . . . Conflict theory is not surprised by . . . upheavals and changes...war or revolution. . . . It sees social order as maintained by forces of domination that cling to the status quo and attempt to legitimate it by traditional ideals; but leaves tremendous stores of social energy locked up in latent opposition, capable of being suddenly released by a catalytic event. (Collins, 1988, p. 118)

The state not only actively participates in these struggles, but also reflects various forms of the interests of the most powerful. A variety of neo-Marxist (O'Connor, 1973; Offe & Keane, 1984) neo-Weberian (Alford & Friedland, 1985; Habermas, 1975), and neo-Gramscian theories (Hall, 1996; Sassoon, 1987) of the state fall within this perspective. A contrasting view of society emerges from the *social order theoretical approach,* built on consensus theories that posit that society is held together by shared values and broad agreement across different groups in society about the way society is organized and functions (Parsons, 1951). Two major theories within the social order paradigm, liberal political and pluralist theories, portray the state as a neutral entity, operating in the universal interest of all members of society (Estes et al., 1984). Critics of the social order paradigm fault it for idealizing democracy and "public choice" while overlooking the power of big, economically concentrated and dominant interests. Schattschneider (1960) introduced the concept of the "mobilization of bias" to describe how these powerful dominant interests are built (i.e., structured) into the way interest group politics and the state operates.

## Critical Theories

> Critical theory is "designed with a practical intent, to criticize and subvert domination in all its forms" (Bottomore, 1983, p. 183). It is a critical perspective on all social practices [that is] . . . preoccupied by a critique of ideology—of systematically distorted accounts of reality which attempt to conceal and legitimate asymmetrical power relations . . . [and how] social interests, conflicts and contradictions are expressed in thought, and how they are produced and reproduced in systems of domination . . . to enhance awareness of the roots of domination, undermine ideologies and help to compel changes in consciousness and action. (Bottomore, 1983, p. 183)

The work of Antonio Gramsci is particularly relevant in three regards: his work on the theory of ideological hegemony (ruling or dominant ideas of the period), on the role of intellectuals, and on the "theory of praxis" in which thought and action (research and policy or practice) are linked. Often described as a member of the Frankfurt School, Gramsci was concerned with the divergence between people's ideas and their economic conditions. He argued that a critical examination of popular culture and beliefs was crucial, and that ideas can have the weight of material (economic) force.

## Feminist Theories

Another set of theories constituting the critical approach to social policy and aging are feminist theories. Feminist theories, which are complementary and often related to or included in the political economy perspective, emphasize the importance of gender by examining the gender biases in social science research and the production of knowledge and practice. Gender is a crucial organizing principle in the economic and power relations of societal institutions as well as of social life throughout the life course. Gender therefore influences and shapes the experience of aging (Calasanti, 1993; Calasanti & Zajicek, 1993; Diamond, 1992; Estes, 1998; Ginn & Arber, 1995; McMullin, 1995) and the distribution of resources in old age to men and women.

In the United States feminist theorists have attended to the state (Acker, 1988; MacKinnon, 1989; Orloff, 1993) but, with a few exceptions (Calasanti, 1996; Calasanti & Zajicek, 1993; Estes, 1991, 1998; Harrington Meyer, 1990, 1996; Quadagno, 1988), have not generally focused on old age. There is little consensus on the paradigm of feminist theory of the state, and the political spectrum has been debated from the "right" to the "left." Janet Saltzman Chafetz (Chafetz, 1997) speaks of the "normative emphasis" in the focus on gender studies and defines feminist theory to include: 1) normative discussions of how societies and relations ought to be structured, their current inequalities, strategies to achieve equity; 2) critiques of androcentric classical theories, concepts, epistemologies, assumptions; and 3) explanatory theories of the relation of gender and social, cultural, economic, psychological, and political structures and processes.

Catherine MacKinnon points out (1989) the strength of a critical and Marxist perspective as a "point of departure" for theorizing about women and the state. She notes that:

> Marxism is . . . the contemporary theoretical tradition that—whatever its limitations—confronts organized social dominance, analyzes it in dynamic rather than static terms, identifies social forces that systematically shape social imperatives, and seeks to explain human freedom both within and against history. It confronts class, which is real. It offers both a critique of the inevitability and inner coherence of social injustice and a theory of the necessity and possibilities of change. (MacKinnon, 1989, p. ix)

Gayle Rubin (1975) contends that Marxian analysis is important for feminist work because it is consistent with the perspective that the sex/gender system is the product of historical human activity. Rubin uses the term, the sex/gender system, to refer to the larger context of male domination and the structures that create and promote domination; it is a set of arrangements by which a society transforms biological sexuality into products of human activity and in which these transformed sexual needs are satisfied. The sex/gender system is reflected in social institutions such as the state and the family (Acker, 1988) and in how these "gendered institutions" (Acker, 1992) reproduce the subordination and subjugation of women (Hartmann, 1981; Walby, 1986) through institutions such as marriage and kinship (Rubin, 1975).

It is widely argued by feminist scholars that the state is a major vehicle for the subjugation of women (Acker, 1988; Connell, 1987; MacKinnon, 1989; Sassoon, 1987) and that the state is in itself a patriarchal institution (Estes, 1998b, 2001). Feminist theories of the state and old age policy address: 1) the two tiers of social policy: social assistance and social insurance; 2) the concepts of the gendered wage and the family wage; and 3) the understanding of how older women's fate in the welfare state is based on her marital status and her husband's work history and how the traditional autonomous nuclear family is inculcated into law and social policy (Estes & Associates, 2001; Harrington Meyer, 1990, 1996). The state and the institution of medicine are seen as vehicles of social control confronting women across the life course, with serious effects on the life situation of old women. Joan Acker proposes two key social processes of the state: *relations of distribution* and *relations of production*. Personal relations (particularly marriage), wages, and the state are each locations of gendered distribution that are vitally affected by the dominance of market relations as the basis of distribution. Fruitful topics of research from the feminist perspective on aging in the United States are the specification of gendered policy, the processes and structures in and through which policy operates, and the gendered outcomes.

## Cultural Studies

*Social constructionism* is a theory within the broader "family" of cultural studies at the micro-level, and linked to the macro-level through processes of social interaction (Estes, 1979; Gubrium & Holstein, 1999). In my earliest proposal of a political economy theory of aging, I began with the proposition that,

> The major problems faced by the elderly in the United States, are in large measure, ones that are socially constructed as a result of our conceptions of aging and the aged. What is done for and about the elderly, as well as what we know about them, including knowledge gained from research, are products of our conceptions of aging. In an important sense, then, the major problems faced by the elderly are the ones we create for them. (Estes, 1979, p. 1)

Later, I argue that, "A cornerstone of the political economy of public policy and aging is the social construction of problems and the remedies to deal with them" (Estes et al., 1996, p. 349). As utilized with the political economy perspective, the constructed "problems" of aging and their policy remedies are examined in relation to: (a) the capacity of strategically located agents and interests to define "the problem" and to press their views into public consciousness and law; and (b) the objective facts of the situation (Estes, 1979).

Symbolic interactionist theories (Gubrium, 1967; Rose, 1967) posit that the interactional context and process (environment, persons, and encounters in it) may significantly affect the kind of aging process a person experiences. "Both self and society are seen as capable of creating new alternatives" (Estes, 1979). The social construction of reality perspective provides several useful insights.

The experience of old age is dependent in large part upon how others react to the aged; that is social context and cultural meanings are important. Meanings are crucial in influencing how growing old is experienced by the aging in any given society; these meanings are shaped through interaction of the aged with the individuals, organizations, and institutions that comprise the social context. Social context, however, incorporates not only situational events and interactional opportunities but also structural constraints that limit the range of possible interaction and the degree of understanding, reinforcing certain lines of action while barring other (Estes, 1981, p. 400).

Within the contemporary theoretical landscape, cultural studies are "a dissenting movement" that "helps to understand the mechanisms of cultural power . . . and the means to resist them" (Sardar & Van Loon, 1997, pp. 170-171). Three noteworthy characteristics of recent work here is that it:

(1) aims to examine its subject matter in terms of *cultural practices* and their *relation to power*. Its constant goal is to expose power relationships and examine how these relationships influence and shape cultural practices . . . ;

(2) [seeks] to analyze the *social and political context* within which (culture) manifests itself... [and]

(3) is committed to a *moral evaluation* of modern society and to a *radical line of political action.* The tradition of cultural studies is not one of value free scholarship, but one committed to social reconstruction by critical political involvement. Thus cultural studies aims to *understand and change structures* of dominance everywhere, but in industrial capitalist societies in particular. (Sardar & Van Loon, 1997, pp. 8-9)

Clearly, within the cultural studies tradition, there are differing, if not a dizzying number of, theoretical and methodological perspectives and emphases, including those that consider ideological hegemony as a cultural element that "binds society together without the use of force" (Sardar & Van Loon, 1997, p. 49). For Gramsci, culture is a key site where struggles for hegemony take place. For Hoggart, the dominant elite express power by projecting their "fields of value" as they accord legitimacy and exposure to their cultural forms and practices (Sardar & Van Loon, 1997).

Cultural studies have contributed a political dimension and the study of such fields of value. This work is potentially *empowering* and *emancipating* "by encouraging . . . [people] with the resources to understand the intrinsic relationship between culture and the various forms of power, and thus to develop strategies for survival" (Sardar & Van Loon, 1997, p. 43). With such knowledge among the people, *the potentially revolutionary human subject may act.*

## Ideology

Consciousness is culture. Ideology is culture. It is noteworthy that *"culture is anything but neutral"* (Parenti, 1999, p. 11). An examination of ideology is an essential element of any work under the rubric of moral or political economy. Intellectual arguments and theoretical oppositions are likely to be about whether one subscribes to: 1) a determinacy for the cultural concepts of ideology and/or social norms in producing state policy on aging (and the institution of retirement, etc.)—for example, whether one argues that ideology determines or is merely part of a larger array of influencing factors that shape state policy; and 2) the processes by which phenomena (such as ideology or norms) develop and have their influence. The issue is whether ideology and norms emerge through coercive processes of social struggle and conflict *versus* processes of consensual agreement in society concerning values and norms.

The view advanced here is that: 1) ideology is a crucial (but not the only) element in the framing of state and social action that culminates in social policy on aging; and 2) the consent of the governed occurs through struggle, albeit, political, material, and ideal. Cultural products are contested, emerging, evolving, and problematic. Nevertheless, we must always account for the recursive relations of agency, culture, and structure (Giddens, 1991).

As belief systems, ideologies are competing world views that reflect the social position and structural advantages of their adherents. All political and economic regimes use ideology as the discourse with which to communicate and impose a reflection of the dominant social relations. The perspective advanced here concurs with Therborn's (1980) in rejecting the narrow definition of ideology as false beliefs that may be contrasted with scientific truth or intellectual doctrinal systems. As described by Thompson, Therborn's view is that "Ideologies are social phenomena of a discursive type, including both everyday notions and experience, and elaborate intellectual doctrines; both the consciousness of social actors and the institutionalized thought systems and discourses of a given society" (Thompson, 1986, p. 15).

Ideology is integral to the three processes by which dominant views of social policy and aging are produced and sustained. These processes are: 1) the successful creation of cultural images by policymakers, experts, and the media— e.g., that the elderly are "greedy geezers"; 2) the appeal to the necessities of the economic system—e.g., claiming that the elderly are responsible for the nation's economic problems by "busting the budget"; and 3) the implementation of policy and the application of expertise in ways that transform conflicts over goals and means into systems of rational problem-solving. This focus on rational problem resolution by technical experts serves to obfuscate the substance of class, gender, and racial/ethnicity (George & Wilding as quoted in Manning, 1985) inherent in both the definition of the problem and the "solutions" that attend to those definitions. An example is the purportedly "gender neutral" policy of Social Security that presently is constructed around (and biased in favor of) the autonomous nuclear family. Ideologies of the state, the market, and the sex/gender system have tremendous consequences particularly for those that are most dependent upon the state—women, minorities, the poor, the elderly, and the disabled.

In considering social policy on aging, the challenge with regard to ideology is to: 1) to locate the systems of beliefs and values within specific social formations (such as old age policy) and examine how they articulate with the economic system of capitalism, the state, and class and other gender and race struggles therein; and 2) to investigate these ideological communities, which exist within specific organized collectivities (e.g., nation states, organizations, institutions) and how they mask past social and class struggles and contradictory norms and values (Thompson, 1986, p. 14).

Work in the political economy of aging (Estes, 1991, 1999) deals extensively with the power struggles over ideology and over the legitimacy of both state actions and the state itself. To say it another way for emphasis, legitimating and de-legitimating ideologies and practices are cultural products, and ones over which there are enormous struggles. As such, ideology and other cultural phenomena are both the "*object of study*" and the "*location of political criticism and action,*" consistent with substantial work in what is now called cultural studies (Sardar & Van Loon, 1997)

## APPLYING THE CRITICAL THEORETICAL
## APPROACH TO AGING

The social institutions of the state, the market, and the family (macro level) can be seen as influencing the construction, experience, and condition of aging, while individuals also actively construct their worlds through personal interactions (micro level) and through organizational and institutional interactions (meso-level) that constitute their social worlds and society.

### The Political Economy of Aging

The political economy of aging offers an important approach to understanding the condition and experience of social policy and aging drawing from multiple theories and levels of analysis. Beginning in the late 1970s and early 1980s with the work of Estes (1979), Guillemard (1980), Phillipson (1982), and Walker (1981), these theorists initiated the task of describing the role of capitalism and the state in contributing to systems of domination and marginalization of the aged. Based on the continuing work of these and other authors developing a critical perspective on theories of aging (Marshall & Tindale, 1978) and theories of the welfare state (Myles, 1984; Quadagno, 1988), the political economy perspective is classified as one of the major theories in social gerontology (Bengtson et al., 1997; Bengtson & Schaie, 1999; Hendricks & Leedham, 1991; Marshall, 1996; Phillipson, 1999; Walker, 1999). The political economy perspective is distinguished from the dominant liberal-pluralist theory in political science and sociology by according greater import to the economic system and other social structures and social forces in shaping and reproducing the prevailing power structure of society. In the political economy perspective, social policies pertaining to retirement income, health, and social service benefits and entitlements are products of economic, political, and socio-cultural processes and forces that interact in any given socio-historical period (Estes, 1991, 2000). Social policy is an outcome of the social struggles, conflicts, and the dominant power relations of the period. Policy reflects the structure and culture of advantage and disadvantage as enacted through class, race/ethnicity, gender, and age relations. Concurrently, social policy stimulates power struggles along these structural lines of class, race/ethnicity, gender, and age. Social policy is itself a powerful determinant of the life chances and conditions of individuals and population groups such as the elderly.

As noted earlier, a central assumption of the political economy perspective is that the phenomena of aging and old age are directly related to the nature of the society in which they are situated and, therefore, cannot be analyzed in isolation from other societal forces and phenomena. The power of the state, business, and labor and the role of the economy are central concerns.

The significance of the political economy literature is in its . . . attention to how the treatment of older people in society and the experience of old age itself are related to an economy whose boundaries are no longer limited to the US alone but include worldwide economic and political conditions. . . . The task of the political economy of aging is to locate society's treatment of the aged in the context of the economy (national and international), the role of the state, the conditions of the labor market, and the class, sex, race, ethnic, and age divisions in society. This will require serious consideration of the relationship of capitalism to aging. (Estes et al., 1984, pp. 11-12)

## Feminist Theory of Social Policy and Aging

Any comprehensive theory of social policy and aging must articulate the relations between gender, the household, the state (and public policy that flows from it), and the market or the economy. Several theorists have laid the groundwork for such conceptualization (Dickinson & Russell, 1986; Estes & Associates, 2001; Harrington-Meyer, 1990; O'Connor, Orloff, & Shaver, 1999; Orloff, 1993). A critical feminist perspective on aging seeks to uncover how the state promotes and reproduces the dominant institutions that render older women vulnerable and dependent throughout their life course (Estes, 1982, 1991). Globalization and neoliberalism are two *ideologies* that currently frame the role of the state vis a vis the family and the market. The ideology of individual responsibility is consistent with state policies that define child and elder caregiving as private individual and family responsibility, ignoring the role of that work of social reproduction in contributing to the economic productivity and corporate wealth of society. Social reproduction is a concept that embraces the work of both producing the members of society as educated, healthy, knowledgeable, and productive human beings and the work of setting up conditions by which such production of individuals and society may continue (recur). Historically under capitalism, women's traditional role in reproduction has been seen as the "complement" (rather than defined as a form of production), while a man's role is in production (Mitchell, 1966).

Feminists critique theories that "privilege" the relations of production that men do through paid work and "ignore . . . much of the process by which people and their labour power are reproduced" (Himmelweit, 1983, p. 419), which is the reproduction work that women do that is seen as informal, unpaid, invisible, and devalued. Reproduction takes place on two levels: "the reproduction of labour power both on a daily and generational sense; and human and biological reproduction" (Himmelweit, 1983, p. 419). This privileging of production over reproduction explains the tendency to treat matters of women's and men's relations (the division of caregiving and household work) as private and beyond the scope of state intervention (O'Connor et al., 1999, p. 3). Caregiving, and the ideology of community care, legitimate minimal state activity in long-term care by defining this type of care as belonging to the private sphere of home and family (Cancian & Oliker, 2000; Estes & Zulman, 2001; Estes, Swan, &

Associates, 1993; Pascall, 1986; Walker, 1984). Estes and her colleagues (Estes & Associates, 2001; Estes, Swan, & Associates, 1993; Estes & Linkins, 1997) show that, with increased for-profit medical and managed care and competition, even more caring work is being transferred from the formal (e.g., hospital) to the informal sector as the State continues to be pressured to redirect its resources from meeting human needs to underwriting various aspects of capital accumulation (Binney, Estes, & Humphers, 1993).

Patricia Hill Collins' (1990, 1991) work on "standpoint" in black feminist theory highlights the interlocking systems of race, class and gender oppression (1990; 1991, p. 68) that operate in and through the state and virtually all other social institutions. She illuminates the struggle of oppressed persons for self-definition involving "tapping sources of everyday, unarticulated consciousness [that is] traditionally denigrated in white male controlled institutions" (1990; 1991, p. 28). Critics of feminist work address the failure of "white dominated" feminism to recognize the impact of race (Collins, 1991; O'Connor, 1993); this critique has reached gerontology as well (Dressel, 1988; Dressel, Minkler, & Yen, 1998).

## Moral Economy and Humanistic Gerontology

The development of cultural and humanistic gerontology, sometimes referred to as moral economy, falls within cultural studies. The development of moral economy is part of a broad field of *cultural gerontology*. This approach has gained popularity, as the classical theoretical opposition of structure *versus* agency and culture *versus* structure has given way to an appreciation of the interplay and "recursive" relationships of culture, structure, and agency (Estes, 1999; Giddens, 1991). Cultural gerontology is part of the trend toward theories that reject the sole determinacy of economics in explaining social institutions such as the state and old age policy. There has been a re-formulation of the unidirectional causality implied in the classical "base- superstructure" model of Marxism. What has followed is an intense focus on questions of meaning and experience.

Humanistic gerontology adds still another dimension to critical approaches to aging, by seeking both to critique existing theories and to construct new positive models of aging based on research by historians, ethicists, and other social scientists (Bengtson & Allen, 1993; Cole, Achenbaum, Jakobi, & Kastenbaum, 1993). Moody (1993) identifies several goals for the critical humanistic perspective in gerontology, including:

(1) developing theories that emphasize and reveal the subjective and inter-pretive dimensions of aging; (2) commitment to praxis and social change; and (3) the production of emancipatory knowledge. Consistent with and complementary to both the political economy and feminist theories, this approach centers on the concepts and relations of power, social action and social meanings as they pertain to aging. At the core, this approach is

concerned with the absence of meaning in the lives of the elderly, and the sense of doubt and uncertainty that is thought to permeate and influence their day-to-day lives and social relations. (Moody, 1988a, 1988b, 1997)

In the United States, theories of moral economy have developed largely as part of the political economy of aging (Minkler & Cole, 1999, 1991; Minkler & Estes, 1991, 1999). Building on the work of E. P. Thompson (1963), Martin Kohli (1987), Minkler and Cole (1991), and others examine the social norms and reciprocal obligations and relations and their role in the social integration and social control of the elderly and the workforce. U.S. proponents of this perspective include Minkler and Cole (1999, 1991), Hendricks and Leedham (1991), Moody (1988b, 2000), Robertson (1999), Holstein (1992), and others. The concept of moral economy reflects "popular consensus concerning the legitimacy of certain practices based on shared views of social norms and obligations" (Robertson, 1999, p. 39). Scholars attend to issues of distributive and economic justice and norms such as reciprocity and generational equity.

The cultural and symbolic elements incorporated under cultural gerontology necessarily include the ideas, beliefs, ideologies, norms, and meanings that are an essential part of the construction of old age and old age policy. The institutions of work, retirement, the family, and the state both *reflect* and *affect* these symbolic and cultural elements. These symbolic and cultural elements are and have always been an essential part of the constructionist perspective on aging that Estes first proposed in 1972 (Estes, 1972) and later joined with a political economy analysis in *The Aging Enterprise* (Estes, 1979).

## THEORETICAL MODEL

### The Multi-Level Analytical Framework

The analytic levels of the framework are: (a) financial and post-industrial capital and its globalization; (b) the state; (c) the sex/gender system; (d) the public and the citizen (adapted from McKinlay, 1985) (see Figure 1). For analytic purposes the model is expanded to include a fifth level: (e) the medical-industrial complex and the aging enterprise, which is a product of the relationship between post-industrial capital, the state, and the sex gender system (Estes, 1979). According to conflict theory, the actors engage in struggles with one another, and policies result from the extent to which one actor is able to dominate and control the others.

This theoretical model for social policy and aging provides a framework to understand and analyze these struggles. Based on the political economy perspective, the model utilizes a multi-level analytical framework that addresses the conflicting and competitive multi-directional relationships between post-industrial capital, the state, and the sex/gender system which create and support the

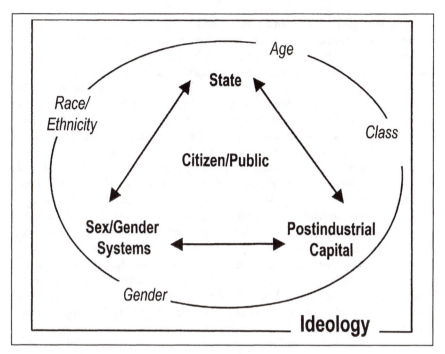

Figure 1. Theoretical political economy model: Estes version.

medical industrial complex and the aging enterprise. The role of the public/citizen is also explored and macro, meso, and micro- levels of analysis are included. The model recognizes that the power struggles between these actors and institutions occur within the context of the "interlocking systems of oppression" of gender, social class, and racial and ethnic status across the life course. Power struggles over ideology reflect the dominant social relations and set the context for defining issues of old age and aging and determining how policies address these phenomena in society.

## CONCLUDING NOTES ON SOCIAL THEORY AND RESEARCH

From a critical perspective, much of gerontology may be appropriately characterized as increasingly theory-less empiricism and "social engineering" as exemplified by applied research on the demographics, health, health care, and health economics of aging that fails to problematize (examine as problematic) or investigate the effects of the surging for-profit and managed-care medical industries on the aging individual (by race, class, and gender) and the society as a whole. The "problem" of aging for the individual and the aging society tend to be defined as *technical* and capable of administrative correction under the continued dominance of medicine and its ever more powerful alliances (and power struggles) with and within profit-making corporations and the scientific disciplines of genetics and economics. Technical and statistical developments including demographic, econometric and actuarial modeling and the availability of national data sets (e.g., Medicare and Medicaid), permit the production (and reproduction) of what appear to be objective and precise value-neutral calculations of the cost-benefits of policy changes. Yet, there is little, if any, consideration of measures of the costs of institutional sexism and racism. Because such calculations are usually made at the individual level and by aggregating individuals, they do not investigate how, or even calculate the types and amount of other social costs that are shifted onto other groups in society. A case in point is the increasing social, economic, and health costs for women of their unpaid informal labor that is essential in the realization of medical care profits as a result of policies that promote shortened lengths of hospital stays and ambulatory surgery.

The current field of health (medical) services research applied to social policy and aging in many ways exemplifies social science "in the service of" reproducing the dominant institutions of society and the unequal distribution of power and material resources. Applications of the policy sciences to aging tend to take for granted the existing systems of medicine and capitalism as scholars work largely within "definitions of the situation" that are framed by economic paradigms, assumptions and models of cost effectiveness and individual level outcomes. The end result is that such investigations consider only a limited array of potentially viable policy options, ensuring the serious consideration of only incremental changes that will do little to alter the basic condition of the old. There is a dearth of critical scholarship in the discipline of economics (for an exception see Rice, 1998). Scholars in the field of health policy and aging generally take-for-granted the assumptions underlying the market, as well as the validity of the theorized and "real" individual preferences and consumer "choices." Dominant economic interests and privilege are preserved by not examining as equally valid options the opposing thought structures of constructing and implementing other systems of governance that would promote the citizen right to universal publicly funded health and health and long-term care, and to an adequate quality of life with economic security.

Challenging these approaches are political-economy theories, critical, feminist, and cultural theories. The substantial intellectual ferment in "political economy," "critical gerontology," and "humanistic gerontology" has, I believe, resulted from a combination of: 1) the infusion of theoretical developments in post-modernism, feminist theory, antiracist theory, critical theory, and cultural studies in science (Estes & Linkins, 1997; Moody, 1998; Phillipson, 1998); and 2) the challenge to the intellectual Left in the wake of the failure of communism, the gold rush of globalization concentrating power and wealth in private hands, and the lack of what are perceived as viable socialist alternatives to the capitalist state. With the global market, the sovereignty of the nation-state is challenged as never before as "more and more of the national economy is owned by international corporations" (Turner, 1999, p. 274), which, in turn, raises more profound questions about the meaning of "the traditional forms of citizenship [that] . . . do not correspond to the idea of an increasingly global market" (p. 274).

These trends have fostered a sense of great urgency on two fronts: first in the need to critically examine aging and social policy and the welfare state at the institutional and world system level in ways that offer some hope of reclaiming or redeeming the citizen and the state from a social rights perspective (Kagarlitsky, 1999; Twine, 1994) and, second, in the need for continuing work challenging the dominant paradigms of knowledge construction.

There is a need for projects in the tradition of the Frankfurt School that are multi-disciplinary and that examine the political, economic, and socio-cultural forces and processes, the situated "knowledges," and consciousness that profoundly shape social policy on old age and aging in any single society and under the globalization.

Required is a commitment not only to a reflexive social scientific approach to the study of social policy but also to praxis—that is, practice and social action that dialectically flow from and into theory and research. At the level of praxis, the goal is to understand and change structures of dominance that produce and reproduce social inequality and injustice (Estes & Binney, 1989).

The overall project of a critical perspective on social policy and aging is to provide alternative theoretical frameworks, a scientific epistemology, concrete information, and emancipatory knowledge that will contribute to a rebalancing of the imperatives of "the market" with a recognition to the social value of, and our capacity to meet human needs across generation, gender, race and social class.

## REFERENCES

Abeles, R. P., Gift, H. C., & Ory, M. G. (1994). *Aging and quality of life.* New York: Springer.

Acker, J. (1988). Class, gender and the relations of distribution. *Signs, 13*(3), 473-493.

Acker, J. (1992). Gendered institutions—From sex roles to gendered institutions. *Contemporary Sociology, 21,* 565-569.

Alford, R. R., & Friedland, R. (1985). *Powers of theory: Capitalism, the state, and democracy.* Cambridge, NY: Cambridge University Press.

Baars, J. (1991). The challenge of critical gerontology—The problem of social constitution. *Journal of Aging Studies, 5*(3), 219-243.

Baltes, P. B., & Baltes, M. M. (1990). *Successful aging: Perspectives from the behavioral sciences.* Cambridge, England; New York: Cambridge University Press.

Bengtson, B. E., & Allen, J. T. (1993). Sociological functionalism: Exchange theory and life cycle analysis. In P. Boss (Ed.), *Sourcebook of family theories and methods: A contextual approach.* New York: Plenum Press.

Bengtson, V. L., Burgess, E. O., & Parrott, T. M. (1997). Theory, explanation, and a third generation of theoretical development in social gerontology. *Journals of Gerontology Series B-Psychological Sciences and Social Sciences, 52*(2), S72-S88.

Bengtson, V. L., & Schaie, K. W. (1999). *Handbook of theories of aging*. New York: Springer.

Biggs, S. (1997). Choosing not to be old? Masks, bodies and identity management in later life. *Ageing and Society, 17*(PT5), 553-570.

Binney, E. A., Estes, C. L., & Humphers, S. E. (1993). Informalization and community care. In Estes, Swan, & Associates. *The long term care crisis: Elders trapped in the no-care zone* (pp. 155-170). Newbury Park, CA: Sage.

Bottomore, T. B. (1983). *A dictionary of Marxist thought*. Cambridge, MA: Harvard University Press.

Calasanti, T., & Zajicek, A. (1993). A socialist feminist approach to aging: Embracing diversity. *Journal of Aging Studies, 7*(2), 117-131.

Calasanti, T. M. (1993). Introduction—A socialist-feminist approach to aging. *Journal of Aging Studies, 7*(2), 107-109.

Calasanti, T. M. (1996). Incorporating diversity—Meaning, levels of research, and implications for theory. *Gerontologist, 36*(2), 147-156.

Cancian, F. M., & Oliker, S. J. (2000). *Caring and gender*. Thousand Oaks, CA: Pine Forge Press.

Chafetz, J. S. (1997). Feminist theory and sociology: Underutilized contributions for mainstream theory. *Annual Review of Sociology, 23,* 97-120.

Cole, T., Achenbaum, A., Jakobi, P., & Kastenbaum, R. (Eds.). (1993). *Voices and visions of ageing: Toward a critical gerontology*. New York: Springer.

Cole, T. R. (1992). *The journey of life: A cultural history of aging in America*. Cambridge, UK; New York: Cambridge University Press.

Collins, C. A., & Williams, D. R. (1999). Segregation and mortality: The deadly effects of racism? *Sociological Forum, 14,* 495-523.

Collins, P. H. (1990). *Black feminist thought: Knowledge, consciousness, and the politics of empowerment*. Boston: Unwin-Hyman.

Collins, P. H. (1991). *Black feminist thought: Knowledge, consciousness, and the politics of empowerment*. New York: Routledge.

Collins, R. (1988). *Theoretical sociology*. San Diego, CA: Harcourt Brace Jovanovich.

Connell, R. W. (1987). *Gendered power: Society, the person and sexual politics*. Stanford, CA: Stanford University Press.

Costa, P. T., & McCrae, R. R. (1980). Still stable after all these years. In O. G. Brim (Ed.), *Life-span develpoment and behavior* (Vol. 3, pp. 65-102). New York: Academic Press.

Dannefer, D., & Uhlenberg, P. (1999). Paths of the life course: A typology. In K. W. Schaie (Ed.), *Handbook of theories of aging* (pp. 306-326). New York: Springer.

Diamond, T. (1992). *Making gray gold: narratives of nursing home care*. Chicago, IL: University of Chicago Press.

Dickinson, J., & Russell, B. (1986). *Family, economy & state: The social reproduction process under capitalism*. New York: St. Martin's Press.

Dressel, P. (1988). Gender, race and class: Beyond the feminization of poverty. *The Gerontologist, 28*(2), 177-180.

Dressel, P., Minkler, M., & Yen, I. (1999). Gender, race, class and aging: Advances and opportunities. In M. Minkler & C. L. Estes (Eds.), *Critical gerontology: Perspectives from political and moral economy* (pp. 275-295). Amityville, NY: Baywood.

Estes, C. L. (1972). *Community planning for the elderly from an organizational, political, and interactionist perspective.* Unpublished Ph.D. dissertation, University of California, San Diego, CA.

Estes, C. L. (1979). *The aging enterprise.* San Francisco, CA: Jossey-Bass.

Estes, C. L. (1981). The social construction of reality: A framework for inquiry. In P. R. Lee, N. Ramsay, & I. VSW Red (Eds.), *The nation's health* (1st ed., pp. 395-402). San Francisco, CA: Boyd & Fraser.

Estes, C. L. (1982). Austerity and aging in the United States: 1980 and beyond. *International Journal of Health Services, 12*(4), 573-584.

Estes, C. L. (1991). The new political economy of aging: Introduction and critique. In M. Minkler & C. L. Estes (Eds.), *Critical perspectives on aging: The political and moral economy of growing old* (pp. 19-36). Amityville, NY: Baywood.

Estes, C. L. (1998, July 29). *Patriarchy and the welfare state revisited: The state, gender and aging.* Paper presented at the The World Congress of Sociology, Montreal, Canada.

Estes, C. L. (1999). Critical gerontology and the new political economy of aging. In C. L. Estes (Ed.), *Critical gerontology: Perspectives from political and moral economy* (pp. 17-35). Amityville, NY: Baywood.

Estes, C. L. (2001). The political economy of aging. In G. Maddox (Ed.), *The encyclopedia of aging.* New York: Springer.

Estes, C. L. (2001). Political economy of aging: A theoretical framework. In C. L. Estes & Associates, *Social policy & aging: A critical perspective* (pp. 1-22). Thousand Oaks, CA: Sage.

Estes, C. L., & Associates. (2001). *Social policy & aging: A critical perspective.* Thousand Oaks, CA: Sage.

Estes, C. L., & Binney, E. A. (1989). The biomedicalization of aging: Dangers and dilemmas. *The Gerontologist, 29*(5), 587-596.

Estes, C. L., Binney, E. A., & Culbertson, R. A. (1992). The gerontological imagination: Social influences on the development of gerontology, 1945-present. *International Journal of Aging and Human Development, 35*(1), 49-65.

Estes, C. L., Gerard, L., Zones, J. S., & Swan, J. (1984). *Political economy, health, and aging.* Boston, MA: Little Brown.

Estes, C. L., & Linkins, K. W. (1997). Devolution and aging policy: Racing to the bottom in long-term care. *International Journal of Health Services, 27*(3), 427-442.

Estes, C. L., Linkins, K. W., & Binney, E. A. (1996). The political economy of aging. In R. Binstock & L. K. George (Eds.), *Handbook of aging and the social sciences* (pp. 346-361). San Diego, CA: Academic Press.

Estes, C. L., Swan, J. H., & Associates. (1993). *The long-term care crisis: Elders trapped in the no-care zone.* Newbury Park, CA: Sage.

Estes, C. L., & Zulman, D. (2001). *The informalization of care and old age policy.* Institute for Health & Aging, San Francisco: University of California, San Francisco.

Geiger, H. J. (1981). Health policy, social policy, and the health of the aging: Prelude to a decade of disaster. In P. R. Lee, N. Ramsay, & I. VSW Red (Eds.), *The nation's health* (1st ed., pp. 389-394). San Francisco, CA: Boyd and Fraser.

George, L. (1990). Social structure, social processes, and social psychological states. In L. K. George (Ed.), *Handbook of aging and the social sciences* (pp. 186-200). San Diego: Academic Press.

George, L. K. (1993). Sociological perspectives on life transitions. *Annual Review of Sociology, 19,* 353-373.

Giddens, A. (1984). *The construction of society: Outline of the theory of structuration.* Berkeley: University of California Press.

Giddens, A. (1991). *Modernity and self-identity: Self and society in the late modern age.* Cambridge, UK: Polity Press, in association with B. Blackwell, Oxford.

Ginn, J., & Arber, S. (1995). Only connect: Gender relations and aging. In J. Ginn (Ed.), *Connecting gender and ageing: A sociological approach.* Buckingham, UK; Philadelphia, PA: Open University Press.

Gubrium, J. F. (1967). *The myth of the golden years: A socio-environmental theory of aging.* Springfield, IL: Charles C. Thomas.

Gubrium, J. F., & Holstein, J. A. (1999). Constructionist perspectives on aging. In K. W. Schaie (Ed.), *Handbook of theories of aging* (pp. xviii, 516). New York: Springer.

Guillemard, A. M. (1980). *La vielless l'etat.* Paris: Presses Universitaires de France.

Habermas, J. (1975). *Legitimation crisis.* Boston, MA: Beacon Press.

Hall, S. (1996). Gramsci's relevance for the study of race and ethnicity. In K.-H. Clan (Ed.), *Stuart Hall: Critical dialogues in cultural studies* (pp. 411-440). London, UK; New York: Routledge.

Harrington-Meyer, M. (1990). Family status and poverty among older women: The gendered distribution of retirement income in the US. *Social Problems, 37*(4), 551-563.

Harrington-Meyer, M. (1996). Making claims as workers or wives: The distribution of Social Security Benefits. *American Sociological Review, 61*(3), 449-465.

Hartmann, H. (1981). The unhappy marriage of Marxism and feminism. In L. Sargent (Ed.), *Women and revolution: A discussion of the unhappy marriage of Marxism and feminism* (pp. 1-41). Boston: South End Press.

Hendricks, J. (1992). Generations and the generation of theory in social gerontology. *International Journal of Aging and Human Development, 35*(1), 31-47.

Hendricks, J., & Leedham, C. (1991). Dependency or empowerment? Toward a moral and political economy of aging. In C. L. Estes (Ed.), *Critical perspectives on aging: The political and moral economy of growing old* (pp. 51-66). Amityville, NY: Baywood.

Himmelweit, S. (1983). Reproduction. In T. Bottomore (Ed.), *Dictionary of Marxist thought* (pp. 417-419). Cambridge, MA: Harvard University Press.

Holstein, M. (1992). Productive aging: A feminist critique. *Journal of Aging and Social Policy, 4*(3-4), 17-34.

House, J. S., Kessler, R. C., & Herzog, A. R. (1990). Age, socioeconomic status, and health. *Milbank Memorial Fund Quarterly, 68*(3), 383-411.

Kagarlitsky, B. (1999). The challenge for the left. Reclaiming the state. In L. Panitch & C. Leys (Eds.), *Social register 1999: Global capitalism versus democracy* (pp. 294-313). New York: Monthly Review Press.

Kohli, M. (1987). Retirement and the moral economy: An historical interpretation of the German case. *The Journal of Aging Studies, 1,* 125-144.

Kohli, M. (1988). Ageing as a challenge for sociological theory. *Ageing and Society, 8,* 367-394.

Lowenthal, M. F. (1975). Psychosocial variations across the adult life course: Frontiers for research and policy. *Gerontologist, 15*(1 Pt 1), 6-12.

MacKinnon, C. A. (1989). *Toward a feminist theory of the state.* Cambridge, MA: Harvard University Press.

Manning, N. P. (1985). *Social problems and welfare ideology.* Aldershot, Hants, UK; Brookfield, VT: Gower.

Marshall, V. W. (1996). The state of theory in aging and the social sciences. In J. H. Schulz (Ed.), *Handbook of aging and the social sciences* (4th ed.). New York: Academic Press.

Marshall, V. W., & Tindale, J. A. (1978). Notes for a radical gerontology. *International Journal of Aging and Human Development, 9*(2), 163-175.

McKinlay, J. B. (1985). *Issues in the political economy of health care.* New York: Tavistock.

McMullin, J. (1995). Age and gender relations which theoretical path is best traveled. In J. Ginn (Ed.), *Connecting gender and ageing: a sociological approach.* Buckingham, UK; Philadelphia, PA: Open University Press.

Minkler, M., & Cole, T. (1999). Political and moral economy: Getting to know one another. In C. L. Estes (Ed.), *Critical gerontology: Perspectives from political and moral economy* (pp. 37-49). Amityville, NY: Baywood.

Minkler, M., & Cole, T. R. (1991). Political and moral economy: Not such strange bedfellows. In M. Minkler & C. L. Estes (Eds.), *Critical perspectives on aging: The political and moral economy of growing old* (pp. 37-49). Amityville, NY: Baywood.

Minkler, M., & Estes, C. L. (Eds.). (1991). *Critical perspectives on aging: The political and moral economy of growing old.* Amityville, NY: Baywood.

Minkler, M., & Estes, C. L. (1999). *Critical gerontology: Perspectives from political and moral economy.* Amityville, NY: Baywood.

Mitchell, J. (1966). *Women: The longest revolution.* Boston, MA: New England Free Press.

Moody, H. R. (1988a). *Abundance of life: Human development policies for an aging society.* New York: Columbia University Press.

Moody, H. R. (1988b). Toward a critical gerontology: The contributions of the humanities to theories of aging. In D. E. Deutchman (Ed.), *Emergent theories of aging* (pp. 19-40). New York: Springer. *

Moody, H. R. (1993). Overview: What is critical gerontology and why is it important. In T. R. Cole (Ed.), *Voices and visions of aging: Toward a critical gerontology* (pp. xv-xxi). New York: Springer.

Moody, H. R. (1997). *The five stages of the soul.* New York: Doubleday.

Moody, H. R. (1998). *Aging: Concepts and controversies* (2nd ed.). Thousand Oaks, CA: Pine Forge Press.

Moody, H. R. (2000). *Aging: Concepts and controversies* (3rd ed.). Thousand Oaks, CA: Pine Forge Press.

Myles, J. (1984). *Old age in the welfare state: The political economy of public pensions.* Boston, MA: Little, Brown.

Neugarten, B. L. (1964). *Personality in middle and late life: Empirical studies.* New York: Atherton Press.

Neugarten, B. L., Havighurst, R. J., & Tobin, S. S. (1968). Personality and patterns of aging. In B. L. Neugarten (Ed.), *Middle age and aging: A reader in social psychology.* Chicago: University of Chicago Press.

O'Connor, J. (1973). *The fiscal crisis of the state.* New York: St. Martin's Press.

O'Connor, J. S. (1993). Gender, class, citizenship in the comparative analysis of welfare state regimes. *British Journal of Sociology, 44,* 501-518.

O'Connor, J. S., Orloff, A. S., & Shaver, S. (1999). *States, markets, families: Gender, liberalism and social policy in Australia, Canada, Great Britain and the United States.* Cambridge, UK: Cambridge University Press.

Offe, C., & Keane, J. (1984). *Contradictions of the welfare state.* Cambridge, MA: MIT Press.

Orloff, A. S. (1993). Gender and the social rights of citizenship: The comparative analysis of gender relations and welfare states. *American Sociological Review, 58*(3), 303-329.

Parenti, M. (1999). Reflections on the politics of culture. *Monthly Review—An Independent Socialist Magazine, 50*(9), 11-18.

Parsons, T. (1951). *The social system.* Glencoe, IL: Free Press.

Pascall, G. (1986). *Social policy: A feminist analysis.* London; New York: Tavistock.

Phillipson, C. (1982). *Capitalism and the construction of old age.* London, UK: Macmillan.

Phillipson, C. (1998). *Reconstructing old age: New agendas in social theory and practice.* London, UK; Thousand Oaks, CA: Sage.

Phillipson, C. (1999). The social construction of retirement. In C. L. Estes (Ed.), *Critical gerontology: Perspectives from political and moral economy* (pp. 315-325). Amityville, NY: Baywood.

Quadagno, J., & Reid, J. (1999). The political economy perspective in aging. In K. W. Schaie (Ed.), *Handbook of theories of aging* (pp. 344-358). New York: Springer.

Quadagno, J. S. (1988). *The transformation of old age security: Class and politics in the American welfare state.* Chicago, NY: University of Chicago Press.

Rice, T. H. (1998). *The economics of health reconsidered.* Chicago: Health Administration Press.

Riley, M. W. (1998). Successful aging. *Gerontologist, 38*(2), 151.

Riley, M. W., Foner, A., & Riley, J. W., Jr. (1999). The aging and society paradigm. In K. W. Schaie (Ed.), *Handbook of theories of aging* (pp. xviii, 516). New York: Springer.

Riley, M. W., Johnson, M., & Foner, A. (1972). A sociology of age stratification. In M. W. Riley, A. Foner, M. E. Moore, B. Hess, & B. K. Roth (Eds.), *Aging and society* (Vol. 3). New York: Basic.

Riley, M. W., & Riley, J. W. (1994a). Age integration and the lives of older people. *Gerontologist, 34*(1), 110-115.

Riley, M. W., & Riley, J. W. (1994b). Structural lag: past and future. In A. Foner (Ed.), *Age and structural lag: Society's failure to provide meaningful opportunities in work, family, and leisure* (pp. 15-36). New York: Wiley.

Robert, S. A. (1999). Socioeconomic position and health: The independent contribution of community socioeconomic context. *Annual Review of Sociology, 25,* 489-516.

Robertson, A. (1999). Beyond apocalyptic demography: Toward a moral economy of interdependence. In C. L. Estes (Ed.), *Critical gerontology: Perspectives from political and moral economy* (pp. 75-90). Amityville, NY: Baywood.

Rose, A. M. (1967). *The power structure: Political process in American society.* London, UK: Oxford University Press.

Rowe, J. W., & Kahn, R. L. (1987). Human aging: Usual and successful. *Science, 237*(4811), 143-149.

Rowe, J. W., & Kahn, R. L. (1997). Successful aging. *Gerontologist, 37*(4), 433-440.

Rowe, J. W., & Kahn, R. L. (1998). *Successful aging.* New York: Pantheon Books.

Rubin, G. (1975). The traffic in women. In R. Reiter (Ed.), *Toward an anthropology of women* (pp. 157-210). New York: Monthly Review Press.

Sardar, Z., & Van Loon, B. (1997). *Introducing cultural studies.* New York: Totem Books.

Sassoon, A. S. (1987). *Gramsci's politics* (2nd ed.). London, UK: Hutchinson.

Schattschneider, E. E. (1960). *The semisovereign people: A realist's view of democracy in America.* New York: Holt, Rinehart and Winston.

Stone, A., & Harpham, E. J. (1982). *The political economy of public policy.* Beverly Hills, CA: Sage.

Therborn, G. (1980). *The ideology of power and the power of ideology.* London, UK; New York: NLB; distributed in the United States by Schocken Books.

Thompson, E. P. (1963). *The making of the English working class.* New York: Vintage.

Thompson, K. (1986). *Beliefs and ideology.* Chichester, West Sussex, London, UK; New York: Ellis Horwood; Tavistock.

Turner, B. (1999). *Classical sociology.* London: Sage.

Twine, F. (1994). *Citizenship and social rights: The interdependence of self and society.* London, Sage.

Walby, S. (1986). *Patriarchy at work: Patriarchal and capitalist relations in employment.* Minneapolis: University of Minnesota Press.

Walker, A. (1981). Towards a political economy of old age. *Ageing and Society, 1*(1), 73-94.

Walker, A. (1984). *Social planning: A strategy for social welfare.* Oxford: B. Blackwell.

Walker, A. (1999). Public policy and theories of aging: Constructing and reconstructing old age. In K. Schaie (Ed.), *Handbook of theories of aging* (pp. 361-378). New York: Springer.

## CONCLUSION

# Where is Theory Headed?

*Simon Biggs, Jon Hendricks,*
*and Ariela Lowenstein*

### NEEDING THEORY

Why, then, do we need theory? By this point readers have drawn their own conclusions. In the introduction, we argued that in gerontology, theory should help us comprehend why we do what we do and make us aware of commonsense assumptions and previously unforeseen implications of contemporary thinking about later life. Theory should:

- Afford a critical awareness of the state of gerontological knowledge. Current thinking should not, in other words simply be accepted as factual or universally true, it should be interrogated to reveal its assumed realities and the limitations to the picture it paints of the world. Links may possibly be made between previously unconnected observations, and by developing alternative perspectives and new syntheses, expand debate.
- Address key issues and contradictions surrounding adult aging. Unfortunately, it is not a simple process to assume that a theoretical endeavor is grounded in its subject matter. Writers often draw, to great effect, on developments in other disciplines or subject matter in order to expand understanding in gerontology. The question is how far it is possible to do this and still be centered on debates relevant to contemporary aging. Theory, in gerontology, should hold the promise of an age-sensitized perspective, rooted in the experience of adult aging.
- Have the power to project gerontological understanding forward, by asking new questions or addressing existing questions in a novel way. Theory, and in particular theory that maintains a critical register, should generate new ways of seeing the world and thereby work toward a series of agendas that link

theoretical development to change in the wider world. In a subject such as gerontology, where so much data is problem-driven and conclusions drawn that will affect the lived experience of older people themselves, the development of ideas should also draw out implications for research, policy, and practice.

## IS AGE INCLUSIVE ENOUGH?

A striking observation that arises as one looks back at the current volume is that contemporary thinking in gerontology draws heavily on the ideas and conceptual frameworks generated from within neighboring disciplines. This raises a key question for gerontology as it enters the twenty-first century. Is age itself inclusive enough to provide sound conceptual grounding? Rather than reflect the dominant techniques and trajectories of other disciplines can the study of aging create its own understandings? The stirrings of this possibility can be seen in the contributions contained here and takes a variety of forms. *First,* it may be possible to reincorporate age into existing theory, to reflexively engage with other disciplines so as to highlight their strengths, weaknesses and habits of thought. The child-centered perspective of much of life-course theorizing or the intolerance of limitation found in post-modern thinking would be two examples of how wider theory might usefully profit from a more substantial engagement with gerontological ideas. The point is that age is more often treated in an atheoretical manner, and beyond gerontology per se is seldom given the consideration it deserves in light of its salience in the life course. *Second,* it may be possible to critically assess existing decision taking on the basis of age. Often concepts, frameworks, and judgments are accepted without questioning whether they themselves contain the assumptive reality of one age over another. This occurs in the domain of ideas as well as in that of aging policy and the work of helping professionals. Some commentators have suggested that focusing upon age as an explanatory factor also has the possibility of being self-serving. At the same time, it can be thought of as a kind of age imperialism whereby the preconceptions and desires of one age-group come to dominate those of another. Who is speaking and who is spoken of in the dominant discourse raises the question of age and voice that can radically alter our perceptions of power and the world in much the same way as gender has already done. *Third,* it is possible that conceptual frameworks and ideas will emerge from the study of aging in and of itself and have broader applicability. If gerontology is to come of age, its practiners should be able to sketch a new understanding of the human condition arising from the experience of adult aging. Age, then, theorized in ways that are embedded in the characteristic and on occasion unique properties and questions generated by later life. Age is a key element in defining social existence and its study should, in time, be able to develop its own original perspectives. We must also be mindful, however, that the meaning of age changes by historical moment and geographical place. The tension between the social contingency of aging and processes that appear to be inherent to it will be a continuing challenge to theoretical development of this field.

## PRACTICAL IMPLICATIONS

Choosing one theoretical perspective over another is not simply a matter of personal preference. An implication of thinking about the world of adult aging in a particular way is that, this itself begins to create a reality. In public policy, for example, whether it is believed that old age is a period of inevitable decline, a period of (almost) inexhaustible social productivity, or of personal spiritual rebirth will lead to diverse public spending plans and the promotion of different social norms. If we are young people caught in aging bodies that are malleable given the right degree of bio-medical progress, this has very different policy and research implications to the view that aging brings maturity and new potentials which are rarely able to be expressed because of social ageism.

Further, the implicit templates we carry around with us about aging will vary depending upon our own age and experience. It is a moot point whether plans for an aging population should best reflect what decision-makers in midlife think they would like in later life, or what contemporary older people say that they want for future generations of older people. Theory should help us engage with such problems at a personal level, as well as at a professional level. Theories of aging influence the narratives of "aging well" that are available as part of social discourse. The attractiveness of these accounts also varies depending upon the age of the person hearing it. Theory is crucial if we are to untangle such questions.

A key issue emerging from the contributions to this book is that the world is becoming a much more uncertain place in which to grow old. Whatever models used to be available and inform anticipated scripts are waning in the face of dynamic global change. The reasons for this are varied and address different facets of macro and micro-analysis. Pressures arising from globalization, increased inequality, competing definitions of identity and successful aging are but a few of the contributory factors. If in the twentieth century aging was over determined and the role of theory was often to channel our ideas of adult aging increasing the likelihood of predictability and external control, the problems of the new millennium appear to reflect a surfeit of fluidity and uncertainty. Good theory should be capable of handling, even anticipating complexity arising from fluid situations, while providing a framework in service of a effective recognition of key issues. It therefore contains a balance between fluidity and fixity that may be essential if contemporary patterns of aging are to be more fully understood. It moves us beyond the what, to ask the how, the who, and the why. We hope that this book reflects the positive pull of multidisciplinarity, the tensions arising from encountering boundaries and diversity, and the need to work toward a coherent understanding of adult aging. It is a contribution to a field that continues to grow and will become increasingly important as it comes of age.

# Contributors

VERN BENGTSON, PhD, holds the AARP/University Chair in Gerontology and is Professor of Sociology at the University of Southern California, Los Angeles, CA 90089-0191, U.S.A., email address: bengtson@rcf.usc.edu

SIMON BIGGS, PhD, is Professor of Social Gerontology at the School of Social Relations, Centre for Social Gerontology, Keele University, Keele, Staffordshire, ST5 5BG, email address: spa04@keele.ac.uk

CHRISTINA BODE is a Post-doctoral Researcher at the University of Utrecht, Department of Health, The Netherlands, email address: c.bode@fss.uu.nl

TONI CALASANTI, PhD, is an Associate Professor of Sociology at Virginia Tech (Blacksburg, Virginia, U.S.A.), email address: toni@vt.edu

FREYA DITTMANN-KOHLI is Professor and Director of Psycho-gerontology at the University of Nijmegen, Department of Psychogerontology, P.O. Box 9104, 6500HE Nijmegen, The Netherlands, email address: dittman@psych.kun.nl

CARROLL L. ESTES, PhD, is Professor of Sociology, Founding and Former Director, Institute for Health and Aging, University of California, San Francisco, Laurel Heights Campus, 3333 California Street, Suite 340, San Francisco, CA 94118, email address: cestes@itsa.ucsf.edu

JON HENDRICKS, PhD, is Dean, University Honors College, and Professor of Sociology, Oregon State University, U.S.A., email address: Hendricj@ucs.orst.edu

STEPHEN KATZ, PhD, is Associate Professor of Sociology at Trent University in Peterborough, Ontario, Canada, email address: SKatz@Trentu.ca

EUGINE LITWAK, PhD, is Professor of Sociology in the Department of Sociology and Professor of Sociomedical Sciences at Columbia University, email address: ell2@columbia.edu

ARIELA LOWENSTEIN is Professor and Head of the Department of Aging Studies—Master in Gerontology, and the Center for Research and Study of Aging at the Faculty of Welfare and Health Studies, the University of Haifa, Israel, email address: ariela@research.haifa.ac.il

CHRIS PHILLIPSON, PhD, is Professor of Applied Social Studies and Social Gerontology, School of Social Relations, Centre for Social Gerontology, Keele University, Keele, Staffordshire, ST5 5BG, email address: spa05@keele.ac.uk

RUTH RAY, PhD, is Professor in the Department of English and Faculty Associate in Gerontology, Wayne State University in Detroit, MI, email address: ab0128@wayne.edu

MERRIL SILVERSTEIN, PhD, is Associate Professor of Gerontology and Sociology at the Andrus Gerontology Center of the University of Southern California, Los Angeles, CA 90089-0191, U.S.A., email address: merrils@usc.edu

EMANNUELLE TULLE, Lecturer in Sociology, Division of Sociology and Social Policy, Glasgow Caledonian University, Glasgow, Scotland, email address: E.Tulle@gcal.ac.uk

HANS-JOACHIM VON KONDRATOWITZ, PhD, is Senior Scientific Researcher at the German Center of Aging (DZA), Manfred Von Richthofen, Strasse 2, 12101 Berlin, Germany, email address: kondrato@dza.de

GERBEN J. WESTERHOF is Senior Lecturer at the University of Nijmegen, Department of Psychogerontology, PO Box 9104, 6500HE Nijmegen, The Netherlands, email address: westerhof@psych.kun.nl

# Index

Acceleration, societal, 50–51
Accompanying and praxeology of social
    constructionist agenda, 60
Achenbaum, W. A., 21, 26
Acker, Joan, 227
Activity theory, 202, 221, 223–224
Actor and context, self/identity and
    interplay of, 65, 77
    *See also* Identity and structured
    inequalities, theory gap between
    experienced
Adaptation processes, 127
Affectual solidarity and intergenerational
    solidarity paradigm, 188
Affinity and intergenerational family
    relations, 190
"After the Fall: New Directions in Critical
    Culture Theory," 15–16
*Ageing Enterprise, The,* 2
Ageism, 21, 145, 175, 206
    *See also* Age relations, theorizing
Agency and self/identity, 64, 65
Age relations, theorizing
    defining terms, 203
    dependence, 214–215
    exploring age relations: centering on
    the old, 209
    fluid and group membership shifts over
    time, age is, 207
    gender relations/identity, 211–215
    identifying age groups, 208
    location, old age as a social, 209–211

[Age relations, theorizing]
    middle-age experiences, limited value
    of theories based on, 199–200
    oppression, a relation of privilege and,
    204–206
    overview, 9, 199–200
    power relation in its own right, old age
    as a, 203–204
    power relations, are age relations the
    same as other, 205–207
    power relations, intersecting, 211–212
    sexuality and gender, 212–213
    successful aging, 200–203
    summary/conclusions, 215–216
Age stratification and the aging society
    paradigm, 223
*Aging and Society Paradigm* (Riley), 223
*Aging Enterprise* (Estes), 234
Aging paradox
    meaning construction, 128–130,
    134–136
    methodological implications, 139
    overview, 9, 127–128
    physical self, 131–132
    positive aspects of aging, 129–130
    practice, implications for, 139–140
    process of meaning construction,
    134–136
    psychological self, 131
    reconsidering the, 136–137
    satisfaction with life and meanings of
    life, 133–134

[Aging paradox]
  self-esteem and meanings of self,
    130–133
  social self, 132
  stability in experience of aging/self/life,
    127, 136
  theoretical implications, 137–138
Appearances and social masking, surface,
    149
Asian societies, changes in filial piety in,
    193
Associational solidarity and
    intergenerational solidarity
    paradigm, 188
Athletes, the body and Masters, 97–103
Austin, John, 21
Authentic words, 38
Authoritarian managerial styles, 213–214
Authority and theorizing age relations,
    206
Autonomization, the complexity of
    knowledge, 58–59
Autonomy, 129, 132, 206
*Averting the Old Age Crisis,* 169


Baudrillard, Jean, 147–150
Beck, Ulrich, 164
Behavioral factors involved with
    aging/health, increasing recognition
    of, 221–222
Benevolent mission practice, avoiding
    relegating critical status to, 20
Bengtson, Vern, 9
Biggs, Simon, 26
Biographical/narrative perspectives
    drawing upon metaphysical humanist
    concepts, 19, 21
Birren, James, 2
Bode, Christina, 9
Bodies, toward a sociology of old
  accessing the sensate body, 96–97
  age relations, theorizing, 206, 207
  aging paradox, 131–132
  capital, the body as, 101–103
  corporeality and later life, 93–97
  decline, age-related, 129

[Bodies, toward a sociology of old]
  deploying the body, 97–103
  disciplining the body, 98
  injuries, 99–100
  mapping the discourse of old age,
    94–95
  overview, 8–9, 91–92
  realization of age, 100
  resisting age, 101
  running and Masters athletes, 97–103
  sociology, the bodies of, 92–93
  successful aging, 200–203
  summary/conclusions, 103
  widening the discursive grid, 95–96
Bonding and creating meaning,
    self-boundary, 75–76
Bourdieu, Pierre, 16, 21–22
Braudel, Fernand, 47
Browne, Collette, 36
Butler, Judith, 150–151
Butler, Robert N., 21


Calasanti, Toni, 9, 36
Capital, dimensions of human/social,
    67–70
Capital, the body as, 101–103
Capitalism, disorganized, 165–166
  *See also* Globalization and
    reconstruction of age
Capitalism, turbo-, 167–168
Capital mobility and globalization, 174
"Case for a Critical Gerontology, The"
    (Phillipson & Walker), 18
Cassell, John, 222
Chafetz, Janet S., 226
"Challenge of Critical Gerontology, The:
    The Problem of Social Constitution"
    (Baars), 25
Change in old age, meaning and, 78–80
Child's surroundings and social
    constructionism, 47
China, 193
Choice making and criticisms of social
    constructionism, 52
Cohen, Lawrence, 20
Cole, Thomas R., 21, 37

Collins, Patricia H., 233
Communist power, fall of Soviet, 15
Competence and theorizing age relations, 206
Conflict theories, 225
Congo/Zaire, 136
Consensual solidarity and intergenerational solidarity paradigm, 188
Consultations and praxeology of social constructionist agenda, 60
Consumer, the gray, 146–147, 149, 202
Context protocols and praxeology of social constructionist agenda, 60
Contextual-dialectical process, 67
Continuity theory, 221
Contrasting and praxeology of social constructionist agenda, 60
Corporations, multi-national, 168, 174, 175
   See also Globalization and reconstruction of age
Counterreading and praxeology of social constructionist agenda, 60
Critical Condition (Gubar), 35
Critical gerontological theory
"After the Fall: New Directions in Critical Culture Theory," 15–16
   approaches to, numerous, 15
   benevolent mission practice, avoiding relegating critical status to, 20
   biographical/narrative perspectives drawing upon metaphysical humanist concepts, 19
   data-rich but theory poor, 17, 33–34
   defining terms, 34
   "Gerschenkron Effect, The," 22–23
   humanistic path as supplement to political economy perspectives, 19
   inequalities, social, 18–19
   intellectual fieldwork and the life of ideas, 20–22
   limits to critical theory, 34
   metaphorical development and terminology, 19
   multidisciplinarity, alternatives to, 16–17

["After the Fall: New Directions in Critical Culture Theory"]
   nomadic qualities, 23–26
   overview, 8
   policy toward aging, social/economic, 223–230
   political economy of aging, 17–18
   soul-less/mind-less/theory-less gerontology, countering danger of, 27
   structural problems, society's widespread, 18–19
   summary/conclusions, 26–27
   See also Globalization and reconstruction of age; Perils/possibilities of theory within gerontology; Policy toward aging, social/economic; individual subject headings
Critical Gerontology: Perspectives from Political and Moral Economy (Minkler), 18, 19
Critical Perspectives on Aging: The Political and Moral Economy of Growing Old, 19, 25
Culture, impact of
   aging paradox, 135–136
   cultural studies perspective, 46, 47, 228–229
   family forms, cultural beliefs/ideologies guiding, 183
   humanistic gerontology, 233–234
   lag, cultural, 19
   performance, identity as, 150
   policy toward aging, social/economic, 228–229
   redefining later life, cultural processes, 19
   self/identity/agency as culturally relative constructs, 64
   See also Social constructionism for social gerontology

Data-rich but theory poor, gerontology as, 17, 33–34
Deacon, Bob, 168–169

Debt repayments, globalization and, 168, 174

Decline, age-related, 129

Decline-of-family proponents, 189

Deleuze, Gilles, 16

Denmark, 118–119

Dependence/gender and theorizing age relations, 214–215

Deregulation and globalization, 170, 174

Detached type of intergenerational family relations, 190

Developing countries, 168, 181, 193

Disaggregated, body as a sociological concept needs to be, 92

Discourse, theory as, 34–35

Discourse analysis and social constructionism, 47–48, 52–53, 59–60

Disengagement theory, 17, 221, 223–224

Ditmann-Kohi, Freya, 9

Dualism and aging concepts, 145–147

Dubois, W.E.B., 21

Education and an emancipatory pedagogy, 39–43

Elaboration and praxeology of social constructionist agenda, 60

Emancipatory agenda, 37–43

*Emergent Theories of Aging* (Birren & Bengtson), 3, 17

Emptiness, social masking and personal, 149

Enfeeblement, body understood through a framework of, 95

Entrepreneurialism, 214

Environmental factors involved with aging/health, increasing recognition of, 221–222

Environmental press, 79

Epistemological radicalism of social constructionism, skepticism voiced at, 51–53

Estes, Carroll, 2, 9–10, 17, 18, 168

Ethnic inequalities, critical gerontological theory underscoring, 18, 213–214

Ethnomethodological approach, 55

European Convention on Human Rights, 175

Exercise and the body, 95–103

Extended family, 183, 187–188

Families, modernization and changes faced by aging
conflict in modern family, solidarity and, 189–191
cultural beliefs/ideologies guiding family forms, 183
extended family, 183, 187–188
filial obligation toward the elderly, 183
government systems, shifting balance between informal groups and formal, 181–182
modernization theory, 182
new family forms, 181
nuclear over the extended household, rise in prominence of the, 183
overview, 9
solidarity paradigm, intergenerational, 183, 188–191
task-specific theory, 183–188
theoretical integration, 191–194
theoretical principles guiding our understanding of, 182
Western paradigm of elder care and support, 193–194

Family, theoretical perspectives on aging and the
familial level of family identity, 116–118
family development theory, 107–108
identity: we element of families, 112–121
individual level of family identity, 114–116
intersecting individual-family circles, 115–116
life course perspectives, 108–112
overview, 9, 107
social-familial resources and the experience of aging, 74–75
societal level of family identity, 118–119

[Family, theoretical perspectives on aging and the]
   testing the family-identity framework, 119–121
   transformed, multiple facets of family life have been, 105–106
*Fatal Strategies* (Baudrillard), 149
Featherstone, Mike, 19
Feiffer, Jules, 33
Felt identity, 114
Feminist criticism as cautionary tale, 35–36
   *See also* Perils/possibilities of theory within gerontology
Feminist theories constituting critical approach to social policy, 226–227, 232–233
Fertility and public/private trade-off for elder care, 193
Fiduciary resources and the experience of aging, 70, 71–73
Field theory, 79
Fieldwork, intellectual/philosophical, 20–22
Filial obligation toward the elderly, 182, 183, 193
Fragmented body of work on aging, 220
Frankfurt School, 237
Freire, Paulo, 38
*French Modern: Norms and Forms of the Social Environment* (Rainbow), 22
Functional exchange and intergenerational family relations, 190
Functional solidarity and intergenerational solidarity paradigm, 188

Gee, James P., 34–35
Gender
   age relations, theorizing, 210, 211–215
   bodies, toward a sociology of old, 95
   feminist theories, 35–36, 226–227, 232–233
   globalization, 168
   inequalities, 18

[Gender]
   managerial styles, 213–214
   performances, culturally enforced, 150
   Social Security, 230
General Agreement on Trade in Services (GATS), 170
German Aging Survey, 134–135, 140
   *See also* Aging paradox
Germany, 54, 135, 136
   *See also* Social constructionism for social gerontology
Gerontology. *See* Critical gerontological theory; Theory in gerontology, the need for; *individual subject headings*
Gerotranscendence, 7, 146
"Gerschenkron Effect, The," 22–23
Gibson, Rose, 36
Giddens, Anthony, 164
Glascock, Anthony, 50
Globalization and reconstruction of age
   family, new era of the aging, 105
   feminist theory of social policy and aging, 232
   individualization of risks attached to the life course, 174, 176
   institutionalizing old age, 164–167
   international governmental organizations, 168–171
   overview, 9, 163–164
   respect for images/institutions associated with supporting older people, 165
   responsibility, emergence of new politics of global social, 174–175
   runaway world, older people maintaining a sense of security/identity in a, 175–176
   summary/conclusions, 177
   supranational organizations, 168–171
   theory, the need for social, 171–177
   transnational networks and relations, 167–171
   uncertainties that surround old age, 176
Government systems, shifting balance between informal groups and formal, 181–182

[Government systems, shifting balance
between informal groups and formal]
*See also* Families, modernization
and changes faced by aging;
Globalization and reconstruction
of age
Gramsci, Antonio, 226
Grandmothers and theorizing age
relations, 215
Grey market, consuming in the, 146–147,
149, 202
*Growing Old: The Process of
Disengagement* (Cumming &
Henry), 6
Guattari, Félix, 16

Habermas, Jurgen, 18
Hall, G. S., 21
*Handbook of Theories of Aging* (Bengtson
& Schaie), 3
Health issues
critical gerontological theory, 223–224
feminist theory of social policy and
aging, 233
globalization, 169–171
health maintenance organizations, 27
healthy side of aging, emphasis put on,
50
policy toward aging, social/economic,
236
privatization of health care, 168, 170
public/private trade-off for elder care,
193
social/behavioral/environmental factors
involved with health, increasing
recognition of, 221–222
socioeconomic status and health
outcomes, 70
Western paradigm of elder care and
support, 193–194
Health maintenance organizations
(HMOs), 27
Held, David, 171
Henderson, Lawrence J., 21
Hendricks, Jon, 8
Hepworth, Mike, 19

History and sociology of (social) sciences,
47
History as part of the familial identity,
118
Homogeneity among older actors,
assumptions of, 63–64
Hooks, Bell, 40
Human capital, 68
Humanistic gerontology, 19, 233–234
Humanistic *vs.* humanitarian pedagogy,
39

Identity, negotiating aging
age relations, theorizing, 213–214
Baudrillard and social masking/fluid
aging, 147–150
Butler and aging/identity/performance,
150–151
dualism and aging concepts, 145–147
family, we element of families,
112–121
identity theory, 113
masquerade and aging, 151–155
overview, 9
self, age/identity theorizing creating
meeting point for social/personal
construals of, 146
summary/conclusions, 155–158
theory, critical state of aging, 145–147
Identity and structured inequalities, theory
gap between experienced
agency/roles/social context, 64–67
capital, dimensions of human/social,
67–70
change in old age, meaning and, 78–80
meaning, creating, 75–78
memory-endowed sequencing, sense of
self anchored in, 65
overview, 8
personal resources and the experiencing
of, 71–75
roles, social, 66–67
self, shaping the, 63–64, 78
self and identity, four themes
characterizing contemporary
accounts of, 65

[Identity and structured inequalities, theory gap between experienced]
self-boundary bonding and creating meaning, 75–76
self-referential interpretation and creating meaning, 76–78
summary/conclusions, 80–81
*See also* Age relations, theorizing
Ideology and social/economic policy toward aging, 229–230
Images and theorizing age relations, 210
Improvisational, perception of life course as increasingly, 6–7
Individual and the social, aging explained through tension between the, 5–6
Individual focused on as primary unit of analysis, 220–221
Individualism, 64
Individualization of risks attached to the life course, 174, 176
Inequalities, critical gerontological theory underscoring, 18–19, 205–207
*See also* Age relations, theorizing; Identity and structured inequalities, theory gap between experienced
Infirm side of aging, pressure put on, 50
Informalism, 214
Inhelder, B., 47
Injuries, running, 99–100
Institutionalizing old age, 164–167
Intellectual fieldwork and the life of ideas, 20–22
Interactionist approach, 47–48
Intergenerational conflict and globalization, 170–171
Intergenerational relations and social/economic policy, 139
Intergenerational solidarity paradigm, 182
*See also* Families, modernization and changes faced by aging
International governmental organizations (IGOs), 168–171, 174, 175
International Labour Organisation (ILO), 169
International Monetary Fund (IMF), 168, 175

Interpersonal relationships and the experience of aging, 74–75
Intimate-but-distant type of intergenerational family relations, 190

James, William, 21
Japan, 193
Joachim, Hans, 8
*Journal of Aging and Identity,* 18
*Journal of Aging Studies, The,* 18, 25, 36
*Journal of Critical Gerontology,* 36
*Journal of Women and Aging,* 18, 36
Jungian psychology, 154

Kafka, Franz, 24
Katz, Stephen, 8, 48
Kinship systems, 191
*See also* Families, modernization and changes faced by aging
Knowledge, utilization of social science, 47, 53–57
Knowledge autonomization, the complexity of, 58–59
Korea, 193
Kotarbinski, Tadeusz, 59

Labor
age relations, theorizing, 202, 206–207, 211–212
inequalities of status/money, 206–207
successful aging, 202
task-specific theory, 184–185, 194
Languages, distinction between major and minor, 24–25
Leaders, making of gerontological theory from lives of, 21
Less developed countries, 168, 181, 193
*Liberated Man, The* (Farrell), 33
Life course perspectives, 108–112, 149–150, 222
Life cycle theory, 221

Lifespan theories, 127
Litwak, Eugene, 9
Location, old age as a social, 209–211
Loneliness, 129
Lowenstein, Ariela, 9
Lyotard, Francois, 23

MacKinnon, Catherine, 227
Macro *vs.* micro perspectives, 220
*Making PCR: The Story of Biotechnology*
    (Rainbow), 22
Malleability of biological/behavioral
    phenomena, 221
Managerial styles, gender identities and,
    213–214
Manufacturing industry and disorganized
    capitalism, 165–166
Marginalization of critical thought, 26
Marshall, Barbara, 22
Marshall, Victor, 2, 17, 26
Marxism, 15–18, 227, 233
Masculine discourses/practices that
    underlie managerial styles, 214
Masquerade and aging, 151–155
    *See also* Identity, negotiating aging
Mayo, Elton, 21
Meaning(s)
    aging paradox and meaning
        construction, 128–130, 134–136
    changes in old age, 78–80
    examination of age-based, 210–211
    how do people create, 75–78
Medicare, 221
Memory-endowed sequencing, sense of
    self anchored in, 65
Metalanguage, 34–35
Metaphorical development and
    terminology, 19
Metchnikoff, Elie, 21
"Metropolis and Mental Life, The"
    (Simmel), 21
Micro *vs.* macro perspectives, 220
Middle-age experiences, limited value of
    theories based on, 199–200
    *See also* Age relations, theorizing
Minkler, Meredith, 17

Modernity and postmodernity, debates
    over, 6–7
    *See also* Families, modernization and
    changes faced by aging; Identity,
    negotiating aging
Modified-extended family, 187–188
Money and experience of aging, 70,
    71–73
Monocratic bureaucracy and task-specific
    theory, 184
Moody, Harry R., 17, 18, 36
Moral discourse surrounding successful
    aging, 201
Moral economy and humanistic
    gerontology, 233–234
Moral economy underpinning an extended
    life course, 164–165
Motivation and task-specific theory,
    185–186
Multidisciplinarity, 4–5, 16–17, 60
Myles, John, 17

National societies, growing sense of
    interconnectedness among, 59
    *See also* Globalization and
    reconstruction of age
Neoliberalism, 232
Netherlands, 135, 136
Neugarten, Bernice, 21
Nomadic qualities of critical
    gerontological theory, 22–26
Normative solidarity and
    intergenerational solidarity
    paradigm, 188
Norway, 118–119
Nuclear over the extended household, rise
    in prominence of the, 183
Nudity, psychological, 149

Obligatory type of intergenerational
    family relations, 190
Ogburn, William F., 19
Opportunity structure and
    intergenerational family relations,
    190

Oppression/privilege and theorizing age relations, 204–207
Organization for Economic Cooperation and Development (OECD), 171

Paradox of aging. *See* Aging paradox
Parsons, Talcott, 21
Pensions, 164, 169, 172, 187
Perception, meaning making and reflexive self-referential, 76–79
Performance as vehicle for establishing personal identity, 150–151
Perils/possibilities of theory within gerontology
    critical gerontology, the role of, 36–38
    discourse, theory as, 34–35
    emancipatory pedagogy, toward an, 38–43
    Feiffer, Jules, 33
    feminist criticism as cautionary tale, 35–36
    overview, 8
    theory and critical theory, distinguishing between, 33–34
Personal identity, 114
Personal resource model, 64, 71–75, 79–80
    *See also* Identity and structured inequalities, theory gap between experienced
Phenomenology and its different research strategies, 46, 137
Phillipson, Chris, 9, 17
Philosophical fieldwork, 21–22
Physical capital, older bodies as, 101–103
    *See also* Bodies, toward a sociology of old
Physical self and the aging paradox, 131–132
Piaget, J., 47
Policy toward aging, social/economic age relations, theorizing, 207
    age stratification and the aging society paradigm, 223
    anti-ageist rhetoric, 146

[Policy toward aging, social/economic age relations, theorizing]
    concluding notes on social theory and research, 235–237
    conflict theories, 225
    critical perspectives/theory, 223–230
    cultural studies, 228–229
    feminist theories, 226–227, 232–233
    globalization, 168–172, 174–175
    health services research, 236
    ideology, 229–230
    individualization of risks attached to the life course, 174
    intergenerational relations, 139
    life course, theories of the, 222
    moral economy and humanistic gerontology, 233–234
    multi-level analytical framework, 234–235
    new politics of global social responsibility, 174–175
    overview, 9–10, 219–220
    political economy of aging, 231–232
    prevailing gerontological theories and their limitations, 220–224
    supranational organizations, 168–171
    values (societal) and support of society's dependent members, 193
    *See also* Families, modernization and changes faced by aging
Political economy of aging, 17–18, 228, 231–232, 234
Positive aspects of aging, 129–130
    *See also* Aging paradox
Postmodernity, debate over, 6–7
    *See also* Families, modernization and changes faced by aging; Identity, negotiating aging
*Postmodernity and its Discontents* (Bauman), 176
Power relations based on age, 199, 203–204
    *See also* Age relations, theorizing
Praxeology of the social constructionist agenda, toward a, 59–60
Praxis as theory-in-action, 38
*Prison Notebooks* (Gramsci), 20

Privatization, 170
Productivity of older individuals and positive image of aging, 221
Psychological centrality, 113
Psychological-physiological resources and the experience of aging, 73–74
Psychological professionals and aging paradox, 139–140
Psychological self and the aging paradox, 131

Qualley, Donna, 42

Race
  age relations, theorizing, 208, 210–212
  feminist theory of social policy and aging, 233
  health outcomes, institutional racism producing negative, 222
  inequalities, critical gerontological theory underscoring racial, 18
Rainbow, Paul, 22
Ray, Ruth, 8
Reagan, Ronald, 206
Reality (outer) and criticisms of social constructionism, 51–52
Reconstructing Old Age (Phillipson), 19
Regional inequalities, critical gerontological theory underscoring, 18
Representation, social, 46
Representations detached from a base in material reality, 148
Representations of old age, gerontological knowledge and, 48–51
Research affiliated with government to responsibilize a new senior citizenry, 26–27
Resources and the experiencing of aging, personal, 71–75
Respect, 129, 165, 167
Retirement, 164, 165, 167, 169, 171, 221
Reversibility of biological/behavioral phenomena, 221
Rhetoric and theorizing age relations, 210

Rights becoming more fragmented/individualized, late modernity and, 174
Rituals and family identity, 117
Riviere, Joan, 153
Roles, family, 116
Roles and self/identity, social, 66–67, 77
  See also Identity and structured inequalities, theory gap between experienced
Routines and family identity, 117–118
Running (exercise) and the body, 95–103

Satisfaction with life, aging paradox and, 133–134
Science, nomad, 23–26
Science knowledge, utilization of social, 47, 53–57
SELE-instrument, 128
Self as culturally relative construct, 64
  See also Identity listings
Self-esteem/meanings of self and the aging paradox, 130–133
Self-structure dialectic, 166
Senescence: The Last Half Life (Hall), 26
Sexuality, 150, 212–213
Shock, Nathan, 21
Silverstein, Merril, 9
Simmel, George, 21
Simmons, Leo, 50
Situationalism, 67
Sociable type of intergenerational family relations, 190
Social capital, 68–70
Social causation hypothesis, 70
Social constructionism for social gerontology
  autonomization, the complexity of knowledge, 58–59
  body, the, 92–93
  child's surroundings, 47
  criticisms, 51–53
  cultural studies approach, 47
  discourse analysis, 47–48
  heritage of different approaches, 45–48

[Social constructionism for social gerontology]
individual and the social, aging explained through tension between the, 5–6
knowledge, utilization of social science, 53–57
nomad science, 23–26
overview, 8
phenomenology and its different research strategies, philosophical, 46
praxeology, 59–60
representations of old age, gerontological knowledge and, 48–51
subjective orientation/meaning/context, 46
Social factors involved with aging/health, increasing recognition of, 221–222
Social-familial resources and the experience of aging, 74–75
Social gerontology, 25
Socialism, 15
Social location, old age as a, 209–211
Social order theoretical approach, 225
Social representation, 46
Social Security, 164, 187, 221, 230
Social self and the aging paradox, 132
Socioeconomic status and health outcomes, 70
Solidarity paradigm, intergenerational, 182
See also Families, modernization and changes faced by aging
Stability in experience of aging/self/life, aging paradox and, 127, 136
State science, 23–24
Stoller, Eleanor, 36
Structural problems, society's widespread, 18–19
See also Identity and structured inequalities, theory gap between experienced
Structural solidarity and intergenerational solidarity paradigm, 188
Structure and theorizing age relations, 210

Structure of Social Action, The (Parsons), 21
Subjective orientation/meaning/context and social constructionism, 46
Successful aging, 50, 200–203, 221
Supranational organizations and social policy, 168–171
Sweden, 118–119
Symbols and theorizing age relations, 210

Task-specific theory, 182
See also Families, modernization and changes faced by aging
Technical abilities and task-specific theory, 184
Theory in gerontology, the need for advancing theoretical formulations, 7–8
chapters in book, overview of, 8–10
characteristics of gerontology, key, 4–7
globalization, 171–177
identity, negotiating aging, 145–147
inclusive enough, is age, 246–247
practical implications, 247–248
summary/conclusions, 10
what is theory and why should we care, 1–4, 245–246
See also Age relations, theorizing; Critical gerontological theory; Perils/possibilities of theory within gerontology; individual subject headings
Thompson, E. P., 19
Thousand Plateaus, A (Deleuze & Guattari), 23
Tight-knit type of intergenerational family relations, 190
Transnational networks and relations, 167–171
See also Globalization and reconstruction of age
Trust and theorizing age relations, 206
Tulle, Emmanuelle, 8–9
Turbo-capitalism, 167–168
Twardowski, Kazimierz, 59
Twigg, Julia, 26

Urban sociology, 21
Utilization of social science knowledge,
　53–57

Values in action approach to critical
　theory, 37–38
Values (societal) and support of society's
　dependent members, 193
Vanston, Nicholas, 171
*Voices and Visions of Aging: Toward a*
　*Critical Gerontology,* 18, 37
Volunteerism, 202

Walker, Alan, 17
Weber, Marianne, 20–21
Weber, Max, 20–21
Welfare state
　age relations, theorizing, 207
　comparing achievements, 59
　family identity, 118–119

[Welfare state]
　globalization, 169–171
　institutionalizing old age, 164–167
　pensions, 187
　*See also* Families, modernization and
　　changes faced by aging
Westerhof, Gerben, 9
Western paradigm of elder care and
　support, 193–194
*Why Survive? Being Old in America*
　(Butler), 5
Wirth, Louis, 21
Women, state as a major vehicle for
　subjugation of, 227
　*See also* Gender
Woodward, Kathleen, 19
World Bank, 168, 169, 175
World Trade Organization (WTO),
　169–170

Zieleniewski, Jan, 59